THE
COMPLETE
APARTMENT
GUIDE

Ardman THE COMPLETE

APARTMENT GUIDE

Harvey Ardman & Perri Ardman

MACMILLAN PUBLISHING CO., INC. New York
COLLIER MACMILLAN PUBLISHERS London

Macmillan Publishing Co., Inc.
866 Third Avenue, New York 10022
Collier Macmillan Canada, Inc.

Library of Congress Cataloging in Publication Data
Ardman, Harvey.
The complete apartment guide.
Includes index.
1. Apartments. I. Ardman, Perri. II. Title.
TX303.A726 1982   643′.2   82-102
ISBN 0-02-500110-8   AACR2

10 9 8 7 6 5 4 3 2 1

Designed by Jack Meserole

Printed in the United States of America

Contents

Preface

Today, apartment living—like practically everything else—has become increasingly complex, requiring a range and depth of information that the average person can't be expected to possess.

To get the most out of apartment living, to avoid the many pitfalls that apartments present, today's apartment dwellers must know about law, furniture construction, decorating, security, human relations, maintenance, finance, and several other fields—information that can't be acquired easily.

The Complete Apartment Guide was written with the intention of providing all of this information, in one easy-to-read source-book. It's designed to be a guide to every major aspect of apartment living, a book that will give the total novice a measure of genuine confidence, while reaffirming and updating what more experienced apartment dwellers already know—or think they know.

We've written this book for practically anyone who's considering apartment living, who's ready to start apartment hunting, or who's already found (and may be occupying) an apartment, but isn't quite sure what to do next.

Included in this group are:

- Young women (or men) who are moving into their first apartment;
- More mature women (or men) who are moving out of a house, into an apartment, with or without their spouse;
- Apartment sharers of both genders and all ages;
- People who are consolidating two households into one;
- People who've lived in the same apartment for years and who, for one reason or another, are now moving;

- Retirees who are giving up the responsibility of owning a house;
- People who haven't been apartment hunting in years;
- People who feel a little overwhelmed with all they need to know about finding, moving into, decorating, maintaining, and living in an apartment.

The Complete Apartment Guide is, first of all, a *practical* book. It's written for real people, not for movie stars. It's for those apartment dwellers who (like most of us) don't have unlimited budgets, for those interested in getting the most out of their apartments—not those who yearn to live decorating-magazine fantasies.

Second, *The Complete Apartment Guide,* while it's filled with decorating suggestions, is written with the premise that you know what you like and you have no trouble exercising your taste, so long as you're familiar with the alternatives.

And what alternatives will you learn about in *The Complete Apartment Guide?* You'll learn:

- How to find the *right* apartment—the best apartment for you and your family, the best apartment for the money;
- How to work out a favorable lease—and protect yourself against any and all of the legal complications that come with renting an apartment;
- How to move efficiently—how to organize your packing and unpacking, how to quickly and conveniently occupy your new place;
- How to figure out your furnishing needs, and the best places to buy what you want;
- How to get the most out of your kitchen;
- How to make your bathroom as pleasant and as convenient as possible;
- How to paint, paper, or panel your walls;
- How to decorate your ceiling;
- How to buy and install floorcoverings (and decide which is best for you);
- How to choose pictures and other wall decorations;
- How to select houseplants that will thrive in your apartment;
- How to make your apartment safe from burglars, intruders, and fire;

- How to keep everything in your apartment in tip-top shape, and what to do if something goes wrong;
- How to deal with the new people in your life—friends, neighbors, landlords, and superintendents.

In putting this book together, we've drawn on many sources —and the advice and knowledge of experts in many different fields. We've also drawn heavily on our own backgrounds, which include considerable experience in retail furniture and in department-store merchandising.

In addition, we've drawn on our own personal experiences. Over the years, we've rented a combined total of nearly a dozen apartments (and owned four different houses, to boot). We've also drawn heavily on the real-life experiences of our friends, neighbors, and relatives.

The result, we think, is an eminently practical book, filled with information you can apply directly, whatever your situation or circumstances.

We hope that the lessons we've learned over the years and the information we've collected will help you avoid the many apartment pitfalls. And we hope that this book helps make your apartment-living experience truly satisfying.

Harvey Ardman
Perri Ardman

THE
COMPLETE
APARTMENT
GUIDE

Chapter 1

FINDING
THE RIGHT
APARTMENT

There's no question of it. The key to apartment living is finding the right apartment to begin with. If you take the time and care to do that, you'll be guaranteeing yourself a minimum of problems and a maximum of pleasures, at least as far as your residence is concerned.

It may even be that finding the right apartment is among the most important decisions of your life, ranking right up there with finding the right mate, deciding on whether, or when, to have a family, etc.

Fortunately, unlike the other major decisions you must make during the course of a lifetime, choosing an apartment is a science —or very nearly so. If you put enough energy and intelligence into it, you'll wind up with the right apartment.

And the purpose of this chapter is to guide you through all the necessary steps, to teach you the science of apartment hunting. Like riding a bicycle or typing, once you learn this skill it will be with you always. And chances are you'll find several occasions to use it over the years, not only for yourself, but for friends, relatives, and offspring.

But, first things first. Let's begin at the beginning:

Determining Your Options

Before you can start looking for an apartment, you have to figure out your basic needs, added extras you'd like to have, and what you can afford. This information, once calculated, will serve you well, giving you a good idea of the possibilities—and the limitations—that are open to you.

CALCULATING THE BASICS

Every apartment dweller has certain basic residential needs— needs that must be met if he or she is to live decently, needs that should be violated only in times of poverty, during wars, or in the event of natural disaster.

These needs are basic, but they are not the same for everyone. They're determined by a variety of circumstances—your job, your family, your age, your gender, whether or not you have a car, etc. We'll take them one by one.

Your family. This factor, more than any other, will determine what size apartment you need—that is, how many rooms, minimum.

Are you living by yourself? In that case, you can live comfortably in a studio apartment—one which has one large combination living, eating, and sleeping room, plus a bathroom and minimal kitchen facilities.

Are there two of you? It's still possible to live in a studio, unless for one reason or another you need separate sleeping quarters.

Do you have children? Unless you have one child, and it's an infant, you'll need a one-bedroom apartment at least. This term is used to refer to apartments that have separate living and sleeping rooms.

Except in emergencies (or perhaps on trips), adults and children should have separate sleeping quarters, for the sake of privacy and convenience, if not for psychological health.

And if you have several children, no more than two should sleep in a bedroom—and then only if they're the same gender (or very young).

Thus, if you're a man and wife with three children—a boy and two girls—your minimum basic space needs require three separate rooms for sleeping. In a pinch, one of these can be the livingroom. But even so, you'll need a two-bedroom apartment for the five of you.

Of course, you will probably prefer an even larger apartment. And if you can afford one, that's fine. But at the moment we're talking about your minimum needs.

Your family will also dictate, to a degree, the location of your apartment. If you have school-age children, for instance, you'll want to choose a place near decent schools.

Your job. If you work, that too will dictate where your apartment must be located, especially if you can't or don't want to drive or walk to work every morning.

If you must depend on public transportation, you'll have to find an apartment that's within easy walking distance of bus or subway lines. If you have to take a bus and then transfer to a subway line, or if the nearest public transportation is quite a walk from the apartment building, you're making trouble for yourself —perhaps serious trouble.

Likewise, if you drive back and forth from work, you'll need an apartment that's within reasonably easy driving distance to your job. It makes no sense to live on the north side of town and work on the south side. That arrangement will force you to spend time behind the wheel when you could be spending it in more rewarding ways.

Your car. If you own a car, you'll want some place to put it—a parking facility you can count on, within a few steps of your apartment building.

At a minimum, you'll want on-street parking that's almost always easy to find. You won't want to live in a neighborhood where people regularly doublepark because there's no place else for them to put their cars.

Your relatives and friends. Do you have close family ties? Close friends you see frequently? If so, you'll want an apartment that's reasonably close to them. Moving to a distant location could make it difficult for you to visit them and vice versa, seriously affecting your social life and sense of well-being.

Of course if you're changing jobs or being transferred out of town, or if you're willing to leave friends and relatives behind, with the thought of making new social contacts, this doesn't apply to you.

Security. This is, or should be, part of everyone's basic minimum living condition. You shouldn't live in an apartment you feel presents a greater-than-average risk of robbery or other crime, or of fire.

And your basic security needs don't end with the building itself. You should also consider the neighborhood, and the walk between the apartment building and the bus stop. You don't want to feel as though you and your family are running the gauntlet every time you go outdoors.

Shopping. At the minimum, your apartment should be within

easy walking distance of a food store—unless you have an apartment in the suburbs, where everyone drives everywhere. And even then, grocery stores shouldn't be too far away.

Depending on your needs, you might also want other stores nearby—newsstands, laundries, drugstores, banks, etc. Decide what you need, as a minimum.

Recreational facilities. If you're a physical fitness buff, you won't be happy with an apartment that's very distant from any recreational facilities. Depending on your tastes and habits, you'll want nearby jogging paths, bike paths, YMCAs, swimming pools, parks, etc.

Determine your basic needs here, too, taking into account the needs of your other family members, if any. What's the minimum you can accept?

Cultural facilities. Are you an inveterate moviegoer? Do you spend a lot of time in libraries? Are museums your favorite entertainment?

If so, and if these things are important enough to you or to other members of your family, you'll want your apartment to be reasonably near your favorite cultural facilities—or at least well connected by public transportation.

Of course only you can know whether or not proximity to cultural facilities is an "added extra" or part of your basic minimum needs. But at least ask yourself the question.

Health facilities. If you or another member of your family is retired, elderly, or has serious health problems, you may also need to be near a hospital, a drugstore, doctor's office, etc.

Once you've considered all of these factors, you'll have an idea of your minimum apartment needs. You may be surprised to discover how truly modest they are.

Of course what you need and what you want are probably two very different things. A studio apartment reasonably well located in a decent neighborhood may satisfy your needs. But you might—probably will, in fact—want something more luxurious.

Depending on your budget, you may or not be able to afford more than the basic minimum. But at the least you should consider what luxuries might be available to you.

THE ADDED EXTRAS

What makes an apartment luxurious? For most people, it's space—more rooms, larger rooms. Others might say that it's such added extras as swimming pools, etc. Still others would say it's a matter of location—the better the neighborhood, the greater the luxury.

These are factors to consider when figuring out what you want above and beyond the minimum decent housing level. But there are many others.

What follows is a list of the most common luxury factors and a brief evaluation of their importance and their cost:

Location. Landlords are highly sensitive to the character of the neighborhood their buildings are in—and they price apartments accordingly, even if the building itself is no great wonder. Just check out a very expensive studio and you'll see that's it's not much better than an inexpensive one, except for location.

On the other hand, you can sometimes find small buildings with reasonable rents, hidden away in good neighborhoods. Just beware that you won't be the first to search for such a gem.

A good location does have very real value. It usually offers greater safety and security, better city services, better shopping, more entertainment and cultural facilities—and a more prestigous address if you happen to care about that.

If you want a good location—and a bargain—try to identify those parts of the city that are "on their way up." These are areas that were—and to a degree still are—middle-class or perhaps slightly less than middle-class, but are now rapidly improving. Get yourself a lease on a good apartment in an area like this, with an option for a lease extension at the same price, and you may find yourself the envy of your friends.

On the other hand, beware of good neighborhoods that are going downhill. If you lease an apartment in such an area, you may be very unhappy before your lease has expired.

How do you find out whether a neighborhood is going up or down, or staying the same? Ask questions. Talk to shopowners in the area. Speak to tenants in the building you're considering. Ask the cop on the beat. You'll soon get the picture.

Proximity to recreational, cultural, or entertainment facilities. For some, the greatest of all luxuries is to live next to a park with tennis courts, or a golf course, or a public swimming pool, or not far from the local Y.

Others enjoy living close to movie houses, bookstores, libraries, even colleges and universities, where, if they like, they can take a night course in something that interests them.

Most landlords understand the value of this proximity—and charge for it. But if it will significantly improve your lifestyle, it may be worth paying for.

On-site recreational facilities. Many large apartment complexes, especially those in the south and west, or those designed for retirement-age people, offer not only living quarters, but also swimming pools, gyms, recreation rooms, tennis courts, and similar recreational facilities.

These are definitely desirable luxuries—if you can afford them. And indeed, some apartment complexes so equipped offer tenants a choice, letting them buy membership in the recreational facilities or not, as they choose.

Prime apartments. No matter which apartment building you look at, not all of the apartments within it are created equal, not even if their floor plans are identical.

Some of the differences:

- Floor. In general, the higher the floor, the better—and the more expensive. High floors provide better security than lower ones. They also provide better views. (But they do have their disadvantages. They require a longer trip on the elevator —and a much longer trip by stairs, if there's ever a power failure. And if the building's plumbing is improperly designed, they may even have water pressure problems.)
- View. Even two identical apartments on the same floor aren't necessarily identical—not if one looks north, at the lake, and the other looks south, at the factory district.

   Views are something you pay for. And they can have a very positive effect on your quality of life. Beautiful views do wonders for your psyche, especially after a hard day's work.
- Terrace. Some buildings offer apartments with or without terraces. The former are usually more desirable.

   Terraces give you the chance to be outdoors without leaving your apartment. They also give you the opportunity to grow a small tree or two, get a suntan, or enjoy the summer breeze.

On the other hand, in some cities and in certain locations they're not much more than soot collectors. And without a good view they're not much more than slabs of concrete.

Peace and quiet. Every apartment everywhere should offer peace and quiet, but few do. And those few usually charge for the difference.

What do we mean by peace and quiet? We mean an absence of beeping horns, heavy traffic, sirens, noisy playgrounds, etc. We mean a building on a quiet, even out-of-the-way residential street, with a minimum of foot traffic and no stores in the immediate vicinity.

All of this is hard to find in a big city. But if you're the sort who doesn't really thrive without peace and quiet, you'll consider it a great luxury—perhaps even worth the price.

A building of unusual beauty or design. There is something thrilling about living in one of the city's most spectacular new high-rise apartment houses, a building that can be seen from miles away, a building that everyone knows. But you pay a premium for this pleasure.

You also pay a premium for the pleasure of living in a building of unusual historical note, or one designed by a famous architect, or one that uses unusual materials in its construction, or one that has become, for one reason or another, highly favored by society.

Are luxuries like this worth the price? That depends entirely on you. To be sure, they provide extra value of a sort. But the extra value is intangible, while its cost is figured in hard cash.

Superior parking facilities. Better apartment buildings sometimes offer off-the-street parking—either outdoors, in a lot near the building, or in basement garages.

Sometimes these parking facilities are included in the rent; other times they're available at extra cost.

Parking facilities like these are more than simply a convenience and assurance of finding a place to put your car, no matter how crowded the streets might be. They're also a safety factor, especially indoors.

Furthermore, indoor or garage parking within the building sometimes connects with building elevators, which is especially handy if you've been shopping and you're carrying packages.

A doorman. Wait, you say, if there's one luxury I don't need, it's a doorman. I can open the door for myself. Besides, I don't want one more hand reaching for tips or Christmas presents.

If this is your notion of what a doorman is, you have a distorted view. True, doormen do hold the door open for tenants and their guests. And they do whistle up taxis or hold out umbrellas when you're getting out of a taxi in the rain. But they have a far more important job.

Doormen are mainly a security measure. It's their job, if they do it right, to make sure everyone who enters the building and who isn't known to them identifies himself or herself.

It's the doorman's job to notify you that someone has come to see you—a guest or tradesman—and not to admit that person until you've given the go-ahead.

To be sure, doormen aren't cops. They can't do much against a determined intruder, other than to call the police. But they can discourage sneak thieves, robbers, muggers, and other undesirables.

Doormen usually aren't provided by the landlords of basic, minimum-housing apartment buildings. But they are frequently available in better buildings. This is a luxury you should give yourself, if possible.

Doormen have other uses, too, incidentally. They can accept packages, admit guests who are scheduled to arrive in your absence and generally give you a helping hand when none other is available.

A package room. The better apartment buildings offer a small but vital service that some might consider a luxury, others a necessity. It's a package room—a room designed to receive packages that come from stores, or through UPS or parcel post, addressed to tenants.

We've lived in buildings with package rooms and in buildings without them and we've found them to be an enormous convenience. Without a package room, you must somehow arrange for someone to accept any packages you might be expecting. This can be very difficult, especially when you have no exact delivery date.

Unfortunately, very few apartment buildings are equipped with package rooms. They're a luxury worth paying for, in our view.

Incinerators. Many large, high-rise buildings dispose of garbage via large incinerators in the basement. These connect to long chutes that run to the top of the building, usually near the elevator shafts.

To use the incinerator, all a tenant need do is to walk out of his apartment, go down the hall, open up a door, shove his garbage bag into the chute, and forget about it. Some apartments require that, in addition, you remove all cans and bottles and leave them in a paper bag in the incinerator room. But even so, incinerators make garbage disposal practically a pleasure.

Air conditioning. Do you need air conditioning? That depends on where you live. In the south and west, you can hardly do without it—and it's standard in most large apartment houses and in many, many smaller ones.

In northern regions, the case for air conditioning isn't so strong, although most of the north has plenty of eighty-five to ninety degree summer days, when, without air conditioning, you feel as though you're living in a furnace. The question is, is it worth paying for air conditioning year round when you use it only two or three months a year?

Most newer air-conditioned apartment houses have central air conditioning, rather than window or wall units. There are several advantages to this type of unit: It's very quiet (the machinery is in the basement or on the roof); if anything goes wrong, it will probably be repaired very quickly, since malfunctions affect *every* tenant; the electricity costs are probably lower than the costs of individual room air conditioners.

On the other hand, centrally air-conditioned buildings are definitely luxury housing, at least in the north, and you pay accordingly. If the summer heat really bothers you, or if you have health problems that might be made worse by sweltering heat, this is one luxury you should seriously consider.

There is another solution, however. You can always rent a non-air-conditioned apartment and buy a room air conditioner which can be installed through a window. There'll be an initial expense, of course, and the air conditioner might not be quite as efficient as central cooling, but you will be able to take it with you when you move—or sell it.

Of course, if you're renting a multi-room apartment, you needn't buy air conditioners for every room. If you're alone or if there are two of you sharing the master bedroom, you can air-condition that room alone. Or, if you spend most of your day at home in the living room, you can air-condition that room.

Some people today feel that air conditioning is a necessity, but we're not of that school. After all, human beings survived reasonably well without it for several millennia. But we do think air conditioning is worthwhile if you can afford it, since it can be a boon to good health and can make life generally more pleasant.

Cable TV or master TV antenna. Many newer apartment houses offer cable TV connections or master TV antennas. The former is usually an extra-cost option, the latter free (or absorbed in your rent payment).

Whether or not you want or need this particular luxury depends on your local TV reception and on how much you depend on television for entertainment.

A freight elevator. We don't think that anyone should either accept or reject an apartment because the building has or doesn't have a freight elevator. But all other things equal, it's a nice added extra.

Freight elevators are normally larger than passenger elevators. That makes it easier to move large items of furniture into the apartment building. But their greatest advantage is that they eliminate freight and move-in or move-out traffic on the passenger elevator or elevators.

This might not seem like much of an advantage, but in a highrise apartment building, where there are several hundred tenants, it seems that someone is always moving in or out—and tying up the elevator for hours.

Quality maintenance and upkeep. It should be part of your minimum basic requirements that whatever building you choose, whatever apartment you rent, the landlord and/or superintendent keeps the place reasonably clean and in good repair.

But if you're willing to pay for it, you can do better than that. You can rent an apartment in a building that's spotlessly maintained, that's kept in perfect repair at all times.

Is this a luxury worth paying for? That depends on your needs, your current lifestyle, the image you want to present to friends, family, and other guests.

Laundry room. Better apartment buildings have laundry rooms, so you don't have to carry your laundry to the nearest laundromat or find some way to do it in your apartment.

Most laundry rooms are in the apartment building's basement. These are quite satisfactory, providing the building security is good. Other buildings have separate laundry areas on each floor. These are more convenient and safer.

Whether or not you want this added extra depends, at least to some degree, on whether you're doing laundry for yourself or for a fairly large family. The more people you're caring for, the less of a luxury a laundry room is—and the more it's a necessity.

WHAT YOU CAN AFFORD

By now you should have a pretty good idea of what your basic needs are and what luxuries are important to you. The next step is to address the question of what you can afford.

In years past it was more or less a rule of thumb that people could afford to spend one fourth of their gross income on housing. That is, if they earned $1,000 a month, they could afford to spend up to $250 on housing—on rent, or on a house payment.

But in recent times authorities on home budgeting have become more flexible on this subject, perhaps as a result of some truly startling rent increases in some parts of the country. At any rate, some experts are now saying that it may be reasonable to spend as much as one third of your gross income on housing today.

Like all rules of thumb, these suggestions, however well-meant, however well-researched, assume too much. They simply cannot account for individual variations in financial obligations, lifestyles, and other particular circumstances.

How then do you determine what amount you can afford to spend for rent? Well, we think that the smartest way to do that is to draw up a detailed budget for yourself and your family.

There are all kinds of books on family budgeting, but it really isn't a very complicated subject. Its basis is to list all of your expenses, comparing them to your income, then making whatever adjustments may be necessary. (Of course that may be easier said than done.)

The standard list usually includes these items:

• Food (including meals eaten out);
• Clothing (your average yearly expenses divided by twelve);
• Entertainment (movies, concerts, theater, ball games, fees

paid for sports activities, cable TV fees, newspaper and magazine subscriptions);
* Transportation (gasoline, car maintenance, car payments, taxis, public transportation costs);
* Health (doctors, therapists, eye glasses, dentists);
* Insurance (medical, life, auto, renter's insurance);
* Utilities (gas, electric, telephone, heat, water—although some of these might be subtracted from your monthly budget if they're included in your rent);
* Savings;
* Other personal expenses, such as union dues, taxes, debt payments, tuition costs, furniture payments, charitable contributions, contributions to the care of an elderly parent, business expenses, housekeeping expenses, babysitters, vacations.

Our point: list *all* of your monthly expenses, and be as accurate as you can. If you're optimistic, you're asking for financial trouble. If you're pessimistic, you may be unnecessarily restricting your lifestyle. (But it wouldn't hurt to add a bit to the figures you come up with, to take care of inflation, unless you're sure your income will go up accordingly.)

You'll notice that we haven't listed housing among the items to be included. The reason: your housing budget is what's left over when you subtract all of your other monthly expenses from your monthly income. Given your particular circumstances, for instance, you may have a monthly income of $1,500 and a monthly outgo, not counting housing, of $1,000. In that case, you can spend up to $500 on rent—one third of your income.

On the other hand, you may earn the same amount but, given your circumstances, have monthly expenditures of $1,200. In that case, you'll only have $300 to spend on rent.

Of course, most of these budget figures are not inflexible. You can cut down in one area or another to increase the amount you're able to spend on housing, but we don't advise this. If you reduce the quality of your life in order to get a better apartment, you'll find the adjustment difficult to make.

On the other hand, you must somehow get a place that meets your basic minimum needs. And if you have to cut back somewhere to accomplish that, do it. After all, nothing is more crucial to a decent lifestyle than where you live.

APARTMENT SHARING

If after all the figuring and cutting back you still can't afford a decent apartment, there is another way: apartment sharing. This is an increasingly common practice in this age of skyrocketing rents.

You can share an apartment with many different sorts of people: old friends, relatives, siblings, co-workers, even total strangers (or at least people who start out that way).

It's even possible to share an apartment with people of the opposite gender, with no romantic entanglements—if both of you are of the right temperament.

And you needn't limit your sharing to just one other individual. Three or four, occasionally even more, can successfully share an apartment, if it's big enough.

You can even share if you find yourself in a large city in which you have no acquaintances whatsoever—by contacting agencies that specialize in pairing roommates or by finding apartment-sharing ads in the classifieds.

On the plus side, apartment sharing can cut costs, provide companionship and convenience for both parties. And many apartment sharers turn out, in the long run, to be lifelong friends.

On the minus side, some people have innate difficulties sharing an apartment—because they value their privacy too highly, because they're too gabby, too snoopy, or too set in their ways to adjust to living with someone who has different tastes in furniture, friends, music, TV, and food.

If you think sharing an apartment might be satisfactory for you, you may well be right. But if you've never done it, you should know that it's probably more complicated than you think.

The greatest difficulty is not in finding someone suitable, at least not in large urban areas. It's in the two of you making all the necessary adjustments to each other. These are some of the problems you're likely to confront:

- Keeping your food separate in the refrigerator, with both of you honoring agreements not to poach;
- Sharing a single bathroom, with all the waiting and rushing that implies;
- Dividing the household chores (let's hope both of you are equally responsible and domestically inclined);

- Dividing shopping and household expenses;
- Dealing with each other's guests, perhaps even overnight guests;
- Dividing cooking responsibilities;
- Adjusting to each other's late-night comings and goings;
- Determing when the TV goes on, when the hi-fi goes on, what either or both of you play, and when silence is best;
- Caring for the household plants;
- Adjusting to each other's pets (and the pets adjusting to each other);
- Working out sensible rules for opposite-gender (but non-involved) roommates.

And of course this is just a small sampling.

To all of these may be added the entire range of relationship complications if you intend to share an apartment with a romantic partner. If each of you now lives in an apartment, there's the question of who moves where. There's also the question of how you meld your joint household possessions, and what you do with what's left over. Then there's the question of splitting up. You both hope that will never happen, but if it does, who gets what? Who stays? Who leaves?

Despite the problems, however, we believe apartment sharing is a viable alternative—with the right people.

CONDOS AND CO-OPS

If you're among the fortunate, however, you may find yourself with plenty of extra income—enough to rent the apartment of your dreams. You may, in addition, have substantial cash reserves in one form or another.

If this is your situation, you might do well to consider other ways to pay for your living space. In particular, you might consider buying a condominium apartment or investing in a co-op.

Condominiums are owned exactly like private homes, except that in addition to whatever you lay out to buy a condominium (either in cash or on a mortgage basis), you also pay a monthly fee for maintenance.

Condominiums—or condos—aren't cheap. Depending on location, facilities, luxuries, etc., they cost about what you'd pay for a house of the same size—more, if you've choosen a prestige location or building.

Furthermore, maintenance payments, which include janitorial services, doormen, garbage collection, groundskeepers, maintenance on central air-conditioning or other centralized services, can run to $200 or $300 a month, or more.

On the other hand, like ownership in a private house, owning a condo is an investment. If you choose your building wisely, you may someday be able to sell your condo for much more than you paid for it.

There are some pitfalls to condo buying, however, even if you have the funds to do it. For example, if a neighbor in the building defaults on his maintenance payments, all the other occupants will be assessed to make up the difference.

Also, some condo builders or agents tend to underestimate the amount of the monthly maintenance payment. Or other factors might greatly increase that figure, such as the need for substantial repairs, or large increases in fuel costs.

In addition, some condo builders are dishonest. The Federal Trade Commission in Washington, which handles such matters, has received fifteen thousand letters from condominium owners complaining about poor construction—particularly, inadequate soundproofing between apartments.

And some condo builders sell units by making promises they don't intend to keep about tennis courts, swimming pools, and gymnasiums. Others use owners' deposits to start the building, then go bankrupt.

Not all condominiums involve new buildings. Some are simply converted apartment buildings, transformed by landlords who want to rid themselves of unprofitable property.

This isn't necessarily bad, if the building is in good condition. But if you're a rental tenant in such a building, conversion can come as a rude shock and force you to find other living quarters.

Clearly, buying a condominium is a complicated and tricky business, so if you intend to go this route, we strongly recommend that you get some expert advice. Especially seek out a lawyer knowledgeable in the field, to help you decipher the many legal documents condo purchase involves.

Another way to buy an apartment—more or less—is to go the cooperative or co-op route. Co-ops differ from condominiums in that when you buy a co-op, you're really buying a share in a corporation. You don't own the building—the corporation does.

This means that you don't make payments on your own mortgage, for your own apartment, but as your share in the building's mortgage. The same goes for tax payments. It also means that if one of the building's occupants can't make his payments, you have to pick up your share of the difference.

For this reason, and because condominiums offer personal ownership, cooperative apartments aren't as popular as condos.

Should you buy a condo or a co-op? That depends on many factors: Do you have the necessary funds? Do you want a long-term residence? Are you interested in the investment aspects of real estate? Do you prefer to own, rather than rent?

Judging the Apartment

Once you've determined your budget, you're ready to start apartment hunting in earnest. But where should you begin? In our opinion, there's no better place than the classified newspaper ads—particularly on Sunday, if your community has a Sunday newspaper.

If you're a long-time resident of your particular community, if you have a good working knowledge of the city, its neighborhoods, its expressways, its bus and/or subway systems, its chief shopping areas, etc., you'll need nothing more than the paper itself.

If you're a relative stranger, however, or even if you've lived in the city for quite some time but haven't explored it much, you'll need some additional reference material. We suggest that you get hold of a detailed map of the city, showing all the transportation routes, public buildings, hospitals, etc. You might also consider city guidebooks, if they're available. And telephone books are also a good idea.

Of course, there's one piece of information that isn't likely to appear on any map or in any guidebook: which parts of the city are the safest, which neighborhoods are the best. But many police departments issue crime statistics by neighborhoods, and many fire departments do the same for fires.

To get this information, check first with your local library. Police and fire reports like these are usually printed in the newspaper and you may be able to learn what you need to know by checking back issues.

If you can't find what you're looking for this way, call or visit police and fire department headquarters and ask to speak to the community relations officer. Explain that you want to rent an apartment, but don't know the city well. Ask which neighborhoods have a high crime or fire risk. Be sure to mention any special circumstances—young children, elderly or retired people living with you, the need to live close to hospitals, colleges, whatever.

The information you should be seeking from police and fire departments is not which particular building might be right for you, but which neighborhoods are most suitable. For this reason, bring your city map and felt marker if you visit one of these departments, or mark the map yourself if you're making contact by telephone.

READING THE CLASSIFIEDS

Now, it's time to look at those classified pages. Generally the listings are divided into two main categories: furnished and unfurnished. These are further divided into one- and two-room apartments; three-, four-, and five-room apartments; six rooms and over; co-ops and condominiums. In major metropolitan areas, they're also divided by area or by street.

Reading apartment listings is something of an art, since they are masterpieces of condensation, innuendo, and hint. Here's how to read them:

Large display ads (anything more than five lines) are usually for big, new buildings, probably among the most expensive and luxurious in the neighborhood. If you see a large display ad in the classifieds, you can be sure there'll be plenty of vacancies in that particular building, and probably in every size category.

The smaller ads—those composed of only a few lines of type —normally mean that there's only one or two vacancies in the building. This, in turn, means that the building isn't brand new and it probably isn't an enormous high-rise (which almost always has several vacancies).

When a large ad prominently features a price—say, "one-bedroom apartments from $500"—the price refers to the smallest, least desirable one-bedroom apartment in the building, usually on the first or second floor. Other one-bedrooms in the building will be substantially higher;

If a large ad fails to mention price at all, you can be sure the price is astronomical;

The phrase "now renting" is meant to imply that a building is new or nearly new. But we've seen faded "now renting" signs painted on buildings that were a decade old;

Ads that list a selection of apartments in different locations are from rental agencies. Some of these charge fees equal one month's rent for finding you an apartment. When apartments are difficult to find, this fee may be worth paying. When they're not, you're better off doing it yourself;

The phrase "prin only," or principals only, is put in ads to discourage calls from agents. This phrase is usually found in ads placed by individuals or by landlords who own smaller buildings. Sometimes it indicates quality.

The abbreviation "bkr" means broker, or agent;

The phrase "perfect for executive" usually means that the building is near the office district. It may also mean the apartment is expensive;

"Immediate occupancy" means that the apartment is vacant and probably has been for a while;

"Walk up" means that the building has no elevator. You may be facing five flights of stairs here;

"Floor-thru" or "duplex" means two-floor apartment.

"View," "riv vu," or similar word or phrase means that you can see something nice from at least one window. But beware—you may have to crane your neck to do it;

"W/w crpt" means wall-to-wall carpeting;

"A/C" means air conditioning. But large ads that do not mention air conditioning usually refer to centrally air-conditioned apartments;

The phrase "membership plan," in connection with pool and health club, means that you must pay extra to use these facilities;

The phrase "all amenities," can mean practically anything. Usually it means that the building has air conditioning, elevators, pleasant lobbies, and possibly indoor parking facilities;

"Renovated." This word can mean anything from repainted to extensively remodeled;

"Concierge." This usually means that the building has an attended package room;

The word "available" in connection with any luxury feature,

such as cable TV, parking, pool, etc. really means optional. In other words, if you want this feature, it will cost you;

The word "prewar," means that the building was built before 1940. Sometimes the use of this word is an attempt to transform a liability into an asset. But prewar buildings have a reputation for being more solid, better-soundproofed, more secure. Don't expect pools and central air conditioning, however;

The word "cute" means tiny or doll-like;

The word "prestige" means very expensive;

"Estimated maintenance," is a term used in co-op and condo ads. The question is, who made the estimate, and on what basis?

With all this in mind, go through the classified ads carefully, circling likely apartments in pen (not magic marker—it blots on newsprint). First, check the listings in the neighborhoods most likely to suit you. Second, study the space category that meets your minimum needs.

After that, widen your review. Look at somewhat larger apartments than you really need. Look on the fringes of desirable neighborhoods. Look at apartments somewhat more distant from your job than you really wanted.

The object of this wider search is to get a good idea of what's available, and where. You may find, for instance, that you simply can't afford an apartment within fifteen minutes of your job, but that there are plenty within half an hour. Or you may find that you can afford a larger apartment than you thought.

Incidentally, if you see an apartment that's priced substantially below the market, it's probably worth no more than that. Brokers and landlords read the ads, too—with a magnifiying glass. And they stay up nights trying to figure out how to get the maximum rental from each apartment.

On the other hand, there are exceptions to this rule—long-term sublets, for instance, or older buildings where landlords aren't quite as sophisticated, or voracious, as those usually in charge of renting new buildings. If you think you've located a bargain, make that your first stop when you go out apartment hunting. And hope no one has beaten you to it.

One way to get a jump on at least some of your fellow apartment hunters is to get hold of that Sunday real estate section as early as possible. In some cities they're printed up several days before the rest of the paper and can be obtained at the newspaper printing plant.

Once you've gone through the classifieds thoroughly, mark your map with the locations of the likely apartments. Then, study what you have.

First, look at the apartments in terms of transportation. How convenient are they to public transportation? Are they near bus or subway stops? Are they near express or local stops? How convenient are they to major car routes? Are they *too* close to expressways (if an expressway runs right beside the building, the noise can be unbearable). If you're looking at a suburban apartment, how convenient is it to commuter transportation into the city center? If you work, figure out how you'd get from each apartment to your job.

Second, look at the apartments in terms of public facilities. (These should be marked on your map. If not, get a better map or consult a city tourist guidebook. Or get a booklet about the city from a real estate office. These often have maps showing information of this sort.)

Look in particular for parks, libraries, schools, colleges, police and fire stations, post offices, YMCAs, public swimming pools, and the like. This should help you determine which apartments are close to the facilitiles that interest you most.

Third, get out your phone book and check out the location of banks, department store branches, supermarkets, and any other retail outlets that may be important to you. Use another colored marker—perhaps a different color for each type of store—to note these on your map.

Now, eliminate everything that doesn't meet your basic needs, whatever they may be. Next, lay out an apartment-hunting route, neighborhood by neighborhood. (If you do your apartment hunting helter-skelter, it will take you much longer and you won't get a feeling for the neighborhood.)

What you'll probably end up with is three or four different routes, one for each of three or four different neighborhoods. We recommend that you start with the neighborhood with the largest number of apartment vacancies, working down to the neighborhoods with the smallest number, or alternately, the neighborhood with the largest number of potential bargains; but beware —this neighborhood may not be as good as you think.

Now take a large, spiral-bound notebook and prepare it for apartment hunting in the following manner:

Starting at the top of a page, go through the next section—the one describing how to judge apartments—jotting down the qualities listed in the left-hand vertical column. Then divide the page with vertical lines. Leave room across the top of the page to note the apartment's address.

You'll be using this notebook throughout the day to make judgments of various aspects of each apartment you visit, so that you'll be able to remember what you've seen and make comparisons with some accuracy.

Incidentally, at least one couple we know take a Polaroid camera along with them when they go apartment hunting. They take pictures of the outside of the building, the lobby, and parts of the apartment itself, if they find one that they consider right for them. Then, when they sit down to make their final choice, they have no trouble remembering what they've seen. This is an excellent technique, but it's expensive.

Once your notebook is ready, you're ready to begin. We recommend that you set aside an entire weekend for apartment hunting, and that you begin no later than 9:00 A.M. on Saturday.

Since apartment hunting can be an exhausting adventure, however fascinating, we recommend that you get a good night's sleep before you start out.

On Saturday morning, fortify yourself with a good breakfast, dress comfortably but not too informally (you'll want to make a good impression on your potential landlords, if only so they'll take you seriously), put your maps, newspaper ads, and notebook into a briefcase of some kind. Now you're ready to go.

If you're looking for an apartment in the suburbs, by all means take your car. This will speed the process and give you a chance to explore a bit. But if you're looking in the city, walk as much as possible and take public transportation. In our experience, this is the best way to get an accurate impression of the neighborhoods you're visiting.

MAKING THE FINAL DECISION

From this point on, your apartment hunting boils down to a series of judgments, on different practical aspects of the neighborhood, the building, and the apartment itself.

These judgments should be entered in your notebook, in the form of letter (A through F) or number (10 down to 1) grades on each item of interest, for each apartment you're considering.

The following pages list the items we think you should consider. We have mentioned some of these previously, but now is the time to think about them in more detail. But don't hesitate to eliminate those that don't apply to you, or to add other items that fit your particular circumstances.

The Neighborhood

Transporation. Is the neighborhood generally convenient to public transportation? To major highways?

Shopping. Are the grocery stores adequate? Does the area have a full complement of other useful retail stores (drug stores, banks, newsstands, bookstores, clothing stores, or whatever else you like?

Recreation. Are there plenty of parks, playgrounds, tennis courts, swimming pools, golf courses, YMCAs and YWCAs, biking areas, jogging paths, movie houses, discos, or whatever else you like?

Cultural facilities. Are there enough libraries, schools, colleges, concert halls, or whatever else you feel you need?

People. Are the neighborhood's residents reasonably similar to you in terms of age, economic character, family composition, occupation, etc.? If not, you may be uncomfortable here or have trouble finding companionship.

Safety. Does the neighborhood seem to meet your basic requirements for safety and security? Ask the cop on the beat, some local store owners, some local residents, if you're not sure.

Condition. Is the neighborhood run-down, in the process of change, spotless? Match the grade to your needs.

Noise. Is it a heavy-traffic, high-noise area, or a quiet area? The quieter the better, everything else equal.

The Building, Outside

Comparison. Is the building you're considering significantly more luxurious, or less luxurious, than its neighbors? If more, it may be overpriced for the neighborhood. If less, it could be a bargain.

Age and condition. Does the building appear to be in good

shape from the outside? Whether it is or not, this probably reflects the care it's gotten over the years, and the care you can expect it to receive. Generally, if a building is poorly maintained on the outside, it will be poorly maintained inside, too.

The grounds. Are the lawns, shrubs, and walkways well cared-for? This is another excellent indicator of general building maintenance.

Exterior lighting. Are all the entrances well lit? They should be, since this is an essential safety factor.

Pet-walking areas. Even if you don't have a dog, you'll want an apartment building with adequate pet-walking areas. Otherwise, pet owners will be forced to use the streets, which could make walking quite unpleasant.

Parking. If you own a car, or if you expect guests to be arriving by car, this will be important to you. Is there plenty of on-street parking? How about off-street parking?

The Building, Inside

Security. Are there good locks on all exterior doors? Does the building have a doorman, especially a doorman who stops you and asks you where you're going? If not, does the building have a good buzzer system, with an intercom, so tenants can be selective about whom they admit?

Lobby. Is the lobby well decorated, well painted, and generally well maintained? Is it comfortable? (If you ever have to wait for a friend to pick you up, you'll be happy if the lobby has comfortable chairs.) Is it well lit?

Mail facilities. Are the individual mailboxes in good condition? Is there a package room?

Elevators. Are there enough? Are they well maintained? Does the building have a freight elevator?

Stairs. Even if the building has elevators, are its stairways clean, well lighted, and well maintained?

Laundry facilities. Does the building have laundry machines? Are these well maintained? Conveniently located?

Garbage facilities. Does the building have an incinerator? If not, are garbage facilities conveniently located and well maintained?

Garage. Does the building have a garage? Is it well lighted and well maintained?

Storage. Do tenants have individual basement storage lockers? Are these large enough? Conveniently located? Secure?

Luxury facilities. Does the building have a pool, health club, recreation room, tennis courts, or similar facility? If so, is it well maintained, well located, pleasant to use? Is it overcrowded? Are there any safety problems? Is all necessary equipment provided? Is there supervision?

Hallways. Are they well lit and well maintained? Is the paint in good shape? The carpeting?

Other tenants. Are they the sort of people you'd like to have as neighbors, the sort with whom you could be friendly? Would you fit in?

Fire safety. Does the building have adequate fire safeguards? A fire escape on the outside or fire-proof stairways? Smoke detectors or alarms? A sprinkler system in public areas?

If at all possible, engage one or more of the building's tenants in conversation. Ask about the landlord, the superintendent, the neighborhood, building maintenance, and anything else that concerns you, especially items that aren't immediately apparent. You'll be surprised how much information a few friendly questions can turn up.

The Apartment in General.

Location in Building. Is the apartment on a bottom floor? A top floor? Near or far from the elevator? The stairs? The incinerator chute? Do its main windows face south? (The most desirable direction, in terms of sunlight). Is the apartment located away from street traffic or near it?

The cost. What's the monthly rental? Add to this figure the estimated monthly cost of all utilities not included (electricity, gas, heat, water, etc.) This will give you an accurate basis for comparison with other rental figures, and a more realistic figure for budgeting purposes.

Apartment condition. How's the paint job? The plaster? The woodwork? Do the windows work well?

Floors. What are the floors covered with? What's the condition of the floor covering?

Ceilings. Are ceilings higher than usual? Most people consider this a plus, although it means additional heating expense, if heat is not included in your rent payment.

Heating system. How is the apartment heated? Electric heat is the most versatile—and the most expensive, if you're paying for it. Is the heating plant in good condition? Does the apartment have its own temperature control? Are there controls in each room? (If the winters are cold and the building is old, you should definitely talk to another tenant to make sure building heat is adequate.)

Air conditioning. Does the apartment have room air conditioners? How well do they work? Does the building have central air conditioning? Is it in good shape? Are there individual controls in each room? Who pays for the necessary electricity?

Extra space. Some apartments are so tightly designed that they don't have an extra inch for hallways, vestibules, foyers, etc. This is particularly true of newer buildings. Older buildings, on the other hand, often have such "extra space." We think it's a great bonus, since it's the best antidote we know to feeling cramped.

Livingroom

Size. This should be the largest room in your apartment, with adequate room for family, friends, guests. We prefer living rooms with a minimum measurement of 18x12 feet.

Shape. Nonrectangular rooms can present serious problems in terms of furniture arrangement and decorating. So can rooms with all kinds of coves, nooks and crannies, or rooms that are inordinately long.

Entryway. Ideally, your front door should not open directly into your livingroom. It should open into a vestibule or foyer area.

Door. This should be steel-covered, with a peephole. It should fit tightly, against an intruder-resistant jamb. It should open and close smoothly and easily. There should be a bell or buzzer on the outside, with a nameplate holder. Don't worry about locks too much, though, since you'll probably be providing your own.

Closet. Yes, a livingroom should have a closet, by the front door. This is where you'll want to hang your outdoor coats and your guests' coats. It doesn't have to be monstrous, but it should be large enough to do the job.

Windows. Livingrooms should be light and bright. Are there enough windows to accomplish this? Are they so located as not to interfere with furniture arrangement? Do they provide cross-ventilation? Do they have venetian blinds, shades, or drapes?

View. If you can only have a view in one room of your apartment, this is the place to have it. But to mean anything at all, it should be visible at a glance—not something that requires pressing your nose against a corner of the far window.

Terrace. If the apartment has one, the entrance will probably be off the livingroom. The terrace door should be weatherproof, it should work well, and it should not be placed in such a way as to make furniture arrangement impossible. The terrace itself should be open to sunlight and air, overlooking something pleasant, if not actually providing a view. It should be sturdy and in good repair.

Access to bathroom. Your guests shouldn't have to traipse through your bedroom to get to the bathroom. It should be just a few steps from the livingroom.

Soundproofing. You shouldn't be able to hear your neighbors easily, nor they you. Of course, some noise transmission is inevitable. But it should be minimal. In this regard, make sure that the apartment livingroom doesn't abut some other tenant's bedroom, on either side, above, or below.

Light fixtures. At the minimum, the livingroom should have a ceiling fixture near the front door. It's also convenient to have a switched electrical outlet, so you can turn on a floor or table lamp by flipping a switch just inside the door.

Electrical outlets. The livingroom should have an adequate number of electrical outlets, well spaced, to accommodate lights, hi-fi, TV, etc.

Radiators, registers. These should not unduly interfere with furniture placement and they should work properly.

Master TV and/or cable TV outlets. These should be sensibly located, so that you can put your television set in a logical place, in keeping with a normal furniture arrangemnt.

Phone outlets. Some apartments have preinstalled telephone outlets. This is a plus, if they're installed in a sensible place.

Bedroom
Size. Tiny bedrooms are rarely pleasant, even if they have everything else going for them. For this reason, we recommend dimensions of at least 11x14 feet for the master bedroom. Children's rooms can be considerably smaller, although anything below 8x10 feet is cramped for anyone except an infant.

Shape. Once more, rectangular is best.

Entryway. Having a bedroom at the end of a hallway is one of life's little luxuries. It shouldn't be the difference between signing a lease and not signing one, but it's nice to have. But even without a hallway, every bedroom should have a lockable door.

Closets. Every bedroom should have enough closet space, either inside the room or just outside the door, to house all of the clothing of its occupants. These closets should be so arranged as not to interfere with the logical placement of the bed. They should also be lighted on the inside.

Light Fixtures. Each bedroom should have at least one ceiling fixture, plus an electrical outlet controlled from a switch near the bedroom door.

Windows. Are there enough to provide sufficient light? Do they provide cross-ventilation? Do they have venetian blinds, shades, drapes, or curtains? Do they work well? Do they interfere with the logical placement of the bed?

View. It's nice to have a view from your bedroom, but let's face it—it's hardly a necessity. After all, most of the time you're in your bedroom, you're unconscious.

Soundproofing. This, on the other hand, is a vital bedroom quality. Does the bedroom abut someone else's livingroom? If so, you're probably in for trouble. Can you hear conversation through the walls? That's also a bad sign.

Access to bathroom. True, the bathroom should be accessible to the livingroom (and, therefore, to your guests). But it's even more important that it be near the bedroom. Ideally, the master bedroom should have its own bathroom.

Radiators and registers. These should work well, and they should not be located so as to interfere with the logical placement of the bed.

Electrical outlets. There should be a reasonable number of these, in good locations. You'll probably want to plug in a bedlamp or two, a clock radio, and on the opposite wall, perhaps a TV set.

Master antenna outlet. Ideally, if your bedroom has one, it should be on the wall opposite the headboard of the bed.

Telephone outlet. This, on the other hand, should be right next to the bed if there is such an outlet in the room.

Kitchen

Size. Apartment kitchens being what they are, you can't really expect much here. The key aspect of kitchen size is usually whether or not a kitchen table and chairs will fit in comfortably. If so, it's a better kitchen than average.

Shape. There's nothing wrong with an L-shaped kitchen, if the L part is a dining nook. But if the shape somehow makes the kitchen more difficult to work in, it should get a lower score.

Convenience. Ideally, kitchens are arranged for maximum convenience, with appliances, tables, and work surfaces arranged to minimize steps.

Refrigerator. What size is it? How about age and condition? Is it reasonably quiet? Does it work well?

Stove and oven. Are they attractive and in good state of repair? Do they have any annoying eccentricities? Are they large enough for your needs?

Dishwasher. If there is one, is it in good condition? Does it work well?

Range hood. If there is one, is it in good working condition?

Microwave oven. Some luxury apartment houses supply them. If the apartment has one, is it in good working condition?

Garbage disposal. This appliance is also found in some apartments. Is it in good working condition?

Trash masher. Another optional kitchen appliance to check out.

Cabinet space. Is it conveniently located? Is there enough to contain your china, glassware, potsand pans, etc.?

Counter space. Is the counter itself in good condition? Is it adequate to your needs, in terms of area and convenience? Is there a backsplash to protect walls?

Lighting. Kitchen lighting should be bright and plentiful.

Windows. Many apartment kitchens don't have any windows, or they have very small ones. Therefore, any kitchen with large windows—especially those with a pleasant view—deserves a high score, as does any kitchen with windows that provide good ventilation.

Electrical outlets. There should be plenty of these—more than enough for all the small appliances you now own or may buy—and they should be conveniently located.

Diningroom

Size. In too many apartments, the diningroom is just an extension of the livingroom. There is no wall dividing them, although the livingroom is sometimes L-shaped, with the smaller part of the L intended for diningroom use. In apartments occupied by single people or married couples, this doesn't present much of a problem. But if there are children, it leads to difficulties, since they can't sit in the livingroom, watching TV for instance, without interfering with adult activities.

Just how big a diningroom you need depends on how much furniture you intend to put in it, how many people you expect to serve there. For the normal four-person family, a room 10x12 feet is usually quite adequate. But your particular circumstances are more important than averages.

Windows. There's definitely something tranquilizing about eating a meal and gazing out the window. And anything that makes dining tranquil is worth having. Therefore, a diningroom with windows, and even a view, is a definite advantage. Cross-ventilation is also a plus.

Registers and radiators. These should not interfere with furniture placement, and of course they should be in good working condition.

Lighting fixtures. There's no substitute for a diningroom ceiling fixture mounted directly above the center of the diningroom table. If an apartment is lacking such a fixture, it should be appropriately penalized in your chart.

Electrical outlets. The main purpose of electrical outlets in a diningroom is for floor lamps, hottrays, coffee machines, etc. It should have an adequate number, in sensible locations.

Bathroom

Size. Most apartment bathrooms are downright tiny. If you find one that's large and comfortable, that's definitely an advantage.

Shape. There's probably no room in an apartment where room shape matters less than it does in a bathroom. And we've seen some odd-shaped bathrooms in our day. But, no matter—so long as you can conveniently use all the facilities.

Appliances. When speaking of bathrooms, this word refers to sinks, tubs, toilets, showers. Are they all in good working order?

Are they attractive and pleasant to use? Are they reasonably modern?

Extras. Fancy bathrooms often have some extras—goodies such as ventilation fans (to prevent moisture buildup), electric ceiling heaters (to keep the chill away) and hampers, to accommodate dirty laundry. These are all conveniences, and the bathroom that has them should get some extra credit.

Lighting fixtures. However dim you may like other rooms to be, from time to time, there's just no substitute for a well-lit bathroom. At the minimum, bathrooms should have a bright ceiling fixture and a well-lit mirror. We generally prefer flourescents, even though they're somewhat harsh.

Medicine chest. Every bathroom should have one, and the larger the better. Make sure that the shelves are sturdy and that the door opens and closes easily, latching positively.

Towel racks. You'll need them—probably beside the sink for hand towels and wash cloths, and on the door for bath towels and bathmats. Of course, if you find a bathroom without a sufficient number of towel racks, that isn't a fatal flaw. You can add what you need. See the chapter on kitchens.

Electrical outlets. Here's one room where a multitude of electrical outlets don't do much good. But you will probably need some near the mirror, if you use an electric razor or a hair dryer.

Linen closet. A bathroom isn't a particularly good place for a linen closet, since it exposes your spare sheets, towels, blankets, and pillows to mildew-producing moisture. On the other hand, better a linen closet in the bathroom than none at all.

If you jot down a letter or numerical grade every time you visit an apartment that seems a good possibility, by the time you're finished checking out all the ads you'll be in a good position to decide which apartment to rent.

Our advice: Study the chart. Look for those apartments that score high in several areas, especially the areas that are most important to you (and only you know which these are). Then get on the phone and let the landlord or rental agent know your intentions. And put down a deposit as quickly as you can.

Of course, you needn't proceed this way at all. Many people have rented apartments—and been perfectly happy in them—in a far less formal way. They've looked until they've found something they really liked, then decided on the spot.

It takes luck to do that, however. And aside from finding some extraordinary bargain, you needn't rely on luck when apartment hunting. The more rational method we've suggested will almost certainly find you the apartment you need and want.

Apartment Scams

In addition to finding the apartment you want and need, however, you must also take care to protect yourself against the many scams or dishonest practices that some dishonest landlords perpetrate. To be sure, most landlords are honest. But if you happen to deal with one who isn't, you can find yourself in serious trouble, unless you're forewarned.

One common rental scam is to take a deposit from several potential renters and refuse to return the money on immaterial grounds—the applicant has given false information, he or she has poor references, he or she has withheld certain requested information.

If this happens to you, see a lawyer immediately. You can't be denied a deposit refund if you do not rent the apartment. You might also consider going to the police, as this landlord action could be a criminal offense.

Another rental scam occurs when a landlord shows you an apartment "identical" to the vacant one which, he says, he cannot show you because it's still occupied, being painted, or being repaired.

The apartment he shows you, of course, is beautiful. And he tells you that yours is exactly the same. So you sign the lease for an apartment you haven't seen. And when you move in, you discover that your apartment is a total wreck. Are you stuck? Maybe not. See a lawyer immediately, before moving in.

Some friends of ours—Gina and Roger—were taken by another, somewhat more sophisticated rental scam. They found what they thought was the perfect apartment. But the landlord had bad news for them—someone else had already put down a deposit on it. But that potential tenant had said he wasn't quite sure he was going to take it.

Roger and Gina asked the landlord if they could talk to the person who'd put down the deposit. The landlord said he was out of town, but told them he'd give them the apartment if they were willing to pay a little more than the $250 monthly rent the apartment had been advertised for.

Of course he told them he'd have to call out of state to reach the other person and probably offer him a few bucks to forget the deal. Gina and Roger agreed to pay $300 in rent and they slipped the landlord another $100 for his trouble and to cover his expenses.

After they moved in, our friends found out that other tenants in the building had exactly the same story to tell. Gina and Roger confronted the landlord, who denied everything. They then consulted an attorney, who told them that there wasn't much that could be done.

A variation on this theme involves a "low ball" ad in the newspaper, for what seems to be a genuine bargain, which turns out to be unavailable when you get there—but another, higher-priced apartment is vacant. Of course, this may not be a scam. The landlord may be telling the truth. But, whatever he tells you or whatever his circumstances, you can avoid trouble by sticking to your budget.

The Long-Distance Renter

By now it should be perfectly clear that you owe it to yourself to see the apartment you rent before you sign the lease. But in certain circumstances that may be impossible, particularly if you're moving to a distant city.

If this is your situation, don't despair. You can get help— reliable, reputable, professional help—in finding the apartment you want, by calling on one of the real estate brokers or apartment-locating agencies that can be found in practically every city in America.

Of course, if you ask one of these outfits to find you an apartment, you won't be able to exercise your own precise judgment on the matter. But if you communicate your needs specifically enough, you have a good chance of satisfaction.

Normally, brokers or apartment locators charge a percentage of the first month's rent for their serivces. They bill either the landlord or you. And this may vary from apartment to apartment, as some landlords are willing to pay to get a reliable tenant and others aren't.

Because the broker is getting a percentage of the rent (sometimes it comes to a full month's rent), you'll find he's naturally more interested in locating a six-room luxury apartment than a studio walkup in "an up-and-coming part of town." This service, then, is more useful for those seeking larger, more expensive apartments, than it is for the bargain hunters.

Some real estate brokers, in addition to whatever apartments they may list, may actually perform managerial services for certain large buildings, serving as combination landlord and agent. If that's the case, you may find yourself signing a lease with the realtor.

Our advice: If you're renting in some distant town, call several realtors or apartment-locating agencies (ask telephone information for some yellow-page listings). That way, you'll have some choices to consider.

If you're moving to a college town, you may be able to find the place you're looking for through the college itself. The larger institutions often have their own housing agencies. These will often provide you with a list of apartments in your category, even if you're not a student. If you're college age or near it, they may also have a list of potential roommates—students looking for someone with whom to share an apartment.

However, agencies such as these may hand out many copies of both lists, so you may find yourself disappointed unless you act quickly. We recommend telephoning the landlords of the apartments that look interesting.

Before you rent an apartment long-distance, no matter who locates it for you, you should talk to the landlord by phone at some length (and you may have to make several calls if there are two or three apartments you're considering).

Before you call, go back to the section on judging apartments, make up a notebook as though you were going to make a personal visit, then get the landlord on the phone and start asking questions.

Go over all the items you'd examine yourself if you could visit in person. By the time you're finished, you should have a pretty good idea what the apartment is like, even if you're a thousand miles away from it.

Obviously, the most important apartment decision you'll ever make is which apartment to rent. And with this chapter's suggestions in mind, you should at least come very close to getting your ideal apartment, if it's available.

But, important as it is, finding the right apartment is only the first step in the process. The next step: signing the lease—not only *a* lease, but the right lease for you.

Chapter 2

LEGAL
MATTERS

Like it or not, when you rent an apartment you automatically involve yourself in the world of law, lawyers, courts—in fact, the entire mechanism society has set up to make sure that people keep their word and treat each other fairly and justly.

By entering into an agreement of any kind with your landlord —long term or short term, oral or written, complicated or simple —you and he become subject to outside authority which, in the event of any serious dispute, can be called in to decide who's right and who's wrong, and require each party to abide by its decision.

This is the world of leases, of security deposits, of—let's hope not—evictions, of housing code violations, of landlord retaliation against complaining tenants, of discrimination, etc.

It is also a world in which each party has rights—and duties. And this chapter is intended to tell you how you can move easily and confidently within this world, knowing what your rights are and how you can protect them, knowing what you can require of your landlord, and he of you.

Through the ages, landlords have often been disliked and sometimes feared, because—at least in the mind of most tenants —landlords are in the driver's seat. They have the power and they know how to use it.

But the fact is, tenants have plenty of power, too. Unfortunately, few of them know its extent, so few exercise it. Perhaps the legal balance is still somewhat tilted in favor of landlords, but the tilt isn't as great as it once was. And tenants are winning more rights every day, as you will see.

Leases

A lease is an agreement between you and your landlord. It's legally binding on both of you—that is, both of you have to do what you say you're going to do (pay monthly rent; provide an apartment) or one of you can take legal action against the other.

Leases can be written or oral. They can be for thirty days or for five years or any longer or shorter period. But, at the minimum, they must include your name and that of your landlord, the address of the premises in question, the amount of rent, and when rent payments are due.

If you and your landlord agree on a month-to-month rental, orally, this means that either you or he can end the agreement on thirty days written notice. It also means that the rent can be raised, at the landlord's whim, from month to month.

If, on the other hand, the two of you have agreed on a longer lease, its provisions must also be followed. And that usually means the landlord won't be able to raise your rent until it's time to sign a new lease—which you can refuse to do, and move out.

But there can be plenty of items in the lease in addition to the basics we've already mentioned. For instance, your landlord may agree to repaint your apartment, or furnish appliances, or repair a leaky roof, or whatever.

And, on the other hand, you may agree to not have pets, not to put up wallpaper, not to have more than a certain number of people living in the apartment, etc.

The lease might also contain clauses concerning subletting, renewal, and many other items.

With an agreement this complicated, the best way to avoid misunderstanding—or to prove what's been agreed to in court, should the need arise—is to get it all in writing.

And, as with any agreement that requires your signature, you should read it carefully—every word of it—before you sign it. Otherwise, you may be putting your name to an agreement that will do you more harm than good.

LEASE PROVISIONS TO AVOID

Some landlords, unfortunately, load up leases with all kinds of objectionable clauses—clauses that can put you at a severe disadvantage should any disagreements crop up.

Here are some examples:

- Clauses that limit the landlord's liability in the event of accidents or damage to the premises not caused by you;
- Clauses that waive your right to legal notices. These give your landlord the power to throw you out, raise your rent, etc., without giving you the legal written notice required in most states;
- Clauses that prohibit you from subletting your apartment;
- Clauses that force you to pay for maintaining and repairing your apartment;
- Clauses that let your landlord enter your apartment whenever he wants, whether or not you consent;
- Clauses that waive your right to defend yourself against eviction proceedings;
- Clauses that permit the landlord to raise your rent during your lease period if his expenses go up;
- Clauses that prohibit you from "illegal conduct" within your apartment;
- Clauses that prohibit you from "defacing" your apartment—and possibly even from hanging pictures.

All of these provisions restrict your rights in one way or another. Some are illegal and aren't recognized in most jurisdictions, even if you sign your name to them (but this varies from state to state). Many can be used as excuses to evict you if you don't abide by them.

On the other hand, many lease forms, especially those the landlord is likely to have on hand, come equipped with one or more of these clauses. What can you do about them?

Well, you can simply refuse to sign a lease that contains such clauses. And you and your landlord, together, can simply cross out the offending provisions, each of you initialling each change.

This, of course, is a matter of negotiation. And negotiating may be easier than you think. All you have to do is ask for something *you'd* like, but you know the landlord is unwilling to provide—new appliances, wall-to-wall carpeting, a new paint job, storm windows, whatever.

And each time your landlord says no, get him to compromise with you, too, by crossing out one of the clauses you don't like.

SECURITY DEPOSITS

Chances are, your landlord will ask you for a security deposit, a refundable payment equivalent to one or two months rent. The purpose of this payment is to cover any damage you might do to the apartment or to substitute for rent owing, should you leave before the end of the lease period.

In some states landlords are forbidden to mix security deposits with their own money. They must put security deposits into a separate account and give you the name of the bank and the account number if you want it. Some states even require that landlords pay interest on security deposits. The amounts vary.

All security deposits are refundable, if you comply with your part of the lease agreement. And in most states, when your lease period has expired and you've moved out, the landlord must submit a list of deductions to you in writing, within a set number of days, if he isn't returning the entire amount.

If the landlord doesn't return your security deposit in its entirety, or return part, along with a written list of deductions, almost all states give you the right to sue your landlord for the balance, in small claims court. Some states even add money penalties. In New Jersey, for instance, you can get twice the amount of the original deposit if the landlord fails to promptly return the money you have coming.

Of course, just because your landlord came up with a list of deductions doesn't mean you have to accept his figure. You can sue for what you think is yours, either in small claims court or in regular court.

Incidentally, both landlords and tenants have some serious misconceptions about security deposits. Many landlords think that they can deduct for ordinary wear and tear—worn carpeting, warped windows, crumbling plaster, etc. Not so. Most courts have ruled that rent itself, plus tax deductions for repair and depreciation, cover these costs.

And many tenants think that they can use their security deposits to pay their last month or two of rent (depending on how much they'd deposited). This isn't true. It defeats the purpose of a security deposit, which is to guarantee the tenant's performance until he's moved out.

Most complaints, problems, and lawsuits involving security

deposits occur when landlord and tenant disagree about whether or not the tenant has in any way damaged the apartment during his or her lease period. Very often, neither has any proof, which makes confrontations that much more unpleasant.

Yet there are several simple ways to avoid such conflicts. One friend of ours, a young photographer we'll call Steve Smith, routinely takes a set of photos of any new apartment he's about to occupy. He prints them up, then has the landlord sign and date them. Only once did a landlord ever try to keep part of Steve's security deposit. And then a quick look at the pictures changed his mind almost immediately.

Other landlords, Steve speculates, are reluctant even to make the attempt, since they remember that the pictures exist and know they have nothing to match them, should the case ever come to court.

But if you're not photographically minded, you can still protect yourself, by going through the apartment carefully with the landlord or superintendent—inspecting and inventorying its condition—before you move in.

If you do this, you should look at all ceilings, floors, walls, etc., at the paint and the plaster, at doors and windows, at locks, at lighting fixtures and other electrical outlets, at any furnishings that are included with the apartment, including kitchen appliances, air conditioners, etc.

And you should also inspect all sinks, bathtubs, faucets, drains, and plumbing; also the kitchen cabinets, the woodwork, the laundry appliances—in fact, everything about the apartment.

Jot down all faults, all the flaws, all the damage—from cracked windows, to water-stained parquet floors, to crumbling plaster. Use your most critical eye. And remember, if you omit anything from your list, you may find yourself paying for it at the end of your lease period, out of your security deposit.

This is a good time, by the way, to get your landlord to promise to make the necessary repairs. Just write up a list, get him to sign it and make copies for both of you.

Once you have a complete list of all prior damage or needed repairs, get your landlord to sign and date it, and keep it in a safe place. If there's any dispute when it comes time to refund your deposit, all you have to do is to produce the list.

GETTING OUT BEFORE YOUR LEASE HAS EXPIRED

Long-term leases—a year or more—have their value, since they usually mean that your rent will remain the same for at least twelve months. And they also make it somewhat harder for your landlord to evict you—but more on that shortly.

On the other hand, long-term leases can be terribly inconvenient—if you get a new job in another town, if you decide you want to buy a house, if you want to move in with someone else, or for any number of other reasons.

Of course, no matter what your lease says, no one can prevent you from moving out. You rent an apartment—you're not imprisoned in it. But, if you vacate without coming to an agreement with your landlord about the balance of the lease, you'll still be liable for all the unpaid rent payments until the lease runs out.

That is, if you move out, say, with three months remaining on your lease, you'll still owe the landlord that rent—even if you move to Bali. And your landlord will have every right to sue you (although if you move to Bali, he may have quite a time collecting).

But there are several things you can do to limit your liability:

You can negotiate with your landlord and arrive at a compromise about your remaining rent payments;

You can sublet the apartment, assuming your lease permits it. This won't relieve you of your legal responsibility for your rent payments, but if you choose your subletter wisely, he'll make the payments, either to you or directly to your landlord.

Of course, some leases prohibit subletting (and this is a key clause to avoid, if there's any way to do it). Many leases require the landlord's consent in writing, but as far as most courts are concerned, he can't unreasonably withhold his consent.

Of course you can't sublet what you don't have. That is, if you find a tenant who wants a year-long lease and you have only seven months remaining on your lease, you can only sublet for seven months. After that, it's up to your (ex) landlord and the new tenant.

If your subletter turns out to be a deadbeat, the problem is yours, not your landlord's. For this reason, it's wise to investigate references and even do a credit check before signing any agreement with the person who'll take over your apartment.

Usually, landlords don't object to subletting, so long as the tenant doesn't present any problems and the rent continues to come in on time.

Another way out is to find, by yourself or in cooperation with your landlord, a new tenant for your apartment—someone who will take on his own lease, beginning on the day yours ends. In this case, you have no further responsibility for the apartment.

If a reliable new tenant can be found, landlords often prefer this solution, since it allows them to write a new lease and perhaps raise the rent at the same time. But sometimes they'll charge you for repainting the apartment—or attempt to. Unless a repainting fee is part of your original lease, don't let your landlord get away with this.

You can also simply vanish in the night. But if you do this, there will be consequences. First, your chances of getting your security deposit back are just about nil. Second, you might be sued for the balance of your rent payments.

On the other hand, leases are contracts, and according to contract law, aggrieved parties (the landlord in this case) must take all reasonable steps to keep their losses to a minimum. That means that the landlord must try to rent the apartment by himself, without delay, and for the same amount you were paying, at least. If he can't do that, or if he can only rent for a shorter period or a lesser amount than your lease provides for, you'll still be liable—but only for the difference.

To keep even that possibility to a minimum, inform your landlord of your plans to move out as soon as you know yourself. Do it in writing and keep a copy of your letter.

These letters, of course, will be useful should your landlord ever choose to take you to court in an effort to recover the rent you haven't paid.

Further, you can leave your apartment without any liability, if it has become unlivable for any reason—lack of heat, water, serious damage from fire or hurricanes, etc., serious violations of the local housing code. But before you take this step, you should check with a lawyer to make sure you're really within your rights.

ALTERATIONS AND DECORATIONS

Let's say that you like your new apartment well enough, but you want to make some changes. You want to put a window seat in the living room. You want to build in some bookcases. You want to install track lighting in the diningroom. You want to put an air conditioner in the wall. You want to make the second bathroom into a darkroom. You want to make your L-shaped livingroom into two rooms, by putting up a wall.

Can you do all of these things? Any of them? Well, it depends. Most leases usually have a clause prohibiting you from making any alterations without the landlord's written consent. If yours is one of these, whether or not you can make the alterations depends on what kind of a person your landlord is.

Usually landlords will let you make alterations if they don't detract from the value of the apartment. And they're quite willing, in most cases, to have you make alterations that make the apartment more valuable. But don't go by your opinion. Get permission. In writing.

Then there's another question: If you alter your apartment by constructing built-in bookcases, for instance, or installing extra kitchen cabinets, can you take these items with you when you move? Or are they the property of your landlord?

Should this matter come before the courts—and it might, if you decide to rip out those bookcases, or if the landlord tells you that they're now his even though you paid for them—the key factor will be: How much damage will be caused to the apartment by taking out the "improvements"?

Generally, if you can leave the apartment in the same condition in which you found it, you can take your alterations with you, should you so desire.

LEASE RENEWALS AND OPTIONS

Usually, when your lease period is over, you either move out of the apartment or you negotiate a new lease with your landlord. There is another way, however:

Your lease can have a provision entitling you to automatically renew, at your option, for another set period—another year or two, for instance. This renewal option might be for the same rent you're now paying, or it might include an automatic increase.

Naturally, you gain by having a same-rent renewal option in your lease. You might even want to bargain for this provision when you sign the lease initially. Whether or not the landlord is willing to give it to you will depend on your bargaining power, of course.

But if your lease runs out, and you have no such option clause, what happens then? Of course, you can leave. And that's that. You find a new apartment.

But what about staying, if you have no renewal clause? That depends on where you live. Some states say that your landlord can evict you without any advance notice. Others say that you are now a month-to-month tenant, according to the provisions of your original lease and that the landlord can't evict you without thirty days notice.

Your landlord, most likely, will want to negotiate a new lease, especially if you've been a good tenant—that is, paid your rent on time and caused no problems. What its terms will be, of course, depends on how badly he wants you to stay and how badly you want to stay.

But in this day and age, a rent increase is practically inevitable.

Getting Evicted

To anyone who rents, there's no more frightening word than "eviction." It brings to mind a jumble of furniture and clothing sitting out on the curb, complete with distraught (ex) tenant, crying, wondering where he or she will spend the next night— and thereafter.

Certainly, the thought, or threat, of eviction is a disturbing one. But you're not powerless against it. You can only be evicted from your apartment for certain reasons and under certain conditions, and not simply at the whim of the landlord alone.

You can be legally evicted from your apartment for three reasons: nonpayment of rent; your lease has expired, or, if you're a month-to-month tenant, after proper written notice (usually thirty days, but state law generally specifies the period); or, "for cause"—that is, if you violate any of the provisions of your lease, break the law, destroy something in your apartment or in the building, ignore "house rules"—dump garbage in the hallways or refuse to lock the front door, etc., disturb the peace and quiet of your neighbors in the building—or commit other similar, serious offenses.

In addition, you can be thrown out of your apartment without any stated reason at all. For instance, if you are a month-to-month tenant your landlord can give you thirty days notice that he intends to repossess the apartment. He doesn't have to say why he wants you out, and the reasons can include anything you can think of, just or unjust. You can also be evicted if your lease has expired but under no conditions can your landlord physically evict you himself. Only a sheriff or constable can do that, and then only after a court has rendered a judgment.

In most jurisdictions your landlord cannot lock you out of your apartment or seize any of your possessions as a substitute for your rent payment. If he does, he's trespassing or stealing. And while the police are reluctant to intervene in such disputes between tenants and landlords, since they're usually considered civil matters, the courts aren't reluctant at all.

Furthermore, if you're threatened with eviction, you don't have to sit back and accept whatever happens. You can defend yourself in court, at the very least substantially delaying the procedure, and depending on the circumstances, perhaps preventing it altogether.

And whatever happens, the landlord can't tell you in the morning that he intends to have you evicted and complete the procedure by nightfall. It takes time—time in which you can come up with the rent payment, defend yourself in court, or, at least, look for a new place to live.

The landlord must give you at least three days notice—often more—of his intention to begin eviction proceedings against you. The shortest periods apply when the eviction is "for cause"— usually between three and seven days, depending on where you live. Written notice is generally required.

After that there are a series of legal steps, each of which takes time. All in all, no matter how quickly the landlord acts, and even if you do nothing at all in response, it will be about three weeks after you get your eviction notice from your landlord that you find yourself sitting on the curb, beside your possessions.

In addition, you can defend yourself in the court proceedings, with or without a lawyer, and even if you don't win, you can considerably delay your departure from the premises.

Let's say, for instance, that your landlord wants to evict you because you haven't paid your rent. You have at least three grounds for defense. First, you *did* pay the rent (in other words,

he's lying). Second, you didn't pay, but you didn't owe it, because your landlord didn't stick to his part of the lease agreement
—by not providing you with a livable apartment, by interfering
with your quiet enjoyment of the apartment, by leaving your
apartment in a dangerous or unhealthy state of disrepair and
forcing you to make your own repairs (this falls under the "repair
and deduct" right, about which more later). And third, you can
respond by paying—and proving you have paid—during the
"notice" period.

If the dispute centers not around the regular rent payment,
but a rent *increase,* you have other defenses. You can argue that
your landlord had illegal motives for raising the rent (if you're
living in a rent-controlled building, for instance), or retaliatory—
his way of punishing you for complaining about inadequate heat,
for example.

If your landlord is evicting you "for cause"—that is, for some
reason other than nonpayment of rent—you have a right to tell
your side of the story in court. The court will then decide which
one of you is telling the truth and rule appropriately.

Even if the court decides in your landlord's favor, your eviction may not take place immediately. If you pay all the rent you
owe, or if you can't find another apartment, you may get a "stay
of eviction"—a delay sometimes lasting several weeks.

You needn't rely on a judge's word for all this. Some states
permit jury trials. And, as we all know from watching soap operas, jury trials are very slow. But there's one catch here: If you
opt for a jury trial, you have to pay all the court costs in advance,
unless you can prove poverty.

If your landlord has started eviction procedures because
you've made problems for him, particularly if you've reported
building or housing code violations to local agencies, or if you've
complained to your landlord about substantial defects in your
apartment, most states have laws that protect you against eviction.

THE FINAL OUTCOME

In the end, the judge (or jury) will make a decision for you or
against you. If the decision is in your favor, you can stay put.
And if the landlord's eviction proceedings were based on "for
cause" reasons, that's that.

If, on the other hand, it was a money dispute between the two of you, the matter still isn't finished. If the apartment had some serious defect that you repaired, and deducted your costs from your rent payment, you'll simply resume paying regular rent, without having to pay the missing amount. In fact, if the repair was expensive enough, the landlord may owe you money, which you may be able to deduct from future rent payments.

If the judgment goes against you, you may now be kicked out of the apartment, and/or you may be forced to pay back rent. And, as with any civil money judgment, the court can "attach, seize, or garnish" your property to pay your debt, if you don't have enough cash. And if *that* isn't enough, the court can order your employer to use part of your salary to pay the judgment.

On the other hand, your landlord—at least in most jurisdictions—cannot himself walk into your apartment and grab something that belongs to you, to settle a money dispute between the two of you.

In any event, if it all comes down to this: some of your property will be exempt—food and clothing (at least certain items), tools of your trade, a certain amount of your wages, social security, and other similar payments.

Incidentally, if you insist, and the judgment is against you, you can be physically evicted (along with your possessions). "All necessary and reasonable force" can be used by the sheriff or constable.

Substandard Housing

The opposite of eviction, in a way, occurs when the landlord fails to meet his obligations to you—when he doesn't provide an apartment that meets the minimum standards of livability.

In fact, thirty-four states (as of this writing) recognize what's called the "warranty of habitability," which, simply stated, holds that you don't have to pay for decent housing if you don't get it. Unfortunately, renters in the rest of the states must pay their rent, whatever condition their apartment is in.

In these laws, decent housing is defined as that which meets state or local housing codes—statutes that establish minimum standards of health and safety.

Specifically, these codes deal with heat, water, electrical service, plumbing, sanitation (garbage collection, vermin, and rodents), etc. They vary greatly from state to state and some cities have their own. But they exist practically everywhere, although they're not strongly enforced in most big cities.

WHEN YOU HAVE A PROBLEM

What should you do when you have a problem with your apartment? What action should you take if you feel your landlord is shortchanging you in the areas of health or safety?

Well, the first step is to contact the health department or the building safety inspection department or some similarly named agency in city hall. Tell them what's wrong, ask for an inspection, find out when it will take place and be there to point out violations.

Normally, if the building inspector finds something wrong, he'll give a report to the landlord, with orders to repair it within a certain time—thirty to sixty days, for example.

Of course, if you report building code violations, your landlord will probably find out about it. And unless he's the highly moral sort, who's pleased to have such defects called to his attention, he's not going to be happy with you. Your actions will cost him money.

As a result, he may try to get even—by trying to evict you, by decreasing services, by increasing your rent, even by locking you out of your apartment or shutting off your utility service.

Twenty-eight states have laws specifically protecting you against this sort of thing. All this is a matter for the courts. Your landlord can definitely cause you problems if you cause him problems, but the alternative is often worse: living in unsafe and unhealthy housing.

OTHER REMEDIES

If your apartment is truly unlivable and your landlord refuses to fix it, you still have some choices:

- You can move out, without notice and without paying any further rent. This is a doctrine of common law and therefore applies to every state. But since it is subject to interpretation, if you do this you'd better be sure that your apartment is actually unlivable. It should lack heat or water or be severely damaged by fire, flood, etc.

• You can fix the apartment yourself and deduct the cost from your rent payments. That's right. This is a legal remedy in twenty-six states. It's called "repair-and-deduct."

What you do is pay your rent not with cash, but with a bill for repairs, plus any amount that may be left over after the repairs have been paid for. You don't even have to go to court to do this. But you may find yourself in court nonetheless, if your landlord decides to attempt eviction as a result of your nonpayment or partial payment of rent. In such a case, the court will listen to your story. And if it decides that you acted properly, or at least honestly, the chances are you'll win the case. But to use the "repair-and-deduct" remedy, you have to give your landlord a reasonable chance to make the repairs before you do. And just how much you can deduct, and on which occasions, is a matter of local law.

• You can withhold rent payments. This is called a "rent strike," or "rent abatement," or "rent withholding." But this only works in states that recognize the warranty of habitability. Rent-withholding procedures vary from state to state and even in some cities. Some places, for instance, require you to deposit the full amount of your rent payment in an escrow account. All places will review the matter in court to make a final determination of what's just and proper. In determining what's fair, courts look at the fair market value of your apartment, as it stands, how much of it you've lost by the landlord's unwillingness to make necessary repairs, and possibly, how much discomfort and inconvenience you've been subjected to.

Rent abatements, by the way, needn't be used to repair your apartment. When the courts grant them, it's more a matter of reducing your rent, of making you pay less because you're getting less.

Incidentally, you might think that if you move into an already substandard apartment, you give up your right to any of these remedies. Not so, according to the courts.

If you're faced with substandard housing—in fact, if you have problems with *any* of the issues raised in this chapter—find out what the law is in your jurisdiction before you do anything. Or consult an attorney.

State and local laws in all areas differ from one another, as does common legal practice and legal interpretation of existing laws. For this reason, look before you leap, or you may wind up in more trouble than you were in when you started.

For these reasons, the information in this chapter, while as accurate as we can make it, should be considered an informal guide rather than firm legal doctrine.

When You Face Discrimination

Let's say that you've found the perfect apartment. It's in the right neighborhood, it's the right size, it satisfies your need in every important way—and you can afford it.

But, let's say, you're black. Or you're a single woman. Or you're a Moslem. Or you were born in Iran. Or your parents were Russian. Or you're pregnant. Or you have a physical disability. Or you're over sixty-five.

Or, let's say, you don't dress very well, or you're a Democrat, or you're on welfare, or you work at a topless bar, or you're blind, or you have children.

In such cases, can a landlord legally refuse to rent you the apartment?

Well, it all depends on which category you fit, on where you live, and on how vigorously you're willing to defend your rights.

There are three sets of antidiscrimination laws in the United States: federal laws, including the Civil Rights Act of 1866 and the Fair Housing Act of 1968, which prohibit discrimination on the basis of race, color, religion, national origin, and gender; state laws, which usually broaden the antidiscrimination provisions of federal laws (currently, thirty-seven states have such laws on the book, but they vary widely as to their provisions); and local laws, which further broaden antidiscrimination provisions.

Generally, state laws prohibit landlords from refusing to rent you an apartment on the basis of your ancestry, your creed, your marital status, your age, the number of children in your family, and any mental or physical disability you have. But the states differ widely, so you'd better check to see if you're covered.

A few states prohibit discrimination on the grounds of pregnancy, source of income, and blindness. And as of this writing, Washington, D.C.—only—prohibits discrimination on the basis of personal appearance, sexual orientation, family responsibility, matriculation, political affiliation (naturally), place of residence, and place of business.

STANDING UP FOR YOUR RIGHTS

Of course, if you can't get the apartment you want, even on the basis of what you're sure is illegal discrimination, you may have a hard time proving it.

But if you think you have a good case, you can pursue it one of two ways. You can complain to the state or federal agency responsible for enforcing the law. This will take time, but it won't cost you anything. And if you win your case, you will get the apartment you want—sometimes plus damages. Or you can go to court, with a private attorney. This is more expensive initially, but sometimes worth it, since you can often collect more money in damages by suing.

In either case, your main problem will be proving that your potential landlord discriminated against you illegally. One of the best ways to do this is to send another prospective tenant to the landlord, someone who is virtually identical to you in every characteristic except the one you think is the cause of the discrimination.

If the landlord takes the bait—if he rents the apartment to the other person—then you have at least the beginnings of a good case against him.

Once more, if you feel you've been discriminated against, we urge you to take the appropriate action against the landlord. Every time someone accepts illegal discrimination without complaint, he's making it harder for the next person who comes along.

But, as with everything else in this chapter, find out the exact provisions of the law in your jurisdiction before you commit yourself to action of any sort. And if you're unsure, consult the appropriate governmental agency, or a private attorney.

Let's assume, however, that your leasing arrangements go well and that you have no legal problems. What's next: moving out of the old place and into the new. And it's trickier than you may think.

Chapter 3

PACKING
AND
MOVING

You've found the right apartment. You've signed your lease. You're all ready. Right? Well, not quite. You must first survive one of life's most dreaded and most common traumas: packing and moving.

Even if your new apartment is an enormous improvement over your present dwelling, it's a shock to the system to pull up your roots, to leave the comfortable and the familiar, to break a hundred established habits, and to settle somewhere else.

This psychological uprooting is at its most disturbing at the very moment of transition, which begins with the moment you begin to close up shop at the old place and ends with the moment that finishes settling in at the new place.

This chapter is designed to make the change as easy as possible, to help you anticipate the difficulties you'll be facing, to guide you through some of the tough decisions that are part of it all, to make sure that you have what you need at all times, and to help you follow the most sensible order of events.

Making Arrangements

Unless your possessions are limited to the clothing you're wearing and a boy scout cookset, you won't be able to move at the drop of a hat. You'll find that you have arrangements to make. You have to set up a series of events. And if everything is to go smoothly, these events will have to take place in a logical order, slowly but inevitably moving you out of your present dwelling into your new abode.

If you do everything right, there'll be no panic, no midnight calls to the fuel-oil company, no frantic searching for junior's school clothing the morning after you've moved, no desperate hunt for a U-haul or moving man.

What's the first step? It's a matter of checking out . . .

THE MOVING DATE

After you sign your new lease, everything you do will depend on your move-in date. So be sure you and your landlord have agreed, not only on the day of the month, but also on the time of day. Call him twice to confirm it. Mention it every time you talk to him, for whatever reason.

Why? Well, if either of you gets confused, you could show up at your new place at midnight only to find it completely dark, no key under the mat, and no one around to meet you.

If this happens to you, you may find yourself pounding on your own front door and on every other front door within sight, then sitting in your car, waiting for a policeman.

When and if a policeman comes, he will probably call the station, which will call your landlord, who will curse, get dressed, come down to identify you, and let you in. He will not be pleased. Neither will the cop.

Sure this couldn't happen to you? Well, it could and did happen to us on one of our moves, all because we hadn't made as clear an agreement with our landlord about our moving date as we'd thought. Don't you do the same.

Be specific not only about date, but about the time you will move in. In writing, tell your landlord that you will be moving in on Thursday, January 15, at 12:00 noon (or whatever). Mail this note to your landlord and call him to make sure he's received it. Call again the day before you leave. And if you're going to be delayed on the road or if there are any other changes for any reason at all, call him as soon as you know about them.

Also make sure that your old landlord knows when you're leaving. Make these arrangements well beforehand and be sure they're clear. Otherwise it's possible that there may be a knock on your door one night and you will open it to find your apartment's next tenant out in the hallway with his wife, his five children, his mother-in-law, and five rooms of furniture.

A few days before you leave, reach an understanding with your previous landlord about your deposit, any extra rent (or refunds), and any outstanding utility bills. Then, on the morning you leave, give him all of your old keys. Keep his name, address, and phone number handy for reference. You never know when you'll forget that junior's trike is in the basement storage room.

Also, give him your new address, so that he can forward your mail or any packages that may arrive for you at the old address. There's no reason for secrecy.

In fact, we make a policy of giving the soon-to-be-former landlord and superintendent small presents. That way, if we need their help for some reason, they're only too willing to give it.

THE METHOD OF MOVING

Don't wait until a week before you're due to occupy your new apartment before you decide if you're going to move everything yourself or get professional help. The time to decide that question is just as soon as you have a definite move-in date. Why? Because if you choose to get a professional mover, you'll have to reserve his services well in advance.

Moving yourself. If you have a generally calm nature and you're a good driver, with a minimum of children and/or pets, a minimum of personal possessions, and a minimal number of heavy objects such as safes, pianos, etc., you should probably look into hiring a truck, van, or trailer so that you can move by yourself. You may save a bundle.

But, if it will take you more than a day to get to your new place, consider the possibility of heavy traffic, the strain on your car from pulling a trailer, lost sleep, cranky kids or spouse, big bridges and little tunnels, stairways, motels, road conditions— and some big-league lifting and carrying. If you think you can handle all of these stresses well, keep reading. If not, skip to the "professional movers" section.

If you have so many possessions that you're considering renting a truck or a van, our advice is to get professional help. You may move successfully, but unless you've done it before, you have no idea how hard it will be.

If you believe that all of your possessions will fit into a trailer in a single trip, or your apartment is so close to your old that you can make a couple of trips with the trailer and finish the job, moving by yourself may make good sense.

But there are other things to consider. For instance, your driving skill and the size of your car. If you're not a confident, competent driver, or you can't get someone who fits that description to do your driving for you, once more we advise you to contact a professional mover. But if you're good behind the wheel, you may be able to handle that part of the job without undue strain.

The size of your car could do you in, however. Tiny cars can't pull big trailers. They're built to carry four people and a couple of pieces of luggage at the most. Ask them to pull a trailer loaded with beds and couches and chairs, plus ten cartons of books, and you're asking for trouble. We know someone who ruined his automatic transmission by doing just this.

When in doubt, consult your local automobile dealer, or the appropriate repair and maintenance manual. You'll probably be all right if you have a standard-sized car or a station wagon. But even if you don't damage your car, be warned that your gas mileage will be much worse than usual.

If, after considering all of this, moving yourself still seems like a good idea, especially in light of today's commercial moving rates, your next step is to consult a trailer rental agent for guidelines on whether or not your stuff will fit into a trailer—and, if so, how big a trailer you'll need.

The object here is to rent the one that's exactly the right size. A too-small trailer that you have to pack like a suitcase to get all of your possessions inside may wind up overloaded, which is both dangerous and illegal, in most states. A too-large trailer could mean shifting cartons, resulting in breakage and damaged furniture.

The trailer's rental price usually includes insurance on the trailer itself, should you have an accident on the road; but the insurance doesn't ordinarily apply to your possessions inside, unless you get a separate insurance policy. These are sometimes available from trailer rental agencies. If yours doesn't offer them, try your insurance agent.

In addition to the trailer itself, you may have to rent a trailer hitch and an outside mirror for the right side of the car (it's required in many states). Consider buying both items. They're useful and they're not too expensive.

Before you leave the rental lot, make sure that the agent hooks up your car brake lights to the brake lights of the trailer. He'll do this by opening your trunk, detaching your brake light wires, and connecting them to the wires leading to the trailer's brake lights. In most states you can't pull a trailer if it hasn't been hooked up this way. And check the connections from time to time to make sure they haven't pulled loose.

If you can, consider renting the trailer for an extra day—a day in advance of your actual move. This will give you time to practice driving with it, and more than enough time to load it.

Before you load, study the driving instructions in the rental agreement. Then practice backing up, pulling out, turning both right and left, and pulling in.

Try this first where there's little traffic, if any. Then, when you're comfortable with your car/trailer combination, practice again in traffic similar to what you expect during the actual move.

Next, study the loading instructions also usually included with the rental agreement. They'll tell you how to distribute the weight and how to pack everything in. Allow at least two hours for packing the trailer if it's small, more if it's large.

Before you make your move, drive your route in someone else's car, if possible, so you'll be thoroughly familiar with road hazards, toll bridges, roads open only to passenger car traffic, etc. If you can't drive the whole route, check with your state highway departments to see if any bridges or roads will be closed to you.

Make sure, on the day of the move, that you have more than enough cash for gas and tolls—and remember that both are likely to cost more than you think. Your normal gas mileage will be down and road tolls will be up.

If you're young, strong, healthy, and have two or three similar friends who are willing to help, you might consider renting a truck and moving yourself this way.

But there are two additional factors to consider: what to do about your own car, and how to drive the truck.

As for the first, you can usually hire someone to drive your car to your new out-of-state location through newspaper want ads. But if you decide to do this, get good references and check them thoroughly. Also, make sure your insurance covers you.

Otherwise, you can have your car shipped by rail, and possibly even by truck. Ask your car dealer about this. If you're moving from New York to New Orleans or from any other seaport to another seaport, you can have your car shipped by boat.

All of this, of course, is another cost to consider and another worry to contend with. Still, it could work out well for you (we know several people who've done such things with great success) and it could save you a lot of money, given the cost of professional movers.

As for driving your rental truck, if you're a good driver and you rent a vehicle with an automatic transmission, you shouldn't have too much trouble. It's just like a car, only bigger.

However, you'll feel better, and probably drive better, if you do some practicing before the actual move. Backing up is particularly tricky in large vehicles. Learn how to use the large outside mirrors. And don't hurry.

Professional movers. If you have too much to move, or you don't feel up to moving yourself, hire a professional moving company. Call them just as soon as you know your moving date and get yourself a reservation.

While you're at it, also get yourself copies of their packing and moving brochures. These are really helpful in getting all of your possessions together and ready for loading on big moving company vans.

As of this writing, rates for interstate moves are regulated and noncompetitive. But that doesn't mean that every mover is equally reliable, skilled, punctual, etc.

If you're moving an entire household from one state to another, you'll want to find the best mover available, even though the prices will be the same.

To do this, we recommend checking out candidate movers through three sources. One is the Interstate Commerce Commission, which regulates movers. They usually have on file statistics showing performance and complaints in regard to each interstate mover. Another is The Better Business Bureau. This is not a Consumer Reports of moving or anything else, since it's an organization *of, for and by* business people. But since they don't want anyone to give business a bad name, they'll steer you away from any real losers among moving companies. And thirdly, check with your friends, relatives, and neighbors.

National moving companies, such as Allied Van Lines, Mayflower, etc., are actually franchise operations, so that the Allied Van Line mover in your town, for instance, may be considerably better (or worse) than other Allied Van Line movers. So check the individual branch and give that information precédence over anything you may hear about the national line.

But no matter how carefully you check, you'll still be at the mercy of a platoon of estimators, loaders, unloaders, drivers, terminal workers, supervisors, and managers.

The only defense is to know exactly what you own. Make a packing list (see packing section, which follows) and make it accurate and complete. And if you're moving valuables or antiques, pay to have them appraised. Take pictures of them and keep the appraisal records.

Watch out for a favorite moving company scam: the cost estimate. The shady outfits attempt to charge for this service. If a mover asks you to pay, politely refuse and call in someone else.

Estimates, when you get one, are just that. They're an effort by the moving company to give you an idea of how much cash —and the operative work is *cash*, since checks won't do—you'll have to come up with when all of your stuff is dropped off at your new place. As this is written, movers charge by *weight*. And while estimators are usually good at their job, they characteristically underestimate. That's something to keep in mind when you cash a check to pay for moving expenses. On the other hand, moving regulations prevent movers from demanding more in cash than a set percentage above the estimate—10 percent as of now (but this may vary).

You can help make sure your estimate is accurate by going through all of your possessions with the estimator. Leave nothing out. And if you have something particularly heavy—boxes of phonograph records or books, for instance—make sure your estimator knows about that.

Few companies actually overcharge you for moving your possessions. But you're the only one who can check up on them. On delivery, make sure that nothing has been added inadvertently (or otherwise) to your bill, such as wardrobes, cartons, moving pads, etc.

Professional interstate movers aren't cheap. It can cost a couple of thousand dollars to move a houseful of furniture across the country, possibly enough for you to consider selling your old stuff, then buying new once you move.

But assuming you want to hang on to what you already own (and chances are, even if you want to sell some items and buy some replacements, you'll still have quite a bit you need to ship), professional movers can get your household across the country a lot faster than you can and probably with less risk. (And you can buy extra insurance on especially valuable pieces.)

Then too, if you choose to move via a professional mover, you won't have to do any of the heavy work, which can be heavy indeed. All you'll have to do is pack. Depending on how much you have, that can be a relatively uncomplicated job or a massive one.

You can pay to have your goods professionally packed. But, since this is an enormously time-consuming process, it's also very expensive. We don't recommend it, unless money is no object— as is sometimes the case if you're being transferred by your company or you or your spouse is a government or military employee and they're picking up the bill.

If you're not moving interstate, you'll find yourself in a fairly competitive marketplace, with many fewer rules and far less consumer protection.

Intrastate movers normally charge by the man-hour. But some may charge by the job. Check out at least three, getting references from them—names and telephone numbers of people they've moved whom you can talk to.

Once you're ready to make a deal, get everything in writing —a firm estimate, the method of payment, insurance and liability, pickup and delivery dates and times. Things can go wrong, and if they do you'll want the protection of a written agreement.

The key to it all: your move-out and move-in dates. They're the first item of business with any professional mover. Movers have only so many trucks and so many men, so reservations will be necessary. Make them as far in advance as you can, and keep checking to make sure there's been no misunderstanding.

But the move-out and move-in dates also put some responsibility on your shoulders. You must be ready—completely ready —when that moving van pulls up to your building.

Being ready includes having a comprehensive list of what you own (yes, from "green plaid Colonial style sofa and chair" to "forty-two-piece silver service for eight, Oneida pattern Moonlight" to "box of assorted toys, including pink stuffed hippo, Parcheesi game, and set of wooden dominoes"). Give the movers one copy of this list—just so they know you've made one out— and keep the other in a safe place.

Being ready also includes clearly marking on every box and carton just which room in your new apartment it should go in. If you're moving into a large place, you'll speed things up by giving your movers a floor plan.

If you're worried about great-grandmother's wedding china, make it clear that you value this and expect it to arrive in one piece. If you know that the bamboo-legged whatnot won't take any rough handling, warn the men who are doing the moving. They'll pad such items well if their fragility is pointed out.

On moving day itself, you have only one job, but it's a crucial one—to make sure that all of your possessions get onto the truck. This won't require anything other than a sharp eye. Don't do *any* lifting or moving yourself. It's not your job. It could even cause insurance complications.

Once the van is fully loaded, you can head for your new apartment. You'll probably get there long before the truck does. Trucks aren't as fast as cars and some highways are off-limits to them. But be at the new place to greet the movers.

At your new apartment, your job is to watch carefully as your possessions come off the truck—counting your boxes, checking everything against your master list, examining all breakables for damage, directing the flow of boxes to the proper rooms (which will save you a lot of work).

If you discover that something is damaged—or missing— after you begin unpacking, call the trucking agent and tell him you're going to file an insurance claim.

He'll send an appraiser or adjuster to your apartment to note and authenticate the loss. If an item is missing, the firm will put out a tracer. Make sure to stipulate a time limit—two weeks to a month, maximum (for interstate moves).

CHANGING YOUR ADDRESS

After you've made arrangements with your mover—hopefully about six weeks in advance of the actual move—your next step is to notify all of your correspondents, charge accounts, magazine subscriptions, etc., that you're moving.

To do this, get a change-of-address kit from your local post office. It will contain postcards you can send to notify everyone of your new address. At the same time, file a change-of-address card with the postmaster, noting the date of your move.

If you live in a large city, file for all the adults in your household, especially if there are differences in last names. If not everyone at your present address is moving, make it clear on the card (there's a box to check) that only you are moving.

The post office asks you to do this a month in advance of your move, but if this is impossible, arrange for someone at your old address to forward anything that goes there by mistake.

Be especially certain to alert the subscription departments of the magazines which you receive by mail. They need a month to six weeks warning. If you wait too long, you'll be getting your magazines late and paying additional postage when they're sent from your old address to your new one.

SWITCHING UTILITIES

If you're paying for your own utilities, have them stop billing you on noon of the day you leave. Some will send a final bill to your new address, others will insist that you pay before you leave. You may be asked to pay an estimated amount, with overpayments refunded and underpayments billed.

When getting new services connected, be leery of deposit requests. Usually telephone, water, and electric companies can't ask you to make a deposit unless you have an outstanding bill.

If any of these utilities refuse you service without a deposit, call the Public Utilities Commission in your state capital. Explain that you have an emergency situation and that you want immediate satisfaction. Usually just threatening to call the state PUC will get action.

For entirely new telephone service, contact the phone company at least two weeks in advance. Know what type of phones you want and where you want them installed. Ask about installation charges, one-time charges, and monthly charges, so you won't get an unpleasant surprise when the first bill arrives.

If you aren't sure what you want, settle for one phone in a central location. That will take care of you temporarily. Also, in some states, you can save money by having your phones installed where the previous tenants had theirs.

It's convenient to have a phone waiting for you when you arrive, but this could lead to misunderstandings and mistakes, unless your landlord or superintendent knows your wishes and is willing to supervise the phone people.

We've found it's usually best to schedule phone installation for the day after you move in. That way, you'll get your phones put exactly where you want them and without imposing on anyone else. The phone installer won't mind all the boxes and general confusion, and he'll only be there for about half an hour.

If you're moving within the same general area, ask the phone company if you can keep your phone and number. This may save a small part of the installation cost.

Make sure, by the way, that the phone company gives out your new number to friends who may call the old one. We suggest that you test this out yourself, by calling your old number now and then. If you get no answer or a busy signal, contact the phone company business office.

Making arrangements with the electric company is easy. You just tell your old company when to stop billing and your new one when to start. The new company will know if any visits to the premises are necessary. Normally they won't be. All you have to do is make sure, when you get your first bill in the new place, that you're not paying for the last part of the previous tenant's stay.

If your first electric bill seems high, call the business office or customer service department of the utility and find out what the billing dates were. (This information might also appear on your bill.) If you're being billed for days before you occupied the apartment, inform the utility. Yes, they'll usually believe you.

In the case of gas and water companies, have the meter read the day you move in, requesting the reading at least two weeks in advance. If your new place uses bottled gas, have the last bottle taken away and a fresh one put in when you move. This is usually standard procedure.

In some states, the LP gas company can request a deposit on the gas container, which will be refunded either when you move, applied towards your bill after a certain period of time, or refunded directly to you if you remain a client for a while.

Packing

We've had this experience more times than we care to remember: We sign our new lease, and return to our old apartment, elated. Then we begin thinking about packing. We look around the house at the incredible number of possessions we've accumulated over the years. Then the despair sets in. How will we be able to get it all together? How will we be able to pack?

We start pecking away at it, getting rid of what we don't need, obtaining the necessary cartons and boxes, determining packing order, imposing an organization on the entire matter, and figuring out what items we'll need as soon as we move in. And, bit by bit, we accomplish the job, finishing up at least twenty-four hours before the move, so that we can have a day to relax before the unpacking begins. In other words, we manage it somehow.

GETTING DOWN TO THE BASICS

If you're even thinking about moving, the first thing to do is to get rid of everything you don't need—throw it out, sell it, give it away, but get rid of it. Our advice: Start early—and be ruthless.

If you've saved newspapers for that "someday" project (refinishing furniture, making a kite, making something out of papier mâché), just bundle them up and toss them out, or drop them off at the recycling depot. Don't look back.

This goes for all other "found" craft objects and all other items with a "someday" value. Make a bonfire or compact them. And if you're a correspondence saver, but have no prospects of historical fame, throw out all old letters that have no sentimental value. Do the same with magazines. And trashy paperbacks. And paper bags. And secondhand gift wrap. Need we go on? Think of the fire hazard you've been living with!

The same goes for old clothes. Donate them, by the bagful, to a church rummage sale or to the Salvation Army. Look, you're no longer a size five. And even if you lose fifteen pounds and shrink two inches, you'd never let yourself be caught dead in that fuschia and yellow striped miniskirt.

Men, listen too. This is the time to get rid of frayed sweaters and socks with holes (who's going to show up to darn them?), madras or Nehru sport coats, Christmas ties or pegged pants. Use this rule of thumb: If you didn't wear it at all during its last full season of the year, chuck it.

Another thing to dispose of is worn-out furniture. If you have some items that are really shot—broken, puppy-chewed, or just plain worn out—this is the time to get rid of them.

This is even a good time to sell or otherwise dispose of furniture you can't stand any longer—items that just don't fit your personality or lifestyle (if they ever did).

Let's say, for instance, that you bought that neat Colonial plaid livingroom set, just like his Mom's, when you were married six years ago, when you were just out of school and convinced that American eagles were the ideal wall decoration.

Since then, you've befriended a woman who has a fantastic job selecting upholstery fabrics in Scandinavia. She's shown you her collection of original Bauhaus designs and you've loved them.

And since you bought your livingroom set, you've also changed your hairdo, your skirt length, your favorite color, and your perfume. You don't buy wine with screw tops anymore and your husband has learned how to eat with an oyster fork without wincing.

What better time than now to get rid of that old livingroom set. It's easier to dump than bad company and cheaper to part with than an ex-spouse. Try the secondhand furniture store, the classified ads, the Salvation Army—or a tag sale. Or give it to a friend or relative.

(By the way, we have a friend named Harry who sells all of his throwaways at tag or garage sales, but never holds one of his own. He looks for ads in the newspaper, then calls those holding the sale to ask if he can add his stuff to theirs. They're usually delighted, because they want to have the maximum amount of merchandise possible to attract customers.)

Don't get rid of anything truly useful, however, unless you intend to replace it right away. We've kept an ugly piece of steel porch furniture through six different moves. We're not exactly in love with it, but it does its job. And it's indestructible.

Actually, you don't have to take any furniture with you at all when you move. We know one young couple who move this way. They're free of family responsibility and young enough not to mind frequent job changes, so they move quite frequently.

And each time they move, they build or buy secondhand any furniture they need, and they have a large moving sale when they're ready to move on. Their homebuilts usually make them a profit, since they sell for about as much as good secondhand furniture.

There are two main advantages to doing things this way: it saves on moving costs (and packing), and it lets this couple buy just what each apartment calls for, freeing them from yesterday's choices and yesterday's styles and fashions.

On the other hand, most people buy wisely and get at least

somewhat attached to their possessions. If you're this sort, you'll want to bring your furnishings with you when you move to a new apartment. But your furnishings won't be all you're bringing. There are books, clothing, mementos, hobby equipment, collections . . . well, the list goes on forever.

And how do you pack all of this stuff? You pack it in . . .

THE ALMIGHTY CARTON

Ours is a highly mobile society. We move on the average of once every four years. But it's hard to see how we could do this if not for a lowly invention called the cardboard box or the carton.

If you have any sizable number of possessions at all, you'll need plenty of boxes and cartons to hold them. But don't panic. There are many places to find them free. And if you have to, they're easy to buy.

We are convinced that the sturdiest cardboard boxes come from the liquor store. Most of these come with cardboard partitions, which makes them perfect for glassware.

But liquor store boxes are in strong demand, for just the reasons we've mentioned. That means you'd better call the liquor store at least a week in advance and ask them to set some aside for you.

If the store isn't anxious to make such arrangements, ask when they expect to be unpacking their next large shipment, and show up at that time.

Some liquor stores charge a small fee for each box, to cover the time they spend handling them—anywhere from a nickel to fifty cents. But if you're shipping some items, or moving very far, or planning to store part of your gear for a while, they're worth it.

By the way, if you're getting your boxes from a liquor store, make sure the tops haven't been cut off. You can't stack a box if it doesn't have a top.

Another good place to get cartons is the grocery store. Grocery store cartons usually aren't as thick-walled as liquor or wine-bottle cartons, but they're more plentiful. Sizes vary a great deal. And you can get anything from the flimsy boxes bathroom tissues are shipped in, to thick-sided bottle and jar boxes.

Like liquor stores, grocery stores sometimes cut off the tops of their boxes. Don't take any of these. In fact, ask the manager which boxes you can have. Some stores have special days when they give boxes away, or a special location for getting them, behind the store. Call first and ask.

If you don't mind paying for boxes, the five-and-dime store has cardboard chests in decorative colors. These are best for clothes and linens. But beware: The weak, corrugated kind usually collapse when you try to fit the cover on and tape it shut.

On the other hand, the heavier, more expensive paperboard boxes last quite a while. Some are even designed to use as furniture of a sort. You can save these for storage in your new apartment.

You can also buy boxes from a commercial box manufacturer or wholesaler. Practically every city of fifty thousand people or more has a box outlet of this sort. They offer a wide variety of box sizes and weights. But they usually sell boxes in packages of ten or more.

Even if you aren't using a professional mover, you can frequently buy packing cartons from your nearest freight terminal. These are quite sturdy and can be collapsed for reuse.

This is the place to get uniform-sized specialty boxes, including such luxuries as wardrobe boxes. These allow you to pack your closet without taking items off their hangers. That means less wrinkling and much greater convenience, especially if you have to start to work as soon as you get to your new location.

The terminals also have glassware and book boxes available. Both are reusable. One couple we know, by the way, moved their books, including several categories of reference and collectors' editions, in special book boxes.

They then found these boxes fit perfectly on industrial-style steel shelving, and they now use them to store back issues of their professional magazines, as well as equipment for their hobbies and their work. The boxes have held up beautifully over the years, despite hard use.

PACKING ORDER

So you collect all of your boxes—more than you need, you think—and you bring them home and spread them out on the livingroom floor. Then you look at them, and at your possessions, and you choke back a scream.

Where did I get all this junk? you ask yourself. What am I

going to do with it in my new apartment? How do I start packing it? Well, we can't help you much with the first two questions, at least not here. But we can offer some help with the third.

Like so many other things in this world, successful and sensible packing is a matter of logic. Over the years, we've developed a system that works well, at least for us. We'd like to share our packing order with you now:

Storage closets and other storage areas. These are the items you're not using right now. Sort them out and pack them by category—household goods, mementos, sporting equipment, etc. With luck, it's probably pretty much categorized in boxes already, so it won't take long to sort.

Items you know you can live without for a while. Books, records, knickknacks, and pictures fall in this category. But don't pack books or records in large boxes. They can get very heavy. Records, by the way, should be tightly packed to avoid warping.

Stereo and other electric appliances. If you own an expensive component system, it probably came in a sturdy box lined with fitted pieces of foam. That's where you should put it now. What? You say you threw it out? Okay, then get another one. Try the hi-fi shops—they might have an extra. If not, buy the proper-sized box at the freight terminal and get some foam to line it.

This advice goes not only for stereos, but also for toasters, toaster ovens, radios, clock radios, mixers, electric can openers, waffle irons, coffee makers, hotplates, record players, even television sets. But you probably won't want to pack your TV set, coffee maker, or clock radio until the day of departure.

And if you have a large, heavy, color TV set, you'll probably want it treated like your other furniture—taken aboard the truck unboxed, then wrapped in heavy moving pads, and packed in a corner where it can't shift or bump into something.

Mirrors and large pictures. The best way to pack these is in special mirror/picture boxes. You can get them from the moving company. Each item should be wrapped in protective padding before being put into a box.

Pictures shouldn't be stacked on top of each other in a box. Their frames may warp, the glass may crack, or the image may be scratched. Take care.

Out-of-season clothing. Now that your shelves are stripped bare, pack the out-of-season clothing that hangs in your closet. Use large, flat boxes. Ditto for those extra linens, towels, and blankets. If you're not moving too far, you can tuck small, not-too-delicate knickknacks between the layers. But remember they're there when unpacking.

Cookware. As your moving date gets close—within a week or so—pack your cookware. This can become heavy, so pack it in small boxes, padding between each dish so that you don't get stains from ironware, chips in your enamel, or cracks in your glassware or ceramics. Then nest what will nest. Wrap lids to keep them from rattling.

Storage containers can be packed now, too. We occasionally use them as packing material, if we're able to wedge them in place without seriously warping them.

As for tableware, wrap it in sheets of newspaper, in groups of four, then tape closed. Some people tape knife blades, so they won't accidently cut themselves when unpacking.

Your best china should go into its own special box, the one that it came in or a new one bought from a supplier. Crystal needs to be wrapped in tissue paper and set carefully in padded, partitioned boxes.

And be sure to mark "fragile" in big red letters on all sides of every box that contains breakables of any kind. Also, clearly mark which side goes up. This will greatly reduce the risk of breakage. Contrary to popular myth, moving men don't single out such boxes for use in touch football games, etc. They don't *want* to break anything.

Your everyday clothing. Finally, pack what you wear every day. You can pack some items in your suitcases, others in boxes—the last boxes to be loaded onto the truck.

We suggest that you put your shoes in plastic bread wrappers and sort underwear and socks or stockings in plastic bags, then put the bags into cartons. Your bed linens can be packed along with your clothes, so they'll be easy to find.

PACKING FOR INSTANT OCCUPATION

Of course, you don't want to pack *everything.* If you do, you'll have to unpack everything before you can find anything. Ideally, you want to take a few items with you in the car to provide for your immediate needs—to keep you going for, say, three days. This will give you time to settle in and it will make unpacking a bit less frantic.

The following list will help you plan what to keep out and

take·with you. Most of it comes to us from a friend whose husband went to college in one town, medical school in another town, interned two thousand miles away, and then joined the Air Force.

After that, he served a second residency in his specialty three states from his last Air Force base. Of course he didn't stay there. He and his wife have moved twice since he set up private practice near us.

Lis can industriously pack a four-room apartment in about three hours. Once she helped us, even managing to pack up a box of old clothing and newspapers we'd intended to throw away. Thanks, Lis. At any rate, here's Lis's list:

Personal needs. Set aside a suitcase for each member of the family. In it, pack their toilet gear, hairbrush and comb, soap, washcloth, towel, shampoo, deodorant, toothbrush, toothpaste, shaving kit, cologne, makeup, aspirin, antacid, antihistamine/decongestant, tampons, unopened box of tissues, and any personal medications. A collapsible tumbler can go into your pocket or the car's glove compartment.

(If you have several small children, you can group their belongings together in one large suitcase. We've had better luck keeping each child's personal needs separate, however.)

Clothing. Also pack into each suitcase enough clothing for three days, if the moving trip itself is scheduled for one day. If you're moving cross-country, add an additional day's clothing for each day you expect to spend on the road.

When packing, remember slippers, socks, comfortable shirts, sweaters, slacks, and underwear (it's wise to take an extra, in case you're delayed). Keep outer clothing to a minimum. And don't forget nightwear if you're bunking with friends on the road.

Sleeping gear. Carry sleeping bags or blankets with you because there's a very good chance you'll be spending at least one night on the floor, unless you bribe your moving men to set up your bed for you. And even then, you'll need bedding of some sort.

If you're flying, you can check your sleeping bag like luggage. But put it in a rip-proof nylon case and tag it well, inside and out. Tag any luggage that will go by plane.

Kitchenware. Get a large, closable cardboard box or two for your kitchen goods. The first item you should put in is a frying pan, preferably one with a detachable handle or one that's oven-proof. A medium-sized saucepan should go with it. (Or, better yet, pack a nesting camping cookset, if you have one.)

Other kitchen items to have with you: a spatula, a stirring spoon, some paper plates and cups, some napkins, forks, knives, spoons, and a medium-sized kitchen knife.

Also pack the following foodstuffs: packaged soup, crackers, coffee (instant), sugar, powdered or canned milk, cookies, soda, fruit, well-wrapped bread, peanut butter, jelly. Also pack some aluminum foil and, if appropriate, an ashtray. Take this food in your car because you never know if you'll be able to find an open grocery store when you arrive at your new apartment, especially if you arrive at midnight or on a Sunday.

Other kitchem items you might take (although they're not essential) include a teakettle, your favorite teas, canned gourmet foods—grouse, truffles, antipasto, artichoke hearts, baba au rhum, fat candles, split of champagne, plastic champagne glasses.

No, we're not crazy. We just think you might want to celebrate your move, either with your spouse or an interesting friend or neighbor. And with what we've suggested, all you have to do is chill everything (no, not the tea and the candles), drain well and serve a romantic cold supper by candlelight. After what you've just done, you deserve something special.

Papers and documents. Get a large manila envelope, put your name and address on it in at least two places, and mark it "important." Then stuff it with the following:

A copy of your lease, rent and deposit receipts, some form of personal ID (although your driver's license will doubtless be enough), your landlord's address and phone number (or the superintendent's), copies of the agreement you have with your movers or the trailer leasing agency, a road map with complete directions to your new apartment, and the emergency number for police at your new location.

Also, take along two essential books: your old phone book, which will be invaluable to you when you have to reach your last employer, your old drugstore, your former doctor or any utility company you did business with, and your new phone book. Write ahead to the new phone company and get one. You'll need it when you want a drugstore, a locksmith, a doctor, the emergency room, the number of your mother's college roommate, a vet, or a hardware store.

Tape to the inside of this envelope the keys to your new apartment (if you have them) and several dimes for calling your landlord, superintendent, or the nearest motel, in case all else fails when you get there.

All of these items should be put into your car. Hopefully, the trunk will hold most of them. That way, your moving men will be dealing only with the boxes you've packed for later use.

Of course, you will have to deal with those packed boxes yourself eventually. You'll want all of your possessions to be easily accessible. You'll want to be able to find your mixer when you need it, or your raincoat, or little Charlie's blocks. You won't want to rummage around through fifty different boxes. All of this leads us to

PACKING ORGANIZATION

It's a fairly simple matter to mark your packing boxes in such a way that you can quickly find what you need, no matter which box it's in. Here's how we do it:

First, as you pack each box, use a marking pen to list on the outside what you've put inside. Since you never know which way the carton might be stacked at its final destination, we advise you to mark the contents on all sides, if possible, and on the top.

But even this technique doesn't always work. We have a close friend, May Chan-Ellis, who moved just before Christmas. Her mother, who had emigrated from China and doesn't speak or write English, helped her pack. May doesn't read Chinese.

When she started to unpack in her new apartment, she found that all of her boxes were marked, all right, but some in a language neither she nor her husband could understand. It was past New Year's Day by the time they found all of their carefully wrapped and decorated Christmas gifts.

After you've noted their contents, number each box, keeping a list of the numbered boxes and their contents. Give one copy to the moving men and keep the other. It's the best way we know of assuring yourself that everything has arrived in your new apartment.

Next, mark the room destination on each box. This way, your kitchen won't wind up in the livingroom and the tax records won't wind up in the bathroom.

Next, add to your master list the destination of each box.

Now, once the move is complete, to find where something is, all you'll have to do is consult your master list. It will tell you what room and what numbered box to look in. So when the kids start crying for their favorite toy or your spouse is angrily searching for a fresh towel, you'll be able to locate the desired items in a flash.

Your First Night

It's been a long drive, but you've finally arrived. You've had to wait a bit for the moving van, but now it's unpacked—and gone. You're sitting on top of a pile of boxes, wondering just what's happened. It's a confusing moment. What do you do now?

The chances are, you're feeling sticky and grimy and a little out of sorts after the ride and the tension of seeing your possessions moved in and out, etc. Your spouse and children, if any, no doubt feel the same way.

What you all need is refreshment. And there's no surer refreshment, we think, than a bath, shower, or general cleaning up. Take your bath or shower, then give your spouse a chance to do the same. Then scrub up the kids. They may protest, but they'll feel better.

After you've dried yourself off and gotten into fresh clothing, it will probably be time to start looking for something to eat. We recommend that you don't try to prepare anything—not on this first night.

Instead, take the brood (if you've got one) out to the nearest fast-food place. Or, at least, order in a pizza. If your children are older, or if you're alone, or if it's just you and your spouse, this might be the time to splurge a little on a better restaurant. Check the local newspaper or ask a neighbor.

If it's too late for a restaurant, get out your emergency supply of traveling food and let the kids eat what they will—peanut butter, cold cereal, soup, or a whole meal of cookies and milk. Just once won't hurt, and it will calm some frayed tempers. Or order in Chinese food. Or pick up some frozen dinners.

If the children are excited and wild—running around, trying all the faucets, doors, and appliances, and arguing about whose room is whose—distract them with food. Then, once the meal has been eaten, firmly insist on bed, even if bed is nothing more than a sleeping bag. If they're still vibrating, pull out some books and let them read in their rooms until they fall asleep. It won't be long.

Babies have no trouble adapting to new surroundings, but like older children, they're often frustrated by long car trips—and comforted by familiar toys and blankets. So make sure these are available, if you're traveling with an infant.

Animals can be worse than kids, especially cats, who are creatures of definite territories and habits. They're best left with a friend, or even boarded for a few days, until the furniture is in place.

If you can't do this, put out food and water for your pet as soon as you get to the new place. Then put his bed and his toys in plain sight.

Cats will often find a dark corner to hide in. We had one who got behind the toilet and almost couldn't get out. So it's sometimes best to keep them in their carriers until you're ready for them, until you've set up their litter, a bowl of water, and a little food.

Most dogs will get excited and nervous in their new surroundings. They'll sniff the entire apartment the minute they set foot in it. They may have "accidents" simply because they're in unfamiliar territory and they're not sure if the same rules apply.

The best way to handle dogs, we've found, is to walk them hourly on their first day in the new apartment. That familiar routine will greatly reassure them and they'll get a chance to look the neighborhood over and sniff out other dogs.

Also make sure your dog has his food, water, bed, and favorite toys handy. Show him where to sleep and what's off-limits (climbing over the boxes, for instance).

During the next couple of days, don't occupy yourself entirely with Herculean efforts to unpack and set up your household. Spend half a day at a time on that project and the other half day exploring the neighborhood.

Keep in mind that you have to acclimate yourself not only to the new apartment you've moved into, but also to the new building, the new mail box, the new neighborhood, the new parking place, the new stores, the new route to work, perhaps even the new city and the new state.

Our advice: Don't try to do any of this all at once. Explore. Discover it all a bit at a time. Savor the surprises. Enjoy yourself.

Whatever your reasons for moving, you've changed your environment and your life. There's no better time to look around the world and to let yourself experience its scents, sounds, and sights.

Chapter 4

FURNISHING
YOUR
APARTMENT

Furniture. Without it, an apartment is an empty shell—good for keeping you out of the rain, but little else. Furniture makes an apartment livable. It makes it come alive. It gives it a personality.

This chapter is primarily intended for those who own little or no furniture, those who must pretty much start from scratch, with the aim of winding up with an apartment that has all the comforts of home.

Therefore those who already own a reasonably complete set of furniture—those who are moving from one apartment to another, or out of a home into an apartment—can skim the pages that follow, taking from them whatever information they might need.

The same goes for those who are renting a furnished apartment. Furnished apartments are getting less common these days, but they're still useful to those looking for very temporary quarters or those who haven't the capital or the inclination to invest in furniture. Of course you have to live with someone else's taste —or nontaste—but sometimes that's not so bad.

Let's say you're in the market for an apartmentful of furniture. Chances are, if you've given this even a few moments thought, you know how complex a subject furniture can be.

There's the question of style, for example, and the matters of fabric and woods. There are a bewildering variety of sizes and types and constructions of tables, chairs, upholstered pieces, and practically everything else. And then there's the question of where to buy it. There are dozens of different places to buy furniture, ranging from your local discount store to Park Avenue auctions. Where are you most likely to find the furniture you want? Or should you try to build it yourself?

No single chapter in any book can aspire to making those who read it experts on the subject of furniture. However, we hope here to give you a basis for understanding your many different options, so that you can go about the process of selecting furniture with intelligence and a certain amount of confidence.

Furniture Styles, Woods, and Fabrics

Before we start going through your bare apartment, room by room, to give you some idea of your furniture choices, we'd like to start off by giving you a quick, basic grounding in furniture styles, woods, and fabrics—information that will apply to all else in this chapter.

FURNITURE STYLES

Over the centuries, furniture designers have created literally hundreds of different styles, reflecting their own personalities, reflecting the dominant stylistic influences of their era, or in reaction to traditional designs.

Today, depending on how energetically you're willing to search, you can find examples of practically every one of these furniture styles. Or, at the least, you can find pictures in furniture encyclopedias and, if you like what you see, have the item built for you, or build it yourself.

However, of all the styles created over the centuries, only a few remain popular and easily available today. We'll concentrate on these:

Contemporary. This is a catchall word—and a catchall style. It can be used to describe most of the furniture made in the last fifteen years or so, and most of that being made today.

Generally, contemporary upholstered furniture—couches, chairs, sectionals and the like—has simple, uncluttered lines, large loose pillows, and a generally informal look.

The fabrics used on such pieces are generally "tweedy" in appearance, with colors ranging from earth tones to muted blues and browns. Leathers, suedes, and imitation leathers are also frequently used on this style.

Most large upholstered pieces have no wood showing, but some have visible frames—usually of oak, walnut, or teak. Stainless steel frames are also not uncommon. Urethane-foam-filled cushions are common.

Contemporary case goods—dressers, chests of drawers, etc. —are also rather simple in design and "clean-looking." Many designs are derivative of the Scandinavian furniture of the 1950s and 1960s or of eighteenth century American Shaker furniture.

From a stylistic point of view, contemporary furniture is not particularly distinguished, although there are exceptions—items sold by the Roche-Bobois chain, for example.

On the positive side, however, contemporary upholstered goods are usually comfortable and easy to care for, while contemporary case goods are sturdy and functional. And unless the items are the products of a famous design house or designer, they're likely to be moderately priced.

Modern. When applied to furniture, this word is thrown around quite carelessly. In fact, it's been used so many different ways that it's hard to say which is actually correct.

We use the word "modern," however, to refer to classic twentieth century designs. Most of these were either the product of or were inspired by the Bauhaus design school, which flourished in Germany in the 1920s. This school emphasized mass producibility and low cost. It created designs of classic simplicity, many of which are more popular today than when they first appeared.

Among these are such famous designs as the Barcelona chair, the Eames chair, and designs by such architects as Le Corbusier and Mies van der Rohe.

Not surprisingly, these designs often rely on chrome or stainless steel frames, or bent rosewood, with leather covers. Tables are often glass with metal bases. Molded plastic is also used.

The original designs, manufactured by Herman Miller, Knoll, and other high-quality factories, are very expensive. But they've been reproduced by many other manufacturers. The quality usually isn't quite as high, but the prices are much lower.

At a certain indistinguishable point, contemporary and modern furniture join—which is, indeed, fitting, since modern is the major inspiration for contemporary furniture.

Scandinavian. This is the third member of the same general family. It was inspired by Bauhaus design and it, in turn, was influential in the creation of most of today's contemporary designs.

The key word describing Scandinavian (sometimes called Danish modern) furniture is simplicity. There is little complexity, except in interior construction (and even this is rare), and little or no decoration.

The chief decorative elements are textures—the texture of wood, chiefly oiled teak or walnut; the texture of fabric, chiefly hard, flatwoven wools or synthetics.

Scandinavian furniture is still popular and still available in many retail outlets. In fact, it has apparently attained classic status. It is handsome, functional and not terribly expensive.

Shaker. Another family of simple, functional furniture is that designed and built by the American Shakers in the last quarter of the eighteenth century.

The Shakers, a religious group dedicated to communal living and asceticism, created furniture that reflected their conviction that making something was, in itself, a prayerful act, and that form should follow function.

Most Shaker furniture was built of pine or other inexpensive local woods. Chairs sometimes had seats woven of cane or rattan, but fabrics and cushions were rarely used.

Shaker furniture is no longer manufactured, at least by Shakers. It can be found at antique shops or at antique auctions—at prices reflecting its rarity. However, a number of contemporary furniture makers are imitating Shaker designs, or interpreting them. These items are available at reasonable prices, and they mix well with either contemporary or modern pieces.

Period furniture. This is another catchall term. It simply means that the furniture is designed in the style of a certain historical period (and if it's an antique it may even have been made at that time). As it happens, there are more periods than you can shake a stick at.

All of this is intended as a brief introduction to the subject of furniture styles, about which many a book has been written. If you're seriously interested in the subject, we recommend that you spend some time at your local library, in the interior decoration section.

Meanwhile, we hope this will give you at least an idea of what it's all about. But remember, there are at least five times as many styles as we've mentioned here.

WOODS

Furniture has always been made of wood. The vast majority still is, although plastic and metal are gaining. And we think that as long as there's enough wood to do the job, furniture will always be made of wood.

But there are literally hundreds of woods available to furniture makers, whether they're skilled cabinetmakers or commercial furniture factories. And each of these woods has its own characteristics—its own assets and liabilities.

Today, however, there are about a score of woods commonly used in furniture. Here's a brief description of the most important:

Birch. This is a family of woods, rather than a single type of tree. The white and sap birches are soft, while the red, black, and yellow varieties are hard. The harder varieties are strong, work well and polish well—often being used to imitate mahogany and walnut.

Cedar. A fragrant red wood often used to line storage chests for linen and bedding. It protects against moths.

Cherry. A hard, fine-grained, red-brown wood, usually highly polished when used in furniture. Strong, light, and beautiful—and not inexpensive.

Ebony. A heavy, dense, and dark (often black) tropical wood. Usually highly polished when used in furniture. Expensive.

Elm. Dying out in the United States, because of Dutch Elm disease. But because of its rather odd grain it makes beautiful furniture. It's light brown, with a texture similar to oak.

Fir. Too soft and sticky for exterior furniture surfaces, but often used in structural parts.

Fruitwood. This term refers to wood from pear, apple, and cherry trees. The wood is usually hard and it takes a good polish. It is often used in small tables and decorative pieces.

Hickory. A very tough wood, especially useful where strength and thinness are required, or for bent parts.

Knotty pine. A soft, yellowish wood with prominent dark knots, often found in casual furniture, such as that intended for dens. Sometimes used in contemporary "Colonial" furniture. Also found in unpainted furniture. Not very durable—but not very expensive.

Mahogany. A strong, red-brown wood of medium hardness, with a very fine grain. Usually highly polished when used in furniture. A beautiful wood, usually found in formal furniture. Fairly expensive.

Maple. This is a family of woods, ranging from very hard to medium hard, even soft, and from white to yellow-brown in color. It's often found with interesting grain patterns: curly, bird's-eye, etc.

In commercial furniture, especially "Colonial" styles, maple is often stained or glazed to a reddish color. But its natural color is beautiful also.

Oak. A very durable hardwood often seen in late Victorian furniture (from the late 1800s and early 1900s). Whitish-yellow in color.

Philippine mahogany. Not a true mahogany, but similar in appearance (texture, grain, and color). An excellent furniture wood, but not inexpensive.

Pine. A fairly inexpensive soft, white or yellowish wood often used in simple country furniture. Easily worked, easily stained, but not terribly durable—subject to scratching and gouging if not treated carefully.

Plywood. Several thin sheets of wood glued together, with their grains at right angles. Stronger and less likely to warp than solid woods (something to keep in mind when you're offered solid maple, mahogany, walnut, etc.). Often veneered—covered with a thin sheet—of fine surface wood. Various woods are used internally.

Redwood. Too soft for most furniture construction, this reddish wood is most frequently seen in outdoor furniture—picnic tables, benches, etc.

Rosewood. This is a deep red-brown wood, capable of taking on a rich finish, either oiled or polished. It's heavy, dense, and strong. It was used in fine European furniture in the eighteenth century and later on in America. Today, it's one of the popular woods for contemporary furniture.

Teak. Another family of woods, ranging in color from medium brown to light brown, with straight, open grains. Teaks are very resistant to moisture and decay, so they're often used for yacht or sailboat decks and fittings. Light-colored teak is also commonly used in Scandinavian modern furniture.

Walnut. One of the most popular furniture woods of all time. Strong without being heavy, easy to work, takes a fine polish. Available in many colors, textures, and grains. Even now, oiled walnut is often used in contemporary furniture designs.

PLASTICS AND METALS

In addition to wood, furniture is also made of plastic and metal—and both of these deserve a few comments:

Plastic   Various types of plastic are now being used in furniture-making, in a number of different ways:

- Laminated plastics. This is the stuff of kitchen counters. It's also the stuff of case goods and tables, in designs and textures that closely resemble wood, and in bright colors and geometric patterns that make no attempt to disguise the underlying material.
- Molded plastics. In some "heavily carved" case goods—bedroom suites are a good example—the carvings, although they have the look of wood, aren't wood at all, but molded plastic. Unless you're the suspicious type, however, you'll have a hard time realizing that the material isn't wood.
- Formed and shaped plastics. These are often used in the inner shells of Scandinavian modern chairs and couches, sometimes with fiberglass reinforcement. They last forever.
- Plastic piping. Lately, we've seen a surge of upholstered goods—chairs and couches—with visible frames of plastic piping. They're held together with webbing, which provides a foundation for pillows and cushions. Plastic piping is sturdy enough and even attractive, in an industrial way. It's altogether suitable for dens and playrooms. Some casual tables now on the market use the same construction.

Metal   Like plastic, various forms of metal are fairly common in furniture construction, especially in chairs, couches, tables, and lawn furniture. It's a feature of some modern and contemporary items.

Metal has its advantages. It lasts forever. It's usually quite handsome. It gives the furniture heft (except in the case of lawn furniture, where lack of heft can be annoying).

On the other hand, metal can corrode, it can be dented, and it can scratch. Wrought iron can even rust, if not properly painted. Similarly, the chrome on the chrome-plated tubing common to kitchen tables and chairs can peel, irreparably.

For these reasons, you should be cautious about considering metal-frame furniture, especially if you plan to give it the sort of use likely to damage it, since it won't be easy to fix.

FURNITURE COVERINGS AND PADDING

Practically any kind of fabric you can imagine—and probably some you wouldn't dream of—have been used to cover upholstered furniture. The same goes for leathers, furs, and plastics.

Each of these coverings has its specific use and its specific advantages and disadvantages. What follows is a listing of some common upholstered furniture coverings, plus a brief description of their characteristics:

Batik. This is usually figured fabric, made by means of successive dyeings or paintings. It's based on a centuries-old Javanese process.

Brocade. This textile has a woven pattern of raised figures, not unlike embroidery. It has a rich and luxurious feel to it and is widely used in furniture of ornate design.

Brocatelle. This is another heavy fabric, with woven patterns that give the impression of being embossed. It's usually made out of silk.

Burlap. In common usage today, this refers to a flat, rough, fuzzy open-weave fabric usually made of jute, the same fiber used to produce twine and other rope products. It's often used on modern and contemporary furniture. Burlap wears quite well, but some people find it unpleasantly rough to the touch.

Canvas. This is a tough, tightly woven fabric, usually woven of cotton, flax, or jute, usually in at least two plies, with either plain or fancy texture. A flat fabric, it wears well and easily withstands the abuse of normal wear and tear.

Damask. This richly figured, silk fabric originated in what is now Syria, sometime around 1,000 A.D. It was discovered by Europeans in the Middle Ages and quickly spread through the Western world.

Embroidery. This usually consists of decorative needlework, applied to a flat, colored fabric. It's either appliquéd or stitched on. It's related to needlepoint, which is an upholstery covering of woolen threads embroidered on canvas.

Frieze. This term describes a heavy woolen, or linen and cotton cloth used for upholstery, that has a looped nap. In recent times the weave has also been made from rayon, nylon, and polyester. Wearing qualities are related to the specific fiber used, but whatever the fiber, it has a tendency to mat down in hard use.

Gros point. This is a type of embroidery that uses coarse stitching. It was developed in France.

Leather and suede. Both of these upholstery materials have been used since ancient times. Properly cared for, they last forever. Treated badly—allowed to dry out, for instance—they crack and deteriorate quickly. Both are quite expensive.

Suede is a particularly popular covering for modern and contemporary furniture, but it has one serious disadvantage: It creates friction with clothing and makes it hard to move around on the furniture.

Mohair. This is a woven fabric with a pile made—at least in the expensive versions—of the hair of the Angora goat. It has a reputation for toughness.

Satin. This term refers both to a basic weave structure and to a fabric made by this method. It is usually characterized by a smooth surface, with a shiny front and dull back. Originally, satins were made from silk. Now they're made of many different fibers. Satin-woven cotton, for instance, is called sateen.

Tapestry. This term refers to a fabric of wool intermixed with silk or linen to produce a pictorial design. It's an ancient weaving method and has been used throughout history in many different periods.

Velour. This is a fabric term, rather than a specific fabric. However, it usually refers to velvets or plush surfaces of wool or mohair. In recent years, it's been used carelessly to include all cut-pile fabrics.

Velvet. Velvets are tightly woven cut-pile fabrics, usually with distinctly soft surfaces. They can be made of many different fibers, although silk and rayon are the most common. Wear depends on fiber used.

Velveteen. Cotton velvet.

Vinyl. Once largely limited to kitchen chairs, and still popular

there, vinyl plastic is also frequently used today in casual upholstered pieces, as a low-priced substitute for leather.

Not long ago, vinyls were neither handsome nor durable.
Their main appeal was price. But there've been many improvements made in this upholstery material over the last fifteen years.
And today some of the best varieties are so leatherlike it's hard to
tell them apart.

Sold under a variety of trade names—Naugahyde is one of
the bestknown—vinyl wears well, is easy to keep clean, and can
be repaired with considerable success if it becomes punctured
(hardware stores have kits).

One caution, however: If you're considering vinyl-covered
furniture, make sure it's the type that's fabric-backed. You can
usually determine this by unzipping a cushion and looking inside. Fabric-backed vinyl is quite strong, but unsupported vinyl
tears easily.

Over the years, practically everything soft has been used to
stuff upholstered furniture. Here's a sampling of the most common stuffings:

Goose or duck down. This is extremely soft and luxurious when
fluffed, but it has the disadvantage of packing down at the slightest excuse. And it's very expensive.

Cotton batting. One of the least expensive paddings, cotton
batting is much firmer than down, but it also tends to pack down
over time, creating an unwanted firmness. It also has a tendency
to shift, with the result that the center part of the cushion may
have little padding and the edges too much.

Coil springs. Still in common use, coil springs reached the
height of their popularity between 1920 and 1950. They're usually
assembled in squares or rectangles the size of a cushion, sometimes with twine tying the coils together.

Once assembled, the spring units are covered in burlap,
wrapped in cotton (or dacron or even a layer of foam), then covered with fabric. Or, coil spring units are installed in the base of
a chair or couch, directly beneath the cushions, or in chair or
couch backs.

Coil springs provide resiliency. But with hard use they can
sag. Or the twine tying them together can snap. Or the spring
units can break apart.

It is possible to make repairs when this happens, but it can be expensive.

Zigzag springs. These are thin bands of wire, formed in a zigzag pattern. They're not found in cushions, but they are frequently used in chair or couch bases or backs. They provide support for pillows or cushions. Another name for springs of this sort: no-sag springs.

Usually, the zigzag bands are fastened at each end, leaving the center to "spring," and provide resilience. This type of construction is simple and inexpensive—and it works. What's more, about the only thing that can go wrong is that one of the zigzag bands works free on one end. Fixing it is relatively easy.

Foam. Currently, the most popular upholstery padding is foam—foam rubber, urethane foam, or other plastic-based foam. Foam is uncomplicated, inexpensive, and long-lasting. It also provides excellent comfort.

This is not to say that foam has no disadvantages, however. Rubber foam, particularly, can smell when wet. And after a decade or two it can begin to harden, then crumble into dust.

On the other hand, it's easy to make foam in different weights and densities, for different uses. The denser foams are firmer (and more expensive), while the lighter-weight foams are softer (and cheaper).

If you're buying low-priced furniture, the cushions will almost certainly be filled with some variety of foam. If you're buying medium-priced furniture, the foam will probably be wrapped in a dacron batting, to provide a more rounded look to the cushions and a seating surface that is superficially soft, but with a firmer underlying layer.

High-priced upholstered furniture is sometimes stuffed with a combination of dacron batting, a layer of foam, then an innerspring unit, in an attempt to provide the best of all possible worlds.

Horsehair. This is actual hair obtained from horses' manes and tails. The shorter hairs are curled, matted together (sometimes in liquid rubber), and used to stuff upholstered furniture or mattresses.

Horsehair was a common upholstery padding in days past, but it's getting rare now. In fact, it's usually found only in the most expensive, most traditional upholstered pieces these days.

So there we have it: a quick lesson in furniture styles, woods, fabrics, and padding. But, of course, all this is only background information, knowledge to be kept in mind while shopping.

Buying Furniture

Before you actually go furniture buying, you have some decisions to make.

You have to figure out what items you need immediately, and if your budget is limited, which you can put off buying for a while.

You have to decide how much money you can spend, total.

You have to determine how much furniture will fit into the space you have available.

You have to decide which style or styles you like.

You have to figure out the best place to buy what you want.

To help you make these decisions, and many others like them, we're going to go through your apartment room by room, describing how you can determine your needs—telling you what to look for and what to avoid, and showing you how to judge quality.

But first, before you even consider buying a stick of furniture, you have to devise a spending plan.

THE SPENDING PLAN

How much should you spend on furniture? In a way, that's like asking the old vaudeville comedian's question, "How big is a grey suit?"

There is no answer—at least no answer that applies to everyone. It all depends on how big your nest egg is (or, if you're willing to buy on credit, what sort of monthly payment you can meet), on your family's needs, on the size of your apartment, on your taste, and on a hundred other factors.

We can't give you a figure. No one can. But we can give you some useful guidelines. And we can tell you how to arrive at a ballpark figure, taking your needs—and your apartment—into consideration. First, the guidelines:

1. Buy your furniture as though it had to last forever. Whatever your plans, your hopes, or your dreams, you may never get another chance to buy an apartmentful of furniture.

2. Buy furniture that *you* like, not what your friends prefer or what the salesman tells you is popular. After all, you're the person who'll have to live with it.
3. If you can't find a particular item, buy nothing. Wait. Shop around some more. Don't worry about leaving a room partly empty. That's better than buying something "temporary" that might be with you for the next twenty years.
4. Don't let yourself be rushed by bargains, sales, or special buys. And don't let yourself be cowed by a salesman who tells you that the price is good for today only. Sales are like street-cars. If you miss one, don't worry—another one will be along shortly. And that salesman will give you the same price to-morrow, next week, or even next month.
5. Buy quality furniture, but don't spend beyond your means. However beautiful that couch or diningroom set, you won't get much pleasure out of it if you have to go into hock to buy it.

Second, the ballpark figure:

1. Consulting the rest of the chapter, make a list of your basic furniture needs. Make another list of items you'd like, but don't need.
2. Go to the largest, longest-established department store in the area, tell the salesman you're "just looking," and start pricing the furniture you need, item by item. Jot the prices down on your lists. Leave your checkbook and all charge cards at home during this step.
3. Go to a large furniture store—the one that has the fewest sales, the one that advertises least—and repeat the process.
4. Check prices in the big mail-order catalogs, keeping in mind that the furniture they offer is medium-quality at best—per-fectly serviceable, but hardly superior.
5. Total up your lists. If you can handle the combined totals, consider that your furniture budget—and go out and cele-brate. You're in a rare and enviable position. If not, subtract the "extras" list. If that doesn't do the trick, you'll have to start putting off buying some of the necessities.

If you have to do without some of the necessities, we recom-mend that you begin your cutbacks in the diningroom, assuming you have an eat-in kitchen. Diningroom furniture is expensive and you *can* do without it, at least for a while.

What, no diningroom? Then begin your cutbacks in the living-room. Instead of buying expensive upholstered goods, get a good cardtable and four chairs. You'll probably need them later. And, until you can afford expensive, upholstered livingroom furniture, they'll be a reasonably adequate substitute. Large floor cushions also work.

Once you've decided on a furniture budget, don't exceed it, no matter how slick the salesman is, no matter how attractive the prices, no matter—gulp—how much you may love the particular item you can't afford.

Instead, wait until you've paid off your purchases, or have more funds for furniture, then go shopping again. Some people take three or four years to accumulate a complete set of furniture this way—but they keep it for thirty or forty years, until they can scarcely recall the "brief" delay.

What we're suggesting here, simply put, is that you spend a little time and energy preparing a logical furniture-buying plan. This will prevent you from winding up with a beautiful, twelve-piece diningroom suite—and no kitchen table. It will also help you avoid buying a hodgepodge: a wild and unattractive mixture of quality furniture and junk.

All right, now—with guidelines in mind and ballpark figure in hand—let's take a look at your apartment, room by room.

Livingroom   In most respects the livingroom is the main room of your house, the place you'll spend most of your time, the place where you'll entertain your guests. How should you furnish it?

Number of pieces. No matter how many chairs and couches you buy, you can expect that there'll be times when your guests can't all sit down at once. So don't try to buy enough furniture for occasions like that. Just ask yourself what your daily seating needs are.

In our experience, small families can do quite well with living-room seating for four to six persons. Larger families should think in terms of eight to ten seats.

Of course it doesn't really matter how you achieve this seating capacity. But we've found that it's best to have at least one couch,

Seating space is the most important element in any livingroom. This apartment dweller has chosen to handle that with a multipiece grouping of sectional chairs. Quite aside from their beauty, groupings of this sort have the advantage of extreme versatility. If this apartment owner moves, chances are he or she will be able to make use of every piece, no matter what the size or shape of the new livingroom.

supplemented by as many chairs as necessary. Sectionals also work well, since they act as both couches and chairs.

Size and shape of pieces. Tiny room? Don't try to stuff it with seating for twelve. You won't have room to walk around comfortably. Gigantic room? Buy larger pieces—and don't place them against walls, otherwise the place will look half-empty.

If you have a huge room, remember when placing the furniture that it is meant not only to provide seating, but also to bring people close enough together so that they can see each other easily and converse in natural tones.

Style. Styles are not the result of laws passed by legislatures or dictums from religious authorities. They're merely the designs of certain people who worked at certain periods in history or who are working today. There's nothing immutable about them, nothing sacred, nothing you can't change at your whim.

Furthermore, there are no laws about mixing or matching. You can, if you're so inclined, put a Scandinavian modern couch into a room otherwise furnished with Queen Anne, Louis XIV, etc. You may get comments from guests, but if you like it that way, that's what really counts.

In general, however, we've found that the most harmonious rooms, if they mix styles, mix either simple with simple or complex with complex. It's when you cross these boundaries that you get what most people consider odd effects.

Other than this, however, follow only one guideline about style: your own preferences.

Colors. What colors you choose for your room depends, to a large degree, on what effect you wish to create. Do you want your room to be formal? Then choose "cool" colors—blues, greens, yellows. Do you want a casual look? In that case, you'll do better with earth tones—browns, tans, and greys. Other muted colors also achieve this effect.

In our opinion, you should avoid bright colors when choosing furniture. These may be very attractive when you first buy them, but they're bound to pall after awhile.

And we speak from experience. We once bought an orange couch—a very well constructed piece with a tough, nylon basketweave fabric. Ten years later it still reigned in our livingroom—and we could hardly stand to look at it. At that point, we moved into a house and immediately relegated the couch to the basement playroom. After the kids crawled on it for a couple of years, it was, to our great delight, completely destroyed. We then got rid of the thing without a pang.

There's another advantage to muted colors. They go well together, almost regardless of the shades involved.

Patterns. In general, we feel the same way about patterns as we do about colors: The less they dominate, the better.

For this reason, we believe in avoiding the following:

- Strongly contrasting stripes. These are okay, perhaps, for the lobbies of flashy, pretentious hotels. But they quickly pall in private livingrooms;
- Large, dramatically figured patterns. The question isn't, "Do I like it?" The question is (or should be), "*Will* I like it, years from now, when it's still here and my tastes have changed?"
- Brightly colored "plain" patterns. Plain colors are fine, if subdued. But if they're bright, they're an unquenchable beacon.

   On the other hand, subdued solids never offend, never intrude—and don't fight with each other.

So when you start considering patterns, consider the following recommendations:

- If you're torn between the conservative and the far-out, choose the conservative. It will wear better, psychologically speaking.
- If you want to get a variety of patterns in your room, either buy a main piece—a couch, perhaps—in a single, solid color, and accent it with patterned chairs; or get a couch with a subdued pattern and accent it with chairs in solid colors.
- When trying to achieve variety and interest consider choosing solid colors, but in a variety of fabric textures—a mixture perhaps of canvas, tweedy fabrics, and leathers or vinyls.

Incidentally, if you're in doubt, some furniture stores will give you fabric swatches to take home to test against your drapes, carpets, or the furniture you already have. They may even let you borrow a chair or couch cushion overnight. But remember—the smaller the swatch, the less likely you'll be able to get a good idea of how it will look.

Quality. It's no easy job to determine the quality of upholstered goods, since everything is covered up. It's practically im-

It's not only the furniture that sets off a room and gives it a unique personality, it's also the upholstery fabric, texture, and color. This room, for instance, is built around this blue and red couch, a truly lovely piece. It often makes sense to buy one superb piece of furniture immediately and add to it when the budget permits.

possible to detect small quality differences. But you can determine if the piece you're considering is sturdy and well-made. Here's what to look for:

FABRICS   The single most important quality a fabric can have is durability. For this reason, we strongly recommend the synthetics—especially nylon, polyester, and polyolefin. Rayon doesn't wear as well.

On the other hand, if fading is likely to be a serious problem in your livingroom, because of the direct sunlight, rayon is probably the best of the synthetics. Polyolefin is also good.

If stains and dirt are likely to be your most serious problem (if you have several children, for instance, or dogs and cats that can't resist sitting on your chairs and couches), polyolefin is your best bet, although nylon is pretty good, too.

In this case an alternative is to choose a fabric that has been "Scotchguarded," or do the "Scotchguarding" yourself, with a spray-on liquid that makes fabrics stain-resistant.

Natural fibers also have their place—and their advantages and disadvantages. Cotton, for example, is an extremely popular upholstery fabric because it is relatively inexpensive, absorbs dyes well, and doesn't fade easily. But it isn't a good-wearing fabric, and it picks up stains and dirt readily.

Wool, when tightly woven, is another good upholstery fabric. It wears far better than cotton and is somewhat more stain-resistant. But it can be damaged by moths. And ordinary household upholstery cleaners can damage it.

PADDING   The first question is, what material is being used in the piece of furniture you're considering. Check the cushions or beneath the cushions, or look on the bottom of the piece and you'll see a white rectangular tag about the size of a dollar bill. It's there by law and it will tell you the stuffing contents.

In most cases today, furniture is stuffed and padded with plastic or rubber foam—an excellent material. The only problems with it occur when it's too thin or not dense enough.

As a rule of thumb, chair or couch cushions filled with foam should be at least 3½ inches thick. And they should have some heft to them. In fact, if you have a choice between furniture with very lightweight foam cushions and furniture with heavier cushions, choose the latter. It's less likely to pack down.

Paddings to avoid, for various reasons, include moss, kapok, and cotton batting. All pack down quickly and get lumpy. Excelsiors—string-like wood shavings—are worst of all in this respect.

Incidentally, if you're looking at a quality piece, the cushions will have removable covers (thanks to some zippers), so they can be cleaned easily. The padding itself will be contained in a secondary fabric.

SPRINGS   Except for ultra-modern couches and chairs made entirely of foam (and usually convertible into beds, simply by unfolding), most chairs and couches have spring bases and backs.

These springs are constructed in a variety of ways, with coils, with zigzag (no-sag) strips, with arched spring steel, etc. But you won't be able to differentiate between them, since they're hidden inside.

For this reason, what you should look for is firmness, regularity of support, and the absence of lumps, bumps, or humps. Incidentally, if you turn over a piece of furniture and find you *can* see the springs—since there's no dustcover—that's good evidence you're looking at something of low quality.

FRAME   In most upholstered furniture, this is something else you can't see. But you can evaluate it, at least indirectly. Ask yourself the following questions:

Does the piece creak when you sit on it? That's a bad sign, particularly in new furniture.

Is the piece stable—that is, when you sit on it, is there any "give" or wobble? If so, this is another bad sign.

Are the legs strong and tightly attached? If there's wiggle or wobble here, you're bound for trouble. (But if the legs simply turn, that means they're mounted on the frame with a central screw—acceptable construction in medium-priced furniture.)

Type. Couches and chairs come in several different types, each suitable to a different purpose. We can't tell you which type is best for you. That's a matter of your individual needs. But we can briefly describe what's available, so you can decide for yourself:

COUCHES   In general, these are available in the following categories: traditional (one-piece units, capable of seating two to perhaps five people), sectionals (multi-piece units that, together, form couches and separately act as chairs), and convertibles (couches that turn into beds).

One variety—convertibles—deserves further description, since it subdivides into several types. The simplest convertible

The unimaginative way to use these two-compartment boxes would have been to stack them one on top of the other, in a single row. This apartment dweller, however, realized that with the weight properly distributed they could be stagger-stacked. The result: a charming corner unit.

couch is nothing more than a twin-sized mattress and box spring, concealed by some kind of cover or throw and topped off with cushions or bolsters.

Then there are "Hide–a–beds" (a name trademarked by Simmons Mfg. Co.), a style in which a folded mattress is stored inside the body of a couch, along with a pull-out base, usually of flat, springy, interlinked wire. Take off the normal couch cushions, pull out the mattress and base, and you have a bed. Depending on the couch size, this can be anything from a single-sized bed to a queen-sized bed.

Another variation on this theme involves a sofa whose back folds down, presenting a flat surface for sleeping. Couches of this sort are far less expensive than the "Hide–a–bed" variety—and less comfortable, too.

Finally, there are couches made of fabric-covered slabs of urethane foam, the slabs attached with fabric "hinges." To make a bed, all you do is fold the slabs out on the floor. One little tug does it. These are quite comfortable and relatively inexpensive.

CHAIRS   These come in an amazing number of styles, types, and varieties. The most basic is the wooden chair—an unupholstered chair (or one with a completely separate cushion). Normally, these aren't used in livingrooms, although they're common in diningrooms and kitchens. However, one type that is a nice addition to almost any livingroom is the Boston rocker.

Boston rockers are large, handsome, wooden chairs, usually of maple, with wide, shaped seats, high backs, wooden arms, and wooden rocking rails. They're most commonly made in traditional designs, although we've seen some Scandinavian modern designs in teak that are really beauties.

There are many types of upholstered chairs on the market today. Among them are easy chairs—some no more than one-person couches, tilt-back and reclining chairs (sometimes capable of swiveling), wing chairs (so-named because the back has forward-facing extensions, or wings), barrel chairs (so-named because of the shape), and convertible chairs, which make into narrow but serviceable beds.

Other necessities. While chairs and couches represent your major livingroom furniture expenses, there are other items you will need sooner or later: lamps, "occasional" tables, bookcases and record cabinets, stools or hassocks, floor cushions, hi-fi equipment, TV set, etc.

Here's what we recommend, to fill your basic needs:

TABLES   A long, low coffee table to go in front of your couch, to hold magazines, ashtrays, snacks and the like; a small, arm-height table for each major chair, and possibly one for each end of the couch (unless chair and couch are close, in which case they can share).

LAMPS   Enough to illuminate all of your major seating capacity, so that all room occupants are able to read in whatever chair or couch they choose. You'll probably need a couple of floor lamps and a couple of table lamps—especially if your livingroom doesn't have adequate ceiling fixtures.

STOOLS AND HASSOCKS   If you have a Boston rocker, a hassock is practically a necessity. But you don't need stools or hassocks with most upholstered couches and chairs, especially if the chairs recline, rock, or swivel.

FLOOR CUSHIONS   These are strictly an option. But if you're used to having them around, or if you're of the right age, they're a good way to increase seating capacity and create a homey look, simultaneously.

ELECTRONICS   As far as we're concerned, the livingroom is the best place in any apartment for a hi-fi set. It's also a good place for a TV set, especially if you expect to have company to watch a specific show from time to time. But all of this, of course, is a matter of personal discretion, taste—and budget.

DESK AND CHAIR   Even if you don't do any work at home, you'll probably need some central spot for handling bills, checks, and correspondence. If you have a large livingroom, you can put the space to good use by making your office there, in the most out-of-the-way spot you can find.

What kind of a desk should you buy? There are many varieties on the market—from kidney-shaped kneehole desks made out of solid mahogany, to rolltops made of golden oak, to plastic-topped, steel desks designed for office use. It's all a matter of taste, needs, and budgets. But if you're considering a wooden desk, you can determine its quality by applying the same rules you'd use for other case goods (chests, cabinets, etc.) See the sections on diningrooms and bedrooms.

BOOKSHELVES, RECORD CABINETS, ROOM DIVIDERS, ETC.   These are all covered in the section on storage.

Multi-level seating, custom-made platforms—these are the stuff of expensive decorators. But with just a little imagination, you can create such furnishings yourself. The ingredients here: concrete blocks, cardboard boxes, contact paper, plywood slabs, and cotton bathroom carpeting (the latter stapled to the underside of the former).

Diningroom   By their very nature, diningrooms are special places. They're where you share meals with guests, or where the entire family eats the evening meal. They're more formal, but often more comfortable eating places than kitchens.

And yet some apartments don't have diningrooms. Some have dining "els," extensions of the livingroom big enough for minimal diningroom furniture. But some have diningrooms that would do a house proud.

Even if you have no diningroom at all, you can make one— not by putting up a wall, but by arranging your furniture carefully and by choosing items that will fit. If this is your situation, we strongly recommend that you find a way to create a dining area for yourself. It will make important meals far more pleasurable.

A full-blown diningroom has three main types of furniture: a table, a set of chairs, and some cabinets (buffets, hutches, or china cabinets). We'll take them one by one.

The diningroom table. When shopping for a diningroom table, three qualities should be uppermost in your mind: convenience and comfort, durability, and beauty. We can't give you much advice about the third, since that's largely a matter of taste. But we have plenty to say about the other two.

CONVENIENCE AND COMFORT   By definition, a diningroom table is intended to provide a little luxury. Therefore, at the minimum, it should offer a substantial amount of convenience and comfort. And the key to both of these is size and shape.

For instance, the table surface should be about 28 to 29½ inches from the floor. Long experience has shown that this is the most comfortable dining height, and most diningroom chairs are designed with that dimension in mind. Other table heights *will* work, but not as well.

Then there's the matter of dining space. Experts have decided that, for comfort, each person must have a dining space 22 inches wide and 18 inches deep (from the front edge of the table to its center).

Then there's the question of shape. Diningroom tables come, essentially, in three shapes: oval, round, and rectangular. Of the three, the rectangular is the most space-efficient—and the most comfortable. It provides more elbow room and more room for serving pieces.

On the other hand, you may not need a rectangular table and,

In this guise, it's a simple hall table, a kind of a shallow desk, ideal for using as your "mail headquarters." Set against the wall, it occupies hardly any useful floor space.

In this guise, however, the same piece of furniture is a table for four, handsome and convenient. Furniture of this type is ideal for small, crowded apartments.

Here's another fold-up-and-store-away dining table. At first glance, it seems like nothing more than a small cabinet, an item that's more decorative than useful.

Take a closer look, however, and you'll find that it isn't a cabinet at all. It's a completely self-contained dining ensemble. All you have to do is open it up, add food, and wait for guests to arrive.

Compare this with the first picture in the series. There isn't a thing in view—except for the candles—that wasn't stored in that cabinet. It's a setup that's not only practical, but elegant.

for aesthetic reasons, may prefer an oval or a round one. So that's up to you, and to your diningroom needs.

Actually, you may be able to eat your cake and have it too, so far as shape is concerned. Better diningroom tables open up to permit the insertion of a leaf, or even two leaves. So you can buy a table that, in one configuration, is of modest size, and in another is quite large.

If you intend to buy a table with leaves, however, keep these hints in mind: As long as you're getting an adjustable-size table, buy one with two leaves even if your present apartment diningroom can't handle the table when it's fully extended. Your next diningroom may be larger. Also, look for leaves that lock into each other and into the tabletop surface with dowels. That's evidence of quality. And before you buy, have the leaves installed in the table, to see that the slide mechanism is working smoothly and to make sure the leaves' finish and grain matches the table. Finally, when you store the leaves, store them flat—not on edge, not diagonally—otherwise, they may warp.

Another important convenience and comfort factor with diningroom tables: the arrangement of the legs. Diningroom tables come with four legs, with two legs (trestle arrangement), and with a single leg (pedestal arrangement.)

The most stable of these arrangements is the one involving four legs. But in situations where extra chairs are added, those legs can get in the way, particularly if they're inset back from the edges, toward the center of the table.

Trestle tables are the next most stable. And the twin-leg/stretcher arrangement, if properly designed, gets in no one's way. Additional chairs don't cause any problems, either.

Pedestal base tables, either with single or double pedestals, do have the virtue of eliminating all dinner-table leg conflicts. But they often aren't very stable. Furthermore, pedestals often terminate in massive bases, which diners frequently kick, causing gouges and scratches.

DURABILITY   There are two factors to consider when judging the durability of a diningroom table: the materials used (particularly in the top), and the construction (particularly how the legs are attached to the top).

The most expensive tabletops are made of solid wood—usually long pieces of it, joined together at their sides, locked together with cross members at each end. Less expensive (but still sometimes very costly) tabletops are not solid, but veneered. In this process, a thin sheet of beautiful finishing wood is applied to a base of less expensive wood, sometimes plywood. (Incidentally, plywood warps less than solid wood.)

The main problem with veneer is that it's more fragile than solid wood—more likely to peel, crack, or chip. However, if properly cared for and not given hard continuous use, a veneered top can last for decades. Using veneer on diningroom tabletops is particularly acceptable, since these tables rarely receive daily use.

If you do plan to give the table heavy, almost daily use, you should buy fitted table pads, whether your tabletop is solid or veneer. Table pads, which go underneath the table cloth, protect tops against spills and bumps. They even protect china and glassware to some degree. They reduce noise, too. They can be purchased at furniture and department stores.

If you're buying a table with a solid wood top, look for the hardest wood you can find. Also, look for the thickest top you can find. The harder the wood, the less likely it is to mar or dent if something falls on it. The thicker it is, the less likely it is to warp.

When it comes to construction, the only factor that really matters in a diningroom table is how the legs are attached to the top. Normally, this involves a third part of the table, too: the apron, that vertical ring of wood on which the top appears to rest.

Except in the case of trestle tables or pedestal bases, legs are fastened to the table's apron, usually by means of hanger bolts that pierce the apron, go through the leg, and are fastened on the inside of the leg with a nut. The leg is cut so that it tightly abuts the underside of the tabletop and the inside of the apron.

The key to this joint's strength is the cut of the leg. It should fit so tightly that it practically stays in place without the hanger bolt. To check this, just loosen the bolt. If the table promptly collapses—or threatens to—keep shopping.

Trestle and pedestal tables use other methods of fastening legs to tabletops. There's really no need to describe them, since it's easy to test the table. All you have to do is stand at one end and give a little push. If it wobbles to any substantial degree, it isn't strong enough. Single pedestals will wobble no matter how well constructed they are, of course. Here you have to judge what degree of shakiness you're willing to put up with.

Chairs. Chairs come in two basic types: arm chairs and side chairs. They also come in about a thousand different styles and countless finishes and fabrics. How do you choose? How do you decide if you're looking at a chair of good quality? What about fabrics and colors? What about padding? Here are our recommendations:

ARM CHAIRS AND STRAIGHT CHAIRS   Arm chairs *are* more comfortable, but they can be a nuisance. They take up more room than side chairs. And unless they're cleverly designed, they don't really fit under the table.

Our suggestion: Get at least two arm chairs, one for the head of the household, one for any VIP guest who might happen to show up. Such people like to feel important, and somehow chairs with arms have that effect.

STYLES   Normally, if you're buying new furniture, selecting a style isn't any problem at all. You just take the chairs that come with the table, assuming there's nothing seriously wrong with them.

But if, for some reason, you're buying tables and chairs separately, you can still get a good match if you make sure both are made of the same wood and have the same general design complexity. If, for instance, your table is heavily carved, it probably won't look quite right with totally unadorned chairs—and vice versa.

Also, try to broadly match your table's shape and proportions. If you have an oval table, for example, don't settle for chairs that don't have a single curve, or rounded edge. And if your table is massively proportioned, don't buy chairs that seem spun from spiderwebs.

In addition, don't attempt to mix very formalized designs with very informal ones. The mixture will look a little ludicrous—like wearing a swallow-tailed coat with a plaid shirt.

FABRICS   Here the rules are the same as with livingroom upholstered furniture. Choose a fabric that will wear well, in a color and pattern that you can live with—for years. It may not be love at first sight, but at least you'll have a chance to develop a relationship, rather than facing quick boredom.

PADDING   The padding on diningroom chairs is far simpler than the upholstery of livingroom furniture. Generally it consists of a board covered with a modest layer of foam, a thinner layer of dacron batting, then the fabric itself. This board is usually fastened to the chair seat in one of several ways.

The best thing about this system is that even the rankest amateur can reupholster his or her diningroom chairs fairly easily (although different fastening techniques require different levels of skill). At any rate, chair padding is something you really needn't worry about. Just make sure the chairs are reasonably comfortable.

CONSTRUCTION AND QUALITY   As with tables, the key factor in chair construction is how the legs are attached. In quality furniture, the chair seat, like the tabletop, sits on a base, an apron. And the legs fit into this.

You won't be able to tell, by looking, what method of joinery has been used to attach the legs to the apron (some are better than others). But you will be able to see how the apron is attached to the chair bottom. It should be both glued and screwed.

If the chair doesn't have an apron—if the legs are joined directly to the chair base—then it must have "stretchers." These are the thin wooden pieces that connect the legs. Ideally, the stretchers should be rectangular, but not square. Square stretchers usually connect to each other and to the legs with round dowels, so they can turn and loosen. Stretchers with rectangular cross sections usually have rectangular joints, which hold better.

Incidentally, the heavier the chair, the more likely it is to last. Weight usually reflects hardwood construction, and hardwoods are far more durable than softwoods.

Cabinets. A table and chairs are the chief functional pieces of any diningroom, but a complete "set" of diningroom furniture, as furniture manufacturers conceive of it, usually includes some kind of large cabinet, or chest.

These pieces carry many different names, but there are three main types:

SIDEBOARDS OR BUFFETS   These are long (50 inches or more), low (usually no more than 35 inches high), narrow (20 inches is common) cabinets, intended to be placed against the wall.

Usually, they stand on stubby legs and have a combination of drawers—for flatware and serving pieces—and doors, behind which are stored china, serving dishes, table cloths, napkins, and other diningroom equipment.

In addition to the useful goods they store, sideboards also have tops that can be put to work as serving space. Here you can put your hot dishes, your coffee percolator, your dessert platter, etc., protecting the surface with trivets when necessary.

From a style standpoint, it's not necessary that a sideboard exactly match your table and chairs—just that the styles, finishes, and woods don't fight with each other.

As for construction, the main quality to look for is sturdiness. This quality—or the lack of it—is most visible in the legs. Ideally, they should be an integral part of the cabinet itself. Look for strength, weight, and solidity.

If you plan to use the top for serving, you'll want it thick and well finished. You'll also want doors that are well mounted on their hinges and that close firmly. Drawers should open and shut smoothly and should remain level even if pulled out most of the way. (See the bedroom section for more information on drawers.)

Since sideboards are designed to sit flush against the wall, their backs are usually made of unfinished plywood, as are their bottoms. Their sides, made of the same material, are veneered in better pieces. The only real caution here is to make sure the plywood isn't paper-thin, as it is in some inexpensive sideboards.

BREAKFRONTS (OR HUTCHES) These are wide, tall, usually open-faced cabinets designed, like sideboards, to sit against a wall. They usually have two sections (which can be separated in some designs): a sideboardlike base and a somewhat narrower bookcaselike unit that sits on top of it.

Much of what we've said about sideboards applies to breakfronts, of course, but there are some differences. The part of the unit with shelves, for instance, should be tightly constructed and the shelves firmly set in place. And if the upper and lower parts are separate, the top shouldn't simply sit on the bottom—it should lock on in some way.

Incidentally, if you're tight for space, there's one hutch design you should know about: the corner hutch. It's smaller than the standard variety and it's triangular. So if you have a small room —but at least one corner that's unused—this is a good way to get extra diningroom storage space.

CHINA CABINETS OR CHINA CLOSETS These are bookshelflike display cabinets, meant to show off your best china. They're not really storage cabinets.

As far as we're concerned, this is not really a legitimate piece of diningroom furniture. It's a collector's piece, an item that can just as easily go in livingroom or den as in the diningroom.

Since china cabinets rarely do anything more than just sit

there, it doesn't matter much whether they're made of hardwood or softwood, so long as they're well finished.

The key quality points to look out for are these: sturdy legs screwed (not just glued) into the frame; smooth-working hinges and latches on the doors; adjustable shelves; bottoms and backs of reasonably thick plywood.

Kitchen   Most apartment kitchens are anything but large. In most ways, this is an inconvenience. But it certainly uncomplicates the question of kitchen furniture. At the most, that consists of a table and chairs—usually four chairs. And you may only have enough room for a couple of bar stools.

Nonetheless, your kitchen table and chairs will be among the most frequently used pieces of furniture you buy—and it's easy to make mistakes when buying them.

When buying a kitchen table, for instance, you should consider the following factors: size and shape, tabletop material, and table leg construction. We'll take them one at a time:

Size and shape. How big a table you get depends, naturally, on the size of your kitchen and the number of people you intend to seat regularly.

But if you're cramped for space, keep these figures in mind: Adults need about 2½ feet of table space. They also need about the same distance between the edge of the table and the wall, if they're to have enough sitting room.

In addition, you'll need some clearance between the kitchen table and your kitchen appliances—the stove, the refrigerator, the dishwasher, etc.—and between table and work space.

The most efficient table shape, from a space standpoint, is a rectangle. You can seat four people, two to a side, at a rectangular table measuring 22x40 inches. Smaller than that, though, and you have trouble.

You can also seat four people at a square table. But if it's larger than a card table (about 30x30 inches), you'll be wasting kitchen space, since there'll be room at the center of the table you can't use efficiently.

If you have your heart set on a round table, you'll need one 36 inches in diameter to comfortably seat four. Such a table, of course, will take up more space than the square or rectangular table, without giving you any extra table area.

Tabletop material. If you grew up in the American midwest as we did, chances are you ate your breakfast on a plastic-topped table. And, chances are, that's what you'll choose again. But there are other suitable kitchen tabletop materials—wood, glass, and marble. Each has advantages and disadvantages:

PLASTIC Usually, this material is laminated to plywood or chipboard, under such tradenames as Micatex, Formica, and Micarta. It's available in hundreds of patterns and colors, including wood and marble imitations, and you can buy it with a smooth, shiny finish or with a slightly textured "matte" finish.

Plastic is impervious to most spills and stains. It takes a violent hammer blow to break it. It wears practically forever (a good reason to make sure you choose something you like).

But there are two things to watch out for when buying plastic-topped tables. First, bubbles—areas where the plastic isn't firmly bonded to the surface. Tap the tabletop with your fingernails lightly. You'll hear the bubbles, if there are any. Second, edging. Avoid metal edging if you can—food gets into the crevices.

WOOD For many people, there's no substitute for the beauty of wood. But, if you want a wooden-topped table that keeps looking good over the years, make sure you buy hardwoods—walnut, maple, birch, oak. Avoid pine—it mars very easily.

Also avoid veneered plywood tops, especially if they're much less than an inch thick. The thicker, the better—and that goes for hardwood tops, too. Butcherblock tops are fine, since they're almost always made of hardwood. But they're expensive, unless you can buy them separately, at a wholesale outlet.

In addition, we advise that you avoid tops with fancy painted designs. Inevitably these scratch and wear, and are practically impossible to restore perfectly.

GLASS This is a very handsome dining surface, but it's not without its problems. Contrary to what you may think, it scratches. And once scratched, there's no way to restore it. Also, unless you buy very thick glass, it can break if you drop something on it. And thick glass—¾-inch or more—is very expensive.

MARBLE This surface, while beautiful, is expensive and fragile. It can crack, it can stain, it can lose its shine (and repolishing is no easy chore).

If you're going to buy a marble-topped table, make sure the marble is at least an inch thick, preferably resting on a substantial plywood or wooden board top. Otherwise, you're asking for trouble.

Table leg construction. Kitchen tables come with either metal or wooden legs. In either case, the key is how the legs are attached to the top.

METAL LEGS   In the cheapest tables, metal legs simply take an L turn under the tables and are attached to the underside of the top with screws that go through holes in the metal tubing. This is barely adequate. If you're buying a metal-legged table, look for legs with metal plates welded to their tops, and attached to the tabletop with screws that run through the metal plates.

WOODEN LEGS   There are several ways to fasten wooden legs to tabletops. Almost all involve the apron—the strip of wood the top sits on.

For instance, the leg can be fastened to the apron with dowels —short round rods that link both parts—or with a mortise and tenon joint (similar to dowels, except the linking piece is rectangular and it's an integral part of the leg). Mortise and tenon is better.

Another fastening method: hanger bolts. One end of this bolt is actually a wood screw. It goes into the piece holding the apron together at a corner joint. The other end of the bolt takes a nut. The hanger bolt goes through a hole in the leg, which is then locked in place with the nut. It's a very strong system, if the apron is well-attached to the top with glue and screws.

A third method involves bolting the leg to a strip of metal set into the apron. This is fine, if the metal is strong.

Of course, the table may not have four wooden legs at all, but a pedestal or a trestle-leg arrangement. If it's a pedestal, the central pole should be strong and thick and it should be attached to the table with screws and glue. If it's a trestle, test the bracing by pushing against the end of the table. There should be no appreciable "give."

Kitchen chairs. When buying kitchen chairs, you should consider the following factors: size and shape, construction, padding. We'll take them in order.

SIZE AND SHAPE   Kitchen chairs needn't be large. The proper dimension for seats is about 15 square inches. Much deeper than that and you won't be able to sit comfortably against the back.

For this reason, we recommend that you forget about armchairs for the kitchen. They're big, they're bulky, and they're really not any more comfortable than simple side chairs.

If they're made for use as kitchen chairs, the seat height will probably be just right for whatever kitchen table you pick out. If not, look for a seat height of 17–19 inches—no higher, no lower.

CONSTRUCTION Most kitchen chairs these days are made with metal frames—bent and welded tubing, either circular or square in cross-section. Seats and backs are usually screwed on. There's not much to say about this sort of construction, except that you should try to anticipate the weak points and assure yourself that the joints are reasonably strong.

Wooden chairs should be constructed in the same way as wooden tables. This has already been discussed at some length in the diningroom section.

PADDING Most metal kitchen chairs come with padding permanently in place. Wooden chairs may also come this way, or they may have detachable pads. But the principles are the same in any case.

If you're buying new furniture, what you should look for and expect to find is urethane foam padding. And if it's thick enough and dense enough, it does the job just fine.

How to tell if it's thick enough and dense enough? Sit on it. Is it comfortable? Can you feel the seat board? Padding should be thick enough to cushion the hardness of the seat board. If it isn't, you're probably looking at an inexpensive chair—and one that will be uncomfortable to sit on day after day. Keep looking.

Incidentally, practically all upholstered kitchen chairs have vinyl covers. This vinyl is available two ways: supported with a fabric backing or unsupported. The former is much stronger. Try to find a visible edge under the chair so you can determine whether or not the vinyl has a backing.

If the kitchen chair you have your heart set on doesn't come with supported vinyl, however, that shouldn't disqualify it. Most kitchen chair seats and backs are easily recovered, even by novices. But make sure the seats and backs can be taken off the frame without too much trouble. Some backs are practically impossible to move—and, therefore, to recover.

Bedrooms In some respects, bedrooms are the most important room in an apartment. After all, people spend about a third of their lives in bed. For this third, at least, they can make sure they're comfortable.

Bedroom furniture falls into three different categories: mattresses, bedsteads, and case goods—chests, drawers, bureaus, wardrobes, nighstands, vanities, and the like.

Just how much of this furniture should you buy? Well, we recommend that you buy the biggest bed you can comfortably fit into your bedroom (and remember, bedrooms can be fairly full, so long as you leave an aisle around the bed for walking around at night).

We also suggest that you don't stint on chests, dressers, etc. Chances are, your clothing accumulation will grow with the passing years, so it won't hurt to have a little extra space now. And if you buy a bedroom set, you may save a little money and eliminate matching problems later on.

One of the central factors in bedroom comfort is how and where you put your bed. Here's what you should consider:

Is there another apartment on the other side of your bedroom walls? If so, set your bed up against a different wall, to cut down on noise transmission from your neighbor.

Is your neighborhood noisy? If so, don't place your bed in line with the windows that look out onto the street. They're noise conductors.

Must you—because of your room's size or shape—place your bed against a wall? If so, choose an inside wall if you can. Outside walls, even if well insulated, are colder.

Do you have cross-ventilation in your bedroom? Position your bed to take advantage of it. You'll welcome the breeze during hot weather.

Does your bedroom have beautiful parquet floors? By all means, leave a little wood showing, but get some area rugs to step on as you get out of bed. They'll help keep your feet warm in winter and give a luxurious feeling in summer.

As for decorating, we recommend soft, restful colors—pastels, muted greys, and browns. As far as we're concerned, bright colors don't belong in a bedroom. They're too harsh, too nerve-jangling. Of course, this is a matter of taste. And the most important aspect of any decorative scheme is that it please *you*.

Now, let's take that furniture, category by category:

Mattresses. There are several factors to consider when buying a mattress: size, stuffing material and construction, foundations, ticking.

SIZE   Almost everyone, it seems, is confused about mattress sizes. Actually, the subject isn't as complex as you may believe. Essentially, there are four mattress sizes readily available at most furniture and bedding stores:

> Twin or single size (39x75)
> Full size (54x75 inches)
> Queen size (60x75 inches)
> King size (78x80)

This doesn't mean, of course, that you can't buy other sizes. You can. You can buy bedding in practically any size that strikes your fancy. But you'll have trouble finding anything in stock other than the four sizes listed above.

And remember, if you want an odd size, you'll not only have to find the mattress (and spring), but also sheets, blankets, mattress pads, etc. to fit. About the only way to get these is to have them custom made.

Of course, if you wander into a specialty shop, you'll hear about other sizes: youth beds, extra-long singles, extra-long fulls, extra-long queens, even extra-long kings. But none of these are commonly available—and, in our view, none are really necessary, unless you're a basketball player or you hold parties in bed.

There is one other size we haven't mentioned—one that is commonly available: cot size. These are small mattresses, usually 30 or 34 inches wide and 75 inches long (sometimes less) designed for roll-away cots. If you're the sort who's used to sleeping in mummy-type sleeping bags, you might be able to make do with a cot-size mattress. Otherwise, you're going to find yourself rolling out of bed a lot.

STUFFING   While you can buy mattresses with many different types of stuffing, two types almost completely dominate the market: innersprings and foam.

You might think that foam is foam and that's all there is to it. Not so. There are several different types of plastic foam—and, in addition, there's foam rubber.

The most important quality of a foam mattress is not the type of foam used, but its thickness and density. In general, the thicker and denser, the better. Denser foams, in addition, are firmer—and most back experts recommend firm mattresses.

How can you tell foam density? The easiest way is simply to lift the mattress. The heavier it is, the denser the foam.

Of course, only the cheapest mattresses consist solely of a slab of foam, covered in some sort of ticking. In the better variety, the foam is wrapped in dacron batting. This provides a superficial softness—and puts a layer of material between you and the foam, which is helpful since many foams have an odor all their own.

In our view, it's hard to beat a good foam mattress. They're available in a wide variety of firmnesses, they're quite durable, and they're less expensive than all but the cheapest innerspring mattresses.

Innerspring mattresses come in two varieties—those with coils tied or wired together into a single, mattress-sized unit and those with individually-pocketed springs.

Those companies who manufacture unitized mattresses—the Sealy "Posturepedic" is a good example—say their products are stronger and firmer. Those who make the other type—the Simmons "Beautyrest," for instance—say their mattresses conform better to the body's curves.

Of course, there are more than springs in innerspring mattresses. In the better ones, there's also a thin layer of foam, a layer of cotton or dacron batting, and sometimes a pad of horsehair or tough vegetable fiber—sisal—to eliminate all chances of "spring feel."

How can you tell the quality of an innerspring mattress? Unfortunately, that's no easy trick. We recommend comparing the cutaway cushions manufacturers sometimes provide retailers. If these are unavailable, limit yourself to brand names you know (but keep in mind that Sealy, Simmons, and all the rest make many different mattresses).

When all else fails, compare the weights of the mattresses you're considering. The heavier ones are generally better. Also compare the ticking material, the tailoring, and the tufting, if any. (And if you can find a good mattress without tufting, by all means do it. Tufting buttons have a way of sticking into your back in the middle of the night.)

There is one other mattress stuffing that deserves mention here: water. Water beds have gained a certain popularity over the last decade. Frankly, we think they're more trouble than they're worth. They have to be filled exactly to the right level or they're either too sloshy or too firm. The heating unit has to be adjusted perfectly, or they're either too hot or too cold.

But water beds present another problem that makes it impossible to use them in some apartments. Fully filled, they're enormously heavy. They put a tremendous strain on the floor—more than a grand piano.

For this reason, we'd stay away from water beds except in reinforced concrete buildings. And even then, we'd be a little wary. After all, the things *can* split open. What would you do if that happened? Would your insurance cover it?

FOUNDATIONS   Most mattresses are sold with companion pieces—foundations or box springs. These are mattress-shaped units made to sit underneath and support the mattress. Usually, they're made in matching tickings.

Most foundations are constructed very much like innerspring mattresses, although with heavier springs. And these spring units are mounted on a wooden frame.

Does your mattress *need* a foundation? What good function does a foundation serve? The answer to the first question is no. Mattresses don't require foundations. But they do provide a resilient base. And, with legs screwed into the wooden frame, they can eliminate the need for a bedframe.

Like innerspring mattresses, box springs consist of more than just a spring unit covered with ticking. They have a certain amount of padding on top, to prevent spring feel and to protect the mattress. The more padding, of course, the better.

TICKING   This is the least important aspect of any mattress. It's the inside that counts. But furniture buyers are often impressed by beautiful damask or machine-made tapestries. So the makers of medium-priced mattresses habitually dress up their products. And the manufacturers of better mattresses, if only to compete, are often forced to use better tickings than are absolutely necessary.

You should look for two qualities in ticking—and beauty isn't one of them. Instead, make sure, so far as you can, that it's durable and well-made. Also, choose a ticking that's fire-resistant if you have a choice. Nylon and polyester, in particular, are less flammable than cotton.

Bedsteads. If you're satisified with legs screwed into the box spring, you don't have to consider this bedroom furniture category. But most of us want a little feeling of luxury. And that's what a good bedstead can provide.

Bedsteads consist of two main parts: the headboard and footboard, and the railings and slats. The headboard and footboard are purely cosmetic. They're available in all sorts of wood, finishes, and designs. Brass headboards and footboards are also popular.

The most expensive beds consist of a matched set of headboard, footboard, and railings. The railings connect at each end to the headboard and footboard with hooks. Two or three wooden slats are spread between the railings and it's on these that the mattress and box spring rest.

To assure quality, be certain the wood is thick and solid, the joints are tight, the hooks are firmly implanted, the finish is smooth, etc. Also make sure that when the unit is fit together, there's little or no wobble.

In some bedsteads, the handsome wooden rails that match both headboard and footboard have been replaced by angle-iron steel. This isn't as pretty as wood, but it's at least as solid.

A variation on this is the steel bedframe, an angle-iron frame on legs, usually with casters. These are made so that headboards can be bolted to them at one end. Less often, they also have a provision for footboards.

Although some authorities warn against getting a bedframe of the wrong size, most modern bedframes are adjustable to anything from a single- to a queen-sized box spring. They have angle-iron metal arms that meet in the center and act like rails, holding up the foundation.

King-sized beds need a special frame—essentially two twin-sized frames joined together. The reason for this is that king-sized mattresses are usually sold with two box springs, each of which supports half the mattress, widthwise.

Perhaps the most modern bedstead now being offered is the platform bed, which is nothing more or less than the name implies. It's a platform raised off the floor and designed to hold a mattress. Usually there's no provision for—or need for—a box spring.

Platform beds range from the simple and roughhewn to the

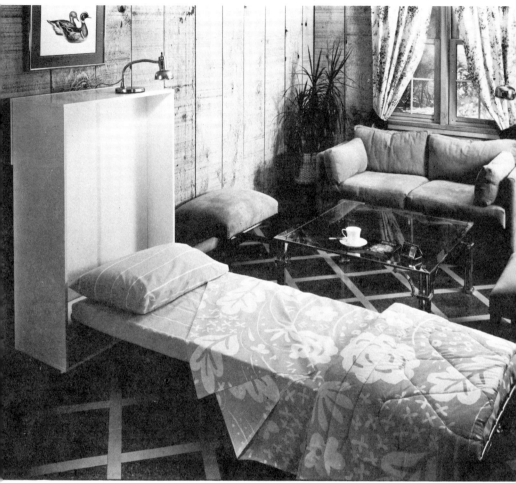

Murphy beds—the sort that folds up into what appears to be a closet—were quite popular in the 1920s and 1930s. They're less well known today, but modern versions, like this one, are excellent ways to handsomely conceal fold-out beds while keeping them ready for almost instant use.

Who says a platform bed has to cost big bucks? All that's really needed is a decent mattress, a piece of plywood (which you can paint or wallpaper), and some small wooden cabinets. Put it all together, and you have what looks like a custom-made unit. Notice also the bookshelves in this photo. They're just slabs of lumber, separated and held up by decorative concrete blocks (available at your local lumberyard).

very fancy, with built-in nightstands, bookshelves, and even stereo centers. They're about as close to a womb as you can get with man-made materials.

Platform beds are pleasant indeed, but they're often a problem for apartment dwellers, since they involve some very large wooden pieces, which, once they're in the door, must usually be fastened together permanently.

Still, if you can find the screw-together type—and a design you really like—platform beds are a good alternative to traditional bedsteads.

Case goods. We can't tell you how many, what size, or what style of chests, dressers, wardrobes, nightstands, and the like to buy. This is a matter of what you like and what you need.

But we can tell you how professionals quickly judge the quality of case goods, as these items are called. It's all in the drawers. Just by carefully examining a single drawer, you can tell if you're looking at high-quality, low-quality, or medium-quality furniture. Here's how:

- Choosing the widest and longest drawer in the piece, slowly pull it out. It should glide easily, without hesitation. It should remain level until you've pulled it practically all the way out.
- Now, add some weight—two or three volumes of the Encyclopedia Britannica would be ideal—and try it again. The action should be just as smooth as before.
- Withdraw the drawer entirely. Look at the wood from which it's made. The best quality furniture is hardwood throughout. Not sure if it's made of hardwood? Turn the drawer over and jab it gently with a ballpoint pen in an inconspicuous spot. You shouldn't be able to dent it easily. Second-quality drawers—good, but not great—use plywood, particularly for drawer bottoms. If this is what you've found, check to see that it's sturdy and reasonably thick.
- Examine the way the sides of the drawer are joined together. Quality furniture is made with dovetail joints (the wooden version of a "d.a." haircut). These are the strongest joints known.

    In very costly furniture, the dovetails may be hand-done. You'll be able to tell because they won't all be exactly the same. The vast majority of dovetailed joints are machine-made and perfectly identical.

If the drawer is nailed—or even screwed—together, the piece isn't of the highest quality (unless it's a geniune antique). Even worse, the drawer is likely to fall apart in no time.

- Look at the bottom of the drawer. Notice how the bottom is fit into the sides. It shouldn't be nailed. Instead, it should fit into grooves incised near the bottom of all four sides.

  Furthermore, it should be reinforced with glue blocks, at least one to a side (preferably more). The work should be neat and solid.

- Examine the guiding mechanism. There are several parts to this. The drawer bottom should have a hardwood rail in the center, screwed in place below the bottom surface, and heavily waxed. There should be a corresponding channel inside the chest. This is called a center guide. Very wide drawers sometimes have more than one guide.

- In addition, at the inside corners of the "bearer," the front railing inside the chest, on which the drawer rests, there should be metal glides—looking like large thumbtacks.

  Very fine furniture also has drawer slides—extenders built into the outside face of the drawer sides. This principle, also used in file cabinets, allows a drawer to be pulled almost all the way out without sagging.

- Now, feel the side rails inside the chest, the pieces on which the bottom side edges of the drawer rest when it's in place. These should be heavily waxed, as should the corresponding edges of the drawer itself.

- Finally, examine the drawer front—the part you see when the drawer is all the way in. Is it well finished? Are the edges well finished? Are the drawer pulls attractive and well mounted? Are they strong enough to do the job when the drawer is full?

  If, by applying these tests, you determine that you're holding a drawer of good quality, you needn't worry much about the rest of the piece. The workmanship will be excellent —and a quick glance should confirm this.

One final word about bedroom furniture: It tends to last forever, far longer than the upholstered furniture you buy for the livingroom, far longer than, say, the kitchen table and chairs, which get heavy wear.

For this reason, we advise you to select it with the greatest care. You don't have to buy the highest quality, although over the years you'll be pleased if you did. But you owe it to yourself to buy something you genuinely like.

This goes double for those bedroom items you'll be using most—your mattress and foundation. Our advice: Ignore whatever the label says about firm, extra firm, etc. Forget about such words as orthopedic.

Instead, lie down on the mattress—right there in the store. Try it out for at least two full minutes (less than that and you won't really be able to get a feel for it.) You needn't test the foundation this way, since the mattress is responsible for 80 percent of the way a bed feels.

When you're sure the mattress will give you the type of comfort you want—and only then—buy it. Otherwise, you're risking a mistake that will plague you every night, for a decade or so.

As for case goods, in addition to the chests and dressers you'll need for your clothing, treat yourself to at least one nightstand —the little one-drawer chest that's designed to sit beside a bed, near its head. You'll need it to hold your lamp, your clock radio, yor nighttime reading matter, your midnight snack, your glasses, etc.

Storage and Closets

Everyone dreams of an apartment with room for everything they own, and everything they hope to accumulate in the future: complete summer and winter wardrobes, a matched set of luggage, several boxes full of extra china, a complete set of sporting gear, a bicycle, several hundred books—well, there's no end to the list.

But what everyone (or practically everyone) actually gets is an apartment with minimal storage facilities—the smallest number of closets the builder or owner can get away with plus, with luck, a tiny locker in the basement for really bulky items.

How can you reconcile dream with reality?

Well, we're happy to report that the wish for extra storage space is one wish that you can make come true. You can make the storage space you need, or you can buy it, or you can do a little of both.

Put briefly, you can add storage space to a cramped apartment in the following ways: with wardrobes, by revamping and reorganizing closets, with bookshelves, with room divider/storage units, and with wall systems. We'll take them one by one.

WARDROBES

What do you do if you simply don't have enough closets? You buy them. Or, if you're handy, you make them. They're called wardrobes. And what they are is large cabinets, usually with full-length, double doors, and a combination of shelves and hanging rods inside.

Wardrobes are available in all steel, with steel bodies and wooden (or composition) doors, or in all wood. The all-wood kind comes in both finished and unfinished varieties.

To use a wardrobe, of course, you need floor space. They're usually about 20 inches deep and they vary in width from 21 inches or so, to as much as 60 inches or so. In height, they range from about 60 inches to as much as 72 inches.

If you don't have enough closets, wardrobes are about your only sensible alternative—other than convincing your landlord to put in more. But in at least one way, wardrobes are better than closets: You can take them with you to your next apartment. And if you move into a house, they're excellent in the attic, for storing out-of-season clothing.

Best of all, they're not very expensive. Current mail-order department store catalogs list wardrobes 3 feet wide for less than $100.

CLOSETS

Another way to increase storage space—without buying or making any additional pieces of furniture—is to make the most of your existing closets.

Now what can I do, you may ask, to make the most of my existing closets, other than to stuff them to the brim? Well, you can buy or make closet organizers that make far better use of the existing space than does the traditional one-rod, one-shelf design.

What you need is a closet with at least two poles for hanging clothes—a high pole for pants or skirts, a low pole for jackets. What you also need is a closet with several shelves, at several different levels, plus a rack for shoes and perhaps compartments for sweaters or folded shirts.

This is more easily achieved than you might think. Department stores and mail-order catalogs sell all kinds of closet organization systems. The simplest of these consists of shelves, poles, and shoe racks mounted on metal poles. These poles are kept in place with internal, spring-tension devices that hold them tight against floor and ceiling.

Such a system can increase useful closet space by nearly 50 percent. If you doubt that, just take a look at your most crowded closet. Note the empty space below your hanging jackets. Note how much of that single high shelf is actually accessible. Look at the jumble of shoes on the floor.

In addition to the spring-tension units mentioned above, there are all kinds of other prefinished, precut, adjustable shelving systems on the market. These come in steel, particleboard, and wood, in every shape, width, and length you can imagine. Most include appropriate hardware and fasteners. You can buy these closet organizers at home center, hardware, and building supply stores.

For the apartment dweller, temporary systems are probably best. Permanent systems may require your landlord's permission before they can be installed—and you won't be able to take them with you when you leave.

BOOKSHELVES

So far as we know, no one has ever calculated the number of different types of bookshelves now available. We doubt anyone ever could, since there are so many.

Basically, however, bookshelves are available in the following general categories:

Wall-mounted shelves. These are planks of lumber that fit onto strips of metal or wood that are screwed into the wall. The shelf supports, which extend from these strips, may be made of either metal or wood. Quality varies enormously, depending on the materials used and their finish.

For apartment dwellers, shelving systems of this sort have several advantages. They can be installed on practically any solid wall. They're available in practically every dimension. And when you move, you can take them down fairly easily. And it's no great problem to fill the screw holes left in the wall.

Free-standing shelves—bookcases. These also come in many different designs, styles, and quality levels, ranging from the finely finished and constructed period pieces with glass doors to unfinished units made of a few pine boards nailed together or industrial steel shelving.

The chief advantage of bookcases is portability. They make it easy, for instance, to rearrange a room. The chief disadvantage is lack of expandability or adjustability (although the better bookshelves can be adjusted internally). Screw-together units are also quite versatile.

Spring-tension shelving systems. In these systems, the bookshelves are mounted on poles that extend from floor to ceiling and have some sort of spring-tension arrangement to keep them in place. The shelves are usually adjustable. Some systems offer units other than just shelves—small cabinets, drawer units, even modest "bars," with pull-down, Formica-covered "counters."

These systems are far more versatile than free-standing bookcases, since you can design practically any configuration you want. And from an apartment dweller's standpoint, they're better than wall-mounted shelves, since they don't require drilling into walls.

The only problem with them is in assembling and disassembling the units if you move frequently. If you've purchased a large, complex unit, that can be quite a task. And you have to worry about small parts, particularly fasteners, during your move itself. Once lost, they can be difficult to replace.

Temporary bookshelves. If all of the above is a bit too formal—or too expensive—for you, you can still have bookshelves galore, without much expense and without much effort.

All you need are some bricks (we prefer the used variety), or some decorative concrete blocks, and some planks. Properly filled with an interesting variety of books, bookshelves made by stacking these elements can be practically as attractive as the more-expensive ready-made sort—because books are the most important decorative element of any bookshelf.

In fact, we've seen some "bookcases" in this category that are no more than stacked wooden apple or orange crates, some with labels still in place. They're rustic, that's for sure, but they do the job and the price is right.

If you like this notion, but are willing to spend a little more money, you might consider the brightly colored plastic "milk" crates now being sold as playroom toy containers. It's easy to stack them three or four rows high—and they certainly add a dash of color to the room.

ROOM DIVIDERS AND WALL SYSTEMS

Many modern apartments have long or L-shaped living-rooms. The builders expect tenants to divide these rooms informally into living and dining areas.

This type of room has given birth to a whole class of furniture —the room divider. Room dividers are nothing more than more or less elaborate variations on free-standing bookcases, or spring-tension wall units.

Normally, room dividers are purchased by the unit—most designs offering at least half-a-dozen different types of units: single shelves, double-shelf units with drawers, base cabinets with drawers or doors.

Another type of room divider consists entirely of a row of widely spaced shelves. This is available in several different widths, or it can be used in multiple units.

Room dividers have a somewhat paradoxical purpose. One of their functions is to separate one part of the room from the other. But another of their functions is to create an openness impossible with a wall, so that each of the two areas can expand, at least visually, into the other.

Both of these functions will be affected by which units you choose to put together and use as a room divider and what use you put them to. For instance, your room divider will be relatively open. On the other hand, if you buy cabinet units or stuff the shelves with books, the two areas you're trying to divide will be more shut off from each other.

The major decorative problem with room dividers has to do with viewing angle. Ideally, they will have no front and no back. They'll be interesting and well-designed whether you're looking at them from the living part of your room or the dining part.

Wall systems are essentially the same as room dividers, except for placement. As you might guess, they go against a wall—usually the longest wall in the room, for they're normally quite wide.

From a storage standpoint, room dividers and wall systems can be a Godsend. With the proper mix of cabinets, there are few household goods they can't absorb—linens, Mixmasters, extra dishes, ice skates, cardboard boxes filled with cancelled checks, the old portable sewing machine, etc.

Unfortunately, the more elaborate the system, the more expensive it's likely to be. Also, the most reasonably-priced units are usually modern or contemporary in style, and built of oiled walnut, teak, or rosewood. Highly-polished period designs, often found in mahogany or cherry, are far more expensive.

OTHER METHODS OF STORAGE

In addition to the above, there are several other types of furniture that provide storage space:

- Livingroom tables that are actually small cabinets;
- Large desks;
- Filing cabinets;
- Flat, drawer-like units that slip underneath a bed;
- Antique steamer trunks;
- Cedar chests (often placed at the foot of the bed);
- Platform beds with drawers below the mattress platform;
- Toychests (they're usually inexpensive—and commodious.

Our point here—and throughout this section: If you find that your apartment simply doesn't have enough storage space, there are many ways to acquire the space you need, ways that will enhance the livability and appearance of your apartment instead of detracting from it.

You can purchase practically everything we've mentioned, in a wood, style, color, or finish that will harmonize with the rest of your furnishings. Or, if you're handy enough, you can consult one of the many do-it-yourself books on the market and build exactly what you want.

One way or another, though, you don't need to live with some of your possessions semi-permanently piled up in a corner or shoved under the bed.

Where to Buy It

For many people, one of the most difficult furniture-buying decisions is where to shop. The choices are legion: conventional furniture stores, used furniture outlets, antique shops, auctions, department stores, catalogs, wholesale houses, decorators, garage sales, flea markets, mail-order catalogs, classified ads, auctions.

Each of these sources has its advantages and disadvantages. Some are good for certain types of furniture, but not others. What follows is a brief guide, so you'll have at least an idea where to start—and what to expect.

CONVENTIONAL FURNITURE STORES

By far, the greatest amount of furniture sold in the United States is marketed through conventional retail outlets. These divide, roughly, into three very different types of stores:

Stores selling low- and medium-quality furniture. These are the outfits with the largest, brightest neon signs, the stores that hold "sales" most frequently, and that fill the newspapers with hyperthyroid advertising. These stores usually allow buying on installment plans.

Stay out of stores like these if you're a sucker for salesmanship, if you're not a smart shopper, or if your friends tell you you're gullible. Otherwise you may wind up with more furniture than you can use in two lifetimes—and payments that your children may have to pick up.

On the other hand, if you're a canny shopper, if you can't be swayed from your stated goal, and if you're a good bargainer (you should be able to get at least 25 percent off the marked price), stores like these are excellent places to find the following:

- Unfinished furniture;
- Durable case goods;
- Mattresses and foundations (but buy *only* nationally advertised brands);
- Appliances (but check prices carefully, using national mail-order catalogs or department store prices as a guide);
- Lamps;
- Kitchen furniture.

But don't go to such stores looking for quality upholstered goods, quality diningroom furniture, or top-of-the-line case goods.

Stores selling higher-priced furniture. Known in the trade as high-tone stores, these are genteel places, with soft-voiced sales-people. Their signage and advertising is quiet and tasteful; their clientele is better-dressed than what you'd find in stores selling low- and medium-quality furniture; and they're the place to go if you're looking for quality upholstered goods and quality dining-room furniture. You'll also find excellent occasional tables and lamps here. But few of these stores carry anything truly distinguished. The very finest furniture, as we shall see, is for the most part sold elsewhere.

Even if you prefer the atmosphere at stores like these, don't shop in them for articles better purchased at stores selling low- and medium-priced furniture. You'll pay through the nose—and you won't be able to bargain, since that's out of the question at most high-tone stores.

Factory outlets. We're using this term here as a catch-all, to refer mainly to stores located at the edge of the city or in some other out-of-the-way place, in a warehouse atmosphere.

These stores offer minimal service—and, very often, minimal furniture. A large proportion of what they sell is imported from cheap-labor countries. Much of it comes disassembled. Some items are close-outs or seconds, some rejects. They often charge for delivery.

You can buy well at stores like these, but we advise you to enter with a suspicious attitude. Be suspicious about the price, the quality, the guarantee, the delivery date—everything. And don't buy anything until you feel completely reassured.

In addition to these three main types of conventional furniture store, there are stores that specialize in particular categories of furniture (the Castro Convertible chain is an example) and stores that specialize in particular design periods, usually contemporary or Scandinavian modern. In addition, there are stores that sell only appliances.

These are good places to shop if you're interested in seeing a large selection of whatever it is they carry. But they subdivide in much the same way full-line furniture stores do, so shop accordingly.

USED-FURNITURE OUTLETS

There is a kind of no-man's land between the conventional furniture store and the antique shop and it's occupied by the used-furniture outlet. They're usually found in the seediest parts of town and they're often shoestring operations (which means you shouldn't place much faith in any guarantee they may offer, since there's no telling if they'll still be there next month).

Sometimes, large, installment-type furniture stores have separate used-furniture outlets (or they even sell used furniture in the main store, well away from the new goods.) This stock is composed mainly of "trade-ins"—furniture taken in trade on new furniture—or of repossessed furniture.

As far as we're concerned, used-furniture stores are excellent sources of decent-quality case goods. But we wouldn't buy upholstered furniture there unless the Pope vouched for it. And, as for mattresses and box springs, forget it. You never know who died—or from what—on a used mattress.

We're also quite wary of buying appliances from used-furniture outlets. Used refrigerators and washing machines have usually been disposed of by the prior owner for good reason— they're shot. Used gas ranges, on the other hand, may be worth the risk, since they're usually easily repaired if not in good working order.

If it's used furniture you're after, for reasons of taste and budget, there are several other places to get it, by the way—all of which are likely to be less expensive than used-furniture outlets (though the prices are usually cheap enough at these places and subject to considerable downward negotiation).

GARAGE SALES

As far as we're concerned, garage sales are an excellent place to find used furniture, especially small case goods: desks, chests, occasional tables, wooden chairs, bookcases, etc. Generally, prices are very low. Upholstered goods aren't terribly common at garage sales, but that's just as well, since you can never be sure that such furniture isn't mildewed, infested with bugs or otherwise unsuitable.

The main problem with garage sales, we think, is lack of selection. Very little truly substantial furniture ever shows up at such sales, unless the person holding the sale is moving or getting divorced. That illustrates a point we've been making about furniture: You keep it practically forever.

FLEA MARKETS

From the furniture buyer's point of view, these are simply garage sales *en masse*. That's all to the good, since it means you're likely to find a fairly good selection of merchandise, if the flea market is well-attended by dealers.

But, once more, stick to wooden pieces here, avoiding upholstered goods unless they're absolutely beautiful. Incidentally, don't pick up a worn upholstered piece with the thought of having it redone. Reupholstery is horrendously expensive and unless the piece is a genuine classic, it's rarely worth the money, even if you're willing to spend it.

CLASSIFIED ADS

Many newspapers, particularly on Sundays, carry columns of "for sale" ads, in which you can find practically every type of furniture or appliance. In addition, most metropolitan areas have entire newspapers that carry nothing else but ads.

We think this is probably the best way to buy used furniture. Usually, the seller is the original owner and, when you go to see the piece, you're also seeing how it's been used and how it's been cared for.

Most of the furniture advertised in the classifieds is relatively new, in our experience. And the sellers are hoping to get a substantial amount of money for it. So, if there's any place to buy used upholstered furniture, this is it. But don't expect the style, color, or covering of your dreams. Be grateful if you can find something that will do the job.

You can even pick up decent used appliances through the classifieds. How so? Because the appliances haven't been traded in on something new, like the used appliances at used-furniture outlets. Furthermore, since the appliances are probably still in use in the seller's home, you'll have no trouble making sure they work properly.

As for price, don't spend more than half of what the piece would cost new. In fact, 25 percent is more like it. And when in doubt, bargain.

Why are we so enthusiastic about the classifieds? Mainly because the seller isn't a dealer. He's not pretending to be an expert, he's not trying to make a profit. And he knows he's dealing with another individual more or less like himself.

But, back to new furniture . . .

DEPARTMENT STORES

Like furniture stores, these come in two general categories: discount stores and standard department stores.

Discount department stores. These outlets don't usually carry a great deal of furniture, but what they stock is apt to be of medium quality at best. More likely, it's of low quality—just above dime-store level.

On the other hand, you can't often beat discount-store prices. So don't hesitate to shop at such places if price is your prime criteria. But, alas, you won't be able to bargain here. The sales-people simply aren't authorized to bargain, even if you can find one.

Standard department stores. Most full-line department stores carry all the furniture you'll ever need. And usually it's quite good—although rarely the equal of high-tone furniture stores.

One of the best aspects of department-store furniture shopping is the price. It's not that the furniture is cheap. It's not. But the prices are legitimate—that is, the mark-ups are fair. (This may not be the case in installment-type furniture stores, which sometimes mark up prices to the sky, so they can appear to cut them dramatically during sales.)

Since a department store's furniture prices are generally legitimate, so are its sale prices. They're actually a reduction in the normal selling price, rather than a manipulation of price tag numbers. So, if you want good furniture at the lowest possible price, we recommend that you watch the department store ads.

MAIL-ORDER DEPARTMENT STORES

In addition to the regular department stores every major city has, there are the mail-order department stores—the ones that also have chains of retail outlets: Sears, Penney's, and Montgomery Ward. The Spiegel catalog falls more or less in the same category.

There are some definite advantages to shopping through these catalogs or at these stores. First, the prices are "legitimate," à la department store. Second, the merchandise is of moderate quality. This means you'll be getting good value for your money here. It also means that sales are genuine, a time for picking up real bargains.

There are also some disadvantages. If you limit yourself to catalog shopping, for instance, you won't be able to examine the merchandise until it arrives at your apartment. You may be satisfied with it, you may not. On the other hand, if you don't like it for any reason, you should have no trouble returning it.

Another disadvantage to shopping at these catalog houses is that you can rarely buy brand-name merchandise. Sears and Ward, in particular, market mainly private-label products—merchandise that may be manufactured by a famous factory, but is identified with a Sears or Ward brand name. This means you'll have some trouble comparison shopping, particularly when it comes to appliances.

Finally, although the furniture sold through these channels is usually sturdy and serviceable, it is the epitome of mass production. From the quality, style, and construction standpoint, it's rarely more than utilitarian.

That doesn't mean it's bad. It's not. It's average, or perhaps a shade better. Of course, the vast majority of America finds that quite satisfactory. But if you buy from one of these firms, be prepared to come across your furniture in friends' apartments. You're not exactly getting one-of-a-kind merchandise.

WHOLESALE HOUSES

If you have the connections—a friend or relative in the business—it is possible to shop in the wholesale houses, particularly if you live in New York, Chicago, or another major city, where furniture is sold to dealers in showrooms.

But beware—if you don't have a genuine connection, you won't be able to get into a genuine wholesale house. They're strictly reserved for the trade. And should you find a place that calls itself a wholesale house, but allows anyone to enter and buy, what you're in is a retail store of some kind—possibly one that specializes in a certain type of furniture, or one that discounts— but a retail store nonetheless.

When you see the price of retail furniture, you'll no doubt wish you could buy wholesale. And you may jump at the chance, if it's offered to you. But, buying wholesale isn't as good as it sounds. We know, since we've been doing it for years.

The advantage is plain enough—it's price. Wholesale prices are about half of department store prices (when merchandise isn't on sale.) A $1,000 couch, then, will cost you about $500 wholesale —maybe less.

Now for the disadvantages:

- If you buy wholesale, you can only buy from manufacturers who supply your friend or relative. They may or may not make the style you want, or offer fabrics you like, etc. And if not, you'll have to compromise.

    It may not be so bad to compromise, if you don't have your heart set on something. But if you do, you'll never really be happy with what you've bought.
- If you buy wholesale, you won't be able to buy exactly at dealer cost—not without costing your friend or relative some money. He'll have to do all the paperwork and processing—a service which, by custom, earns him 10 percent. So if you're being fair, your lowest price will be "cost plus 10."
- If you buy wholesale, you may have delivery problems. Furniture stores are open during normal business hours, so trucks have no trouble delivering furniture to them. But if you have something shipped directly to you, you may have problems connecting with the delivery truck. And you can't have the piece delivered to your friend or relative, for later delivery to you, unless his store happens to be nearby.
- If you buy wholesale and something goes wrong—the furniture arrives broken, or the fabric or style is incorrect—you have a real problem. How do you get the mistake corrected? How much do you want to complain to your friend or relative?

    If you buy wholesale and you have trouble with the furniture, you have another serious problem. Let's say the springs pop, or the joints in the chairs loosen. Who fixes the problem?

Does all of this mean you should never buy wholesale? Not really. If your friend or relative's store is nearby (your apartment is within his delivery area), you're probably all right. But be prepared to ask for further favors if something goes wrong.

DECORATORS

There is no way to pay more for furniture than buying it through a decorator. The mark-ups are astronomical—100 percent, 200 percent, even 300 percent being quite common.

On the other hand, when you buy through a decorator, you're also buying his aesthetic expertise. Certainly that's worth something. But just what it's worth is anyone's guess.

It must also be said that the only way to buy the very highest quality furniture made today is through a decorator (or wholesale, from the manufacturers who make it).

A certain level of manufacturers simply will not sell their products through any retail outlets. They'll sell *only* through decorators. So decorators can show you furniture you just will not find in stores, no matter how high-toned.

Furthermore, if you buy through a decorator, you'll probably have access to all the wholesale showrooms he deals with. He may take you there himself or he may send you to browse by yourself. (But if you go by yourself, don't expect anyone to quote you prices. They leave that part of it to your decorator.)

Should you go the decorator route? That depends on whether or not you're willing to let someone else create your apartment —and on whether or not you have the money that involves.

Frankly, we'd rather do it ourselves. The furniture might not be quite as good, the look not quite as perfect. But the apartment will reflect *our* taste, not someone else's.

AUCTIONS

Furniture auctions are one of America's national pastimes— and have been for decades. At the very least, they're entertaining and educational. At the most, you can pick up some nice pieces of furniture for far less than their market value.

We strongly urge you to find out where the furniture auctions are held in your area (there's hardly any place in the country without them). Then go. Make it a social occasion. Bring friends. But *don't* buy. At least, don't buy the first time you go. In fact, we'd advise waiting until you've sat through at least four or five auctions.

Why delay? Well, if you rush things, you're likely to make mistakes. You may have no trouble determining the quality of a piece, but it will take you awhile to learn the going rate in your area.

As far as we're concerned, half the fun in an auction is buying at the right price. If you do it, you'll be surprised at how much satisfaction it gives you—and how long the satisfaction lasts.

We have, for instance, a golden oak pedestal table that we bought for $25. It was worth at least $100 at the time and who knows how much it's worth now. So we have a piece of furniture that not only fills our needs, it also makes us feel smart. What else could you want?

There are, here we go again, several types of auctions. For the sake of convenience, let's divide them into two: fancy-folk auctions and common-folk auctions. The former deals with quality antiques, even museum pieces. The latter mainly deals in borderline antiques and furniture that's too old to be called used. But it also sometimes handles antiques.

We prefer the common-folk auctions. There's a better chance of getting a good buy. You sometimes find yourself bidding against dealers, to be sure, but that's much better than bidding against the museums and collectors who appear at the fancy-folk auctions.

But, to each his own. If you have the cash, the knowledge, and the inclination, by all means try the fancy-folk auctions. And even if you don't, you owe it to yourself to visit them once and awhile, if only to see what really goes on here.

ANTIQUE SHOPS

There is practically as much disagreement about what an antique is as there is about the definition of "love." The same might be said of "antique" shops. Some are fancy, some middle-brow, and some decrepit. And what they sell usually, but not always, has a similar range.

For us, antique furniture is old furniture that, for some reason, has a value exceeding its utility. That reason might be its design, its construction, the workshop it came from, the people who purchased it, or any of a dozen other factors.

The casual eye, even the educated eye, however, can't do much more than determine the piece's utility and overall quality. To understand its value as an antique, you must have special knowledge.

Unless you have this knowledge, we'd recommend that you don't do your buying in antique shops, at least not antique shops of the fancy variety. If you do have this knowledge, well, you don't need our advice.

If you insist on antiquing, however, we strongly suggest that you follow these rules of thumb:

1. Don't buy something just because it's old. It may be old, but common—and worth a lot less than you'd think.
2. Don't buy something you don't like. Just because it's a valuable antique, that's no reason you have to own it. Besides, if you buy something that's ugly, you may never be able to get rid of it.
3. Don't buy something that's falling apart. Condition is a key factor in the value of antiques. Unless you really know what you're doing, therefore, avoid pieces in poor condition.
4. Beware of anything that's too perfect. Unless you're an expert, you can be easily fooled by a fake, handmade in exactly the same style, finish, etc., as the real thing.

HAND-ME-DOWNS

There is one last source of furniture we haven't mentioned: hand-me-downs from friends and family. For most people starting out, they're a Godsend.

But we have two cautions to offer here:

1. Don't accept things you don't truly need. You may come to resent the giver if you wind up with a breakfront that occupies 60 percent of your livingroom—and stands empty at that.
2. Don't accept anything you don't intend to keep for a while. Otherwise, you may have to do some fancy explaining when the giver comes to visit.

About the only other advice we can give concerning the furniture-buying process is this: take your time and enjoy yourself. You're embarking on an enterprise that doesn't happen very often in each lifetime.

Of course, as important as furniture is, it's only one aspect of decorating an apartment. There are the floors to consider, and the walls, and the ceilings, and the windows. And the finishing touches . . .

Chapter 5

FLOORS

Floors. We walk on them, we put our furniture on them, and most of us don't think much about them.

But floors are one of the four main decorative elements of any room (furniture, walls, and windows are the other three).

Furthermore, what you put on your floors—or don't put on them—can dramatically affect a room's comfort. Floor coverings can make a room quiet or noisy, warm or cold, cozy or business-like.

Basically, there are five different categories of floor coverings: 1) carpets and rugs, 2) linoleum, 3) wood, 4) tile, and 5) "other" —our catchall term for such less commonly used floor coverings as sheepskin, fur, straw mats, rubber or plastic matting, canvas, needlepoint, crocheted rugs, and the like.

Each of these floor coverings has its purpose and place. Each is perfect in some applications, awful in others. Each has its own different complexities, cautions, installation problems, care, and cleaning, etc. Some you can easily take with you—others are permanent. Some are relatively inexpensive, others will cost you a bundle. But every one of them requires your active consideration.

The most common type of floor covering, and the type you'll probably want for at least one room, is . . .

Rugs and Carpeting

Strange but true, the famous "Magic Carpet" of ancient Arabia was not a carpet at all. It was a rug.

That's not nitpicking.

"Carpeting" is a term usually reserved for woven floor coverings that cover an *entire* floor and are fastened down to it with some kind of tacking system or adhesive.

"Rugs," on the other hand, don't occupy an entire room. They're usually not fastened down in any formal way (although people do sometimes tack down their edges to prevent them from slipping, or to make sure people don't trip on them).

Carpets are generally cut to fit (unless you happen to have a room that's exactly the size of a piece of cut carpeting a dealer has in stock). Rugs are precut and prefinished at the edges in most cases.

Other than that, they're identical. Both can be made of a wide variety of fibers, in a wide variety of textures, in a wide variety of constructions, in solids or patterns.

Each has advantages and disadvantages.

Carpeting, for instance, covers a floor completely—and some worn or grungy floors need nothing more. Carpeting gives a room a finished look. It's good at reducing noise within the room and even masking noise coming up through the floor. It has a certain amount of insulation value—and heaven knows, it feels warmer to the tootsies on a cold morning than a plain wood floor.

On the other hand, carpeting is rather permanent. To be sure, you can pick it up when you move and take it with you, but the chances are you'll have to use it as a rug in your new place, or as a wall-to-wall covering in a smaller room.

Carpeting doesn't usually wear as well as rugs do, and this has nothing to do with construction, fiber, etc. Because carpeting is permanently installed, it must be cleaned in place—never as good as sending it out. And ground-in dirt reduces carpet life. Also, carpeting can't be shifted or rotated to equalize wear and fading.

Rugs, however, are totally portable. They can easily travel from room to room or apartment to apartment. Unlike carpeting, they have an independent existence.

Because rugs can be shifted to equalize wear and fading—and sent out to be cleaned—they usually last longer than carpeting, sometimes much longer. That's why rugs sometimes become heirlooms, to be passed down from generation to generation.

Because of their easy portability and long-wearing qualities, rugs are probably better investments than carpeting (although

Here's how parquet floors can be used along with small area rugs. It's hard to match the natural beauty of wooden parquet floors. But softer floor-coverings —a straw mat in this case—add luxury and sound-absorbency.

carpeting can be made into rugs if it's not too worn). For this reason, it's easier to sell a rug than a carpet, and for a better price.

Rugs also have some decorative advantages over carpeting. First, they're what you want if you have a beautiful floor and you want to display part of it. Second, it's no great trick to switch a rug from one room to another, changing your decor completely. You can't do that with a carpet.

On the other hand, rugs aren't as good as carpeting at reducing noise, maintaining warmth, or creating a finished-off look.

In the end, to quote an old saying, "You pays your money and you takes your choice." We have some of each.

FIBERS

Whether you decide on carpeting or rugs, one of the first decisions you're likely to face is which fiber you should buy. None is perfect. Each has different advantageous qualities:

Wool. This is the traditional rug and carpeting fiber—and it has a lot to recommend it. It's warm, durable, strong, and resilient. It cleans relatively easily, although it holds onto stains rather persistently.

But wool is subject to damage from moths and animal urine. It sometimes causes allergic reactions. And it's the most expensive carpet and rug fiber commonly found on the marketplace.

Acrylic (Acrilan, Orlon, Creslan). This term refers to a group of synthetic fibers. Their advantages: They're relatively fade-proof, they release stains fairly quickly—and they're less expensive.

On the other hand, they're not as easy to clean, overall, as wool, and they're nowhere nearly as resilient.

Nylon. Perhaps the synthetic most commonly used in carpets and rugs, nylon is strong, resilient, and durable. It usually shrugs off mildew, insects, and common household chemicals.

Nylon does have some disadvantages, however. It's rather hard and shiny, for instance, which can make for an unpleasant surface except in long, lightweight shags. It's also very prone to produce static electricity, especially in conditions of low humidity.

Polyester (Kodel, Fortrel, Dacron). This is another synthetic frequently used in rugs and carpets. Its advantages: It's resistant to fading and stains and it's luxuriously thick in most cases. Its disadvantages: It isn't very resilient and it doesn't clean all that well. Also, it doesn't wear as well as nylon or acrylic or wool fibers.

Polypropylene (including Herculon and other olefins). These synthetic fibers are essentially different than all the fibers listed above in that they don't have a "wooly" texture. Instead, they're hard —something on the order of synthetic grass. So they're not ideal for bedrooms, bathrooms, or livingrooms, where comfort is a major factor.

But these fibers are extremely stain-resistant and they clean very easily. That makes them perfect for kitchens, playrooms, and other locations where food and beverage spills are common.

Cotton. In general, this is not a good carpeting fiber, since it isn't all that durable, since it's subject to fading, and since it can shrink in some circumstances.

However, cotton is popular in small throw rugs for bathrooms —rugs that can be tossed into the washing machine without doing them any harm. It's also often found, in combination with nylon or by itself, in larger braided rugs—the thick, flat traditional rugs often used with Colonial decor.

TEXTURES

Many of the fibers we've mentioned above are available in a variety of textures, each with a different decorative effect:

Level loop. This is the strongest, most soil-resistant carpet and rug texture on the market. Its surface consists of a series of low, level, tightly woven loops. It's ideal for heavy traffic areas. But it has one disadvantage: The rather flat pile is somewhat on the hard side and not as luxurious as some higher-pile textures.

Sculptured pile. In this texture, different fiber lengths are used to produce repeating patterns in relief, from one end of the carpet or rug to the other. The best of these are quite beautiful, with interesting, subtle, design effects.

Shags. Shag carpeting or rugs have long twisted fibers that are far longer than other weaves and textures, although shags are actually available in many different lengths. Shags come in solid colors, tweeds, even patterns. They're soft underfoot and they have a relaxed casual look that makes them perfect for bedrooms and playrooms, although definitely not first choice for formal livingrooms.

If you like shag rugs or carpeting, you'd better know that they require a special carpet tool for your vacuum cleaner. Otherwise their long fibers can jam up the works.

Random shears. This texture is another way of producing a pattern in rugs or carpeting without the use of varying colors. Here, some fibers are cut, others are looped. The result is a subtle and often very pleasing overall design.

Two-level loop. This is a variation on sculptured piles and random shears. Here, as the name implies, carpets and rugs are woven to two different surface levels, producing an overall pattern in the pile itself. It's second in wearing quality only to level-loop rugs and carpets.

Cut pile (also known as plush and velvet). This texture has a smooth, even surface, with all fibers cut to the same length. It "shades" in use—as the fibers are stepped on or pushed in different directions, subtle color changes are produced. The effect is soft and luxurious (although the color differences drive some people crazy.) This texture doesn't wear as well as the looped textures or shears.

Indoor-outdoor carpeting. This product, usually made out of polypropylene, actually is available in three textures: a flat, felt-like surface; a flat, densely-looped pile; and a shaggy grasslike weave. It's impervious to practically everything, it's relatively inexpensive, it's easily cut, and it's easily installed. But it's anything but elegant, since the surface is often unpleasantly hard to the touch.

Incidentally, while we're talking about carpet and rug terms, three words come to mind that have sewn more confusion here than any others: Broadloom, Axminster, and Wilton. Salesmen often throw them about as evidence of quality. They're not.

Axminster and Wilton are the names of English towns that once manufactured cut-pile or velvet-pile carpeting. The two are manufactured in slightly different ways, with slightly different results. You can ignore the differences.

Broadloom is one of those magic words that reeks with quality —until you examine it. It refers, as it says, to a broad loom. It doesn't refer to quality at all. It's just a way of differentiating between precut carpets or rugs, and roll carpeting, which is made in widths of up to 18 feet these days (more commonly 12 or 15 feet).

This floor covering is the cheapest carpet available—flat surface indoor-
outdoor carpeting. It's essentially indestructible. Neither water nor sun can
harm it much. Here, two colors have been cut into semirectangular carpet tiles
and attached to the underflooring either with two-sided tape or adhesive. The
price is low, the effect striking.

QUALITY

Speaking of quality, how can you, as a layman, tell the difference between good, bad, and indifferent carpets and rugs? Very often, the difference isn't apparent at first or even second glance. Well, there are some clues:

1. Look at the rows of yarn. The closer the weave, the better. This can be checked from the front of the carpet, by bending it backward.
2. Check fiber texture. The firmer, the more tightly twisted the fiber, the better. Fibers with little body just don't stand up.
3. Compare yarn weight. The heavier the better. (But make sure you're comparing yarns of the same fiber. There's no way to cross check, for instance, nylon and wool.)
4. Look at the back. Quality carpeting has a closely-woven, jute backing. Cheaper carpeting has a flat-rubber or foam-rubber backing. We're not saying you shouldn't buy this type of carpeting. We're just saying it isn't very high quality—not suited to formal livingrooms and diningrooms, for instance (but fine for kitchens, playrooms, and bathrooms).
5. Compare fiber length. The longer, the better. Also, unfortunately, the longer the more expensive. But the rule of thumb in carpeting, as in most everything else, is that you can pay a lot for shoddy goods, but it isn't easy to find quality merchandise at a low price.
6. Check the balance of yarn rows and stitches. If the carpetmaker hasn't struck an even balance, the carpet will have a patchy look and feeling.
7. Tug on the fibers (but don't go into your "Hulk" imitation). They should be firmly implanted. If they come out very easily, choose another carpet.

PADDING

While you're in the carpet store, your salesman will doubtless bring up the subject of padding. And, unless you're well informed on this subject, you may think that what he's really trying to pad is your bill. Not so.

The truth is, all carpets and rugs *need* padding. It's the best way we know to extend their lives. Without padding, carpets and rugs are truly stuck between a rock and a hard place: your heel and the floor. In high-traffic areas, it won't take long before unpadded carpets and rugs are ground to pieces.

Several different padding materials are available, each, naturally, with its own particular advantages and disadvantages:

Curled horsehair. This type of pad mixes horsehair with latex. It's flexible, it wears practically forever, it provides good ventilation and it absorbs moisture—all desirable qualities. Its only drawback is that it isn't very soft.

Sponge rubber. Well, it's not rubber anymore, but that's what people still call it. This material usually consists of inch-square bubbles of thin synthetic rubber sheeting on a fiber scrim. Alternatively, it consists of rubber sheeting in a herringbone pattern, again glued to a fiber scrim. This material is soft and bouncy, but it tends to break down with heavy use.

Urethane foam. This padding consists of simple sheets of urethane foam, in various thicknesses and densities. This type is our choice for most rugs and carpeting. It's durable, it's springy, it's easy to handle.

There are other types of padding available, specifically jute and hair mixtures or just plain jute. They work, but not as well as those listed above.

If money is an issue, there is a way to keep costs down and still pad your rug adequately. Just use another rug. An old, worn-out one will do perfectly well. But it should be about the same size as the new rug.

One other type of padding must be mentioned here: the self-padded rug or carpet—one that comes with a rubber pad already glued to the back.

Originally, rugs and carpets with this construction were about the least expensive, lowest-quality woven floorcoverings you could purchase. But in recent years, rubber paddings have been mated with carpets and rugs of better and better quality.

The result is a package that is easy to lay (if you're buying carpeting) and unlikely to unravel, stretch, or wrinkle. Best of all, the thickest varieties of this material don't really need to be tacked down. They simply stay in place.

HOW MUCH DO YOU NEED?

Before you can start shopping for rugs or carpets, you have to know how far your money will stretch. The first step is to figure out what size rug you want or how many square yards of carpeting you'll need.

Rugs. If you have decided, for various reasons, on a rug, measure the area you hope to cover. We advise getting a rug large enough to go at least under the front legs of your major pieces of furniture. Anything less will be a constant annoyance, and it will look somehow shrunken. Your other alternative is to buy a rug that is considerably smaller—one that has at least a one-foot border on all sides between it and your major pieces of furniture.

Not sure which is the right alternative for you? Set up your furniture as you intend it to be and draw in the outline of your yet-to-be-purchased rug, using chalk. When you've got the most pleasing size, measure it. Then take the measurements to the store.

Of course, since rugs come precut and prebordered (sometimes with fringe on each end, or all four sides), you may not be able to get exactly the size you want. In such a case, buy the next-largest size. But leave at least a foot around the edge of the room. Otherwise it will seem as though you've purchased wall-to-wall carpeting but made a measuring mistake.

Carpets. Figuring out how much carpeting you need is simpler in principle, but harder in practice, than determining your rug size. What you do is make a sketch of the room you intend to carpet, including every nook and cranny, every jig and jog, heat registers, trap doors, alcoves, window seats, etc. Then measure the dimensions of everything.

Unless your room is perfectly rectangular and unless one of its dimensions exactly matches the width of the broadloom you're buying, you're going to find you need more square feet of carpeting than you think, to avoid extra seams and patching. But you can have the extra carpet made into throw rugs or save it for potential repairs.

BUYING CARPETING

Chances are, if you live anywhere near a metropolitan area, there are dozens of carpet stores within driving distance of your apartment. We strongly recommend that you check out several before making any buying decision.

We also recommend that you don't listen too closely to the salesman when he starts talking about quality, fiber, manufacturer, texture, popularity, how much carpeting his store sells, etc.

But listen closely when he starts talking about yardage, guarantees, installation charges, delivery and installation dates, extra charges (such as for stairways, bound edges, cutouts for fireplaces, etc.).

If you're not sure about color or texture, most reputable stores —if they think you're seriously interested—will let you take home a swatch or two (sometimes even a sample throw rug) to see how it goes with your furniture. A semi-satisfactory alternate to this is to get some poster board at an art store that matches the carpet color you think you want and bring it home to try it against the furniture.

When you're ready to buy, get *everything* in writing. Be friendly, be polite, but don't be trusting. You'll need:

- The total price of carpet and padding, plus delivery and installation (if you're not laying it yourself);
- The exact terms of the guarantee;
- The name of the carpet manufacturer, his code number for the style, color, and grade of carpeting you're buying;
- A precise description of the padding you're buying;
- The exact yardage of carpet and padding;
- The delivery and installation dates.

Once you have all this information in hand, you can put down a deposit on your carpeting. Note, we said "deposit." Do not pay in full. If you do, and something goes wrong, it may be many months before you get satisfaction. For this reason, don't put down more than 25 percent (but be prepared to pay the rest in cash on delivery and/or installation.)

After the carpeting has been delivered to your apartment— but before it's been installed, check it out. Thoroughly. Like everything else man-made, carpets can have flaws. But you've paid for perfect merchandise, so don't accept anything less.

CARING FOR YOUR CARPETING AND RUGS

Let's face it—most rugs and carpeting don't get very good treatment. After all, people are forever walking on them, getting dirt on them, spilling things on them, and otherwise mistreating them.

But rugs and carpeting will last a great deal longer, and look better in the process, if they're properly cared for. Here's how to do it:

Vacuuming. Your carpet or your rug should be thoroughly vacuumed at least once a week. The experts say that means each part should get seven strokes from the vacuum cleaner. Where traffic is heavy, you should vacuum even more often. For best results, move the cleaner slowly. And make sure it's properly adjusted for the height and type of carpet, if it's an adjustable machine.

Cleaning. There are all kinds of ways to clean your carpet, good and not-so-good, expensive and not-so-expensive. Professional carpet-cleaning is usually excellent, although it isn't cheap. Obviously, the professionals have all the equipment, supplies, and know-how they need to do the job right.

But you can do it yourself, by renting carpet-cleaning machines at the hardware store or floor-covering store. These machines do an excellent job, if their instructions are carefully followed. But the carpet will usually take eight hours to dry after this sort of cleaning.

In addition, there are dry powders and aerosol foams on the market said to clean carpeting and rugs in a trice, wih a drying time that's either very short or nonexistent. They do remove some soil, but they're no substitute for shampooing or steam cleaning your carpet. And at best, they only remove surface soil, leaving underlying grit to be ground further into the carpet every time someone walks over it.

Stain removal. Different types of stains require different treatment, but there are five general rules to follow when removing rug or carpet stains:

- Start from the outside and work toward the center of the stain (if you do the opposite, you may spread it).;
- Blot, don't rub. Rubbing can damage the pile;
- Don't soak the carpet or rug. This can cause additional stains from the jute backing;
- Act immediately. The longer a stain sets, the harder it is to remove.
- Always test the stain remover solution in an inconspicuous area of the carpeting before trying it on the stain. Do this by applying the stain remover, then holding a white paper towel

against it for ten seconds. If the paper towel comes up discolored with carpet dye, try another stain remover.

Carpet dealers and professional cleaners have carpet stain-removal charts (too large to reproduce here) that tell you what stain remover to try on what carpet fiber stained with which type of stain. But we're going to offer a simpler solution to the problem —a four-step escalation of stain removers—to try one after the other.

First, try dry-cleaning fluid (the nonflammable type, please). After testing, apply a small amount to the outer edge of the spot. Blot. Continue until the stain is gone.

Second, if the dry-cleaning fluid doesn't do the job, try detergent solution. Mix ¼ teaspoon of dry powder detergent in one cup of warm water, then proceed as with the dry-cleaning fluid.

Third, if the first two stain removers fail, try an ammoniated detergent solution. Add one teaspoon of household ammonia and ¼ teaspoon of dry powder detergent to a cup of warm water. TEST! Then proceed as above.

Fourth, if the first three solutions haven't worked, try white vinegar solution. Mix one part white vinegar to one part water.

After removing the spot, blot up as much liquid as possible. And when your rug or carpet has dried, brush your carpet gently to restore texture.

Carpet and rug "problems." You look at your new rug or carpet, the beautiful floor decoration for which you spent so much money, and you panic. It's shedding. It's sprouting. It's shading. It's pilling. What can you do to keep it from falling apart?

Actually, you don't really have much of a problem at all, if any. Shedding is common to all new carpeting. It's not a defect. It happens when some of the trimmed fibers fall into the carpeting, then come up with vacuuming or wear.

Sprouting—when a tuft pops up above the surface—isn't serious if it only involves one tuft. It can happen when something snags the carpet or rug. Should it happen to you, don't pull— clip. Cut the tuft down to its proper level. If it happens frequently, check your vacuum cleaner—it may be to blame.

Shading is a natural condition of cut-pile carpeting. It happens when the fibers are pressed in different directions by foot traffic or furniture and then reflect light differently. It's not a flaw. Many think it's a mark of great beauty.

Pilling happens when tiny fiber fuzz-balls form and adhere to carpet tufts. It's particularly characteristic of synthetic fibers. It's not a defect, but it can be annoying. Frequent vacuuming is the best solution.

There are two other carpet problems that are real enough, however: fading and wearing.

Fading occurs when carpeting is exposed to direct sunlight for long periods. The solution: Keep the shades drawn or the blinds pulled when possible.

Wearing occurs from, well, foot traffic. If you have wall-to-wall carpeting, there isn't much you can do about it, except to put down throw rugs or plastic mats over areas where traffic is extremely heavy. But if you have a rug, you can reverse it frequently, to at least equalize wear.

Linoleum

Next to rugs and carpeting, linoleum is America's most popular floor covering (and it's way ahead of rugs and carpeting in kitchens, laundry areas, basements, etc.)

But different people mean different things when they use the word "linoleum." We know of four different types: 1) tile, 2) sheet, 3)pourable liquid, and 4) "rugs"—that is, precut sizes, sold rolled-up.

These differ widely in quality and physical characteristics—some are right for one application but not another, for instance. And there are also wide price variations.

LINOLEUM TILE

As of this writing, you can buy 12-inch squares of linoleum tile for anywhere from 24¢ each to $1.59 each, via the large mail-order chains. The range available in retail stores is even greater.

What's the difference—and what are the similarities—between the lowest-priced and the most expensive linoleum tiles?

Well, first the similarities: They are all 12x12 inches, they all have self-adhesive backs with peel-off paper protecting the sticky stuff, they can all be installed over just about any clean, dry, reasonably even surface (even old linoleum), although not over particleboard or flooring felt. They're all made, at least in part, of vinyl, and their patterns go clear through the tile, from front to back. Most are sold in cartons of 45 tiles and they're also available separately.

Now, the differences: Simply put, the more expensive the tile, the greater variety of patterns available, the thicker the tile, the more likely that the surface is textured or embossed, rather than smooth. The best tiles, for instance, are ⅛-inch thick, while the least expensive are 1/16-inch thick.

The least expensive tiles are available in three or four marblized patterns—and that's it. The most expensive are available in every pattern you can imagine and in textures reminiscent of brick, flagstone, ceramic tile, wood block, etc.

Then too, the more expensive tiles have "no-wax," urethane finishes—hard, shiny coatings that require practically no care at all other than the occasional damp-mopping. The cheaper tiles must be waxed if you want a shiny look.

Calculating your needs. If you want linoleum tile for your room, your first step is to figure out how much you'll need. That's easy. Measure the length and the width of your room, then multiply. The result is the number of tiles you'll need. If you have alcoves, do the same, then add the two figures together. Next, add another 10 percent, for trimming or replacement. When you order, order by the carton, to assure color match.

Just to give you an idea, if you're tiling (measuring in feet) a 5x9 vestibule, for instance, you'll need 45 tiles. A 9x10 kitchen or bathroom will take 90 tiles. A 9x15 kitchen (good-sized for an apartment) will need 135 tiles. A family-sized 12x15 kitchen will take 180 tiles. Your tile store will be able to provide you with detailed installation instructions that fit your circumstances.

Of course, before you do put down tile—before you even buy it—check with your landlord. Chances are, he'll be more than pleased to see his property improved. But you never know. Also, consider the fact that whatever tile you put down on the floor this way won't be going with you when and if you move. It's there to stay, more or less.

SHEET LINOLEUM

This material is very similar to linoleum tile, except that the more expensive varieties have a soft, cushiony surface of dense vinyl foam.

Here, two different types of floor covering are used in combination: a braided cotton rug and seamless linoleum, with matching cove strips. Care has been taken to make sure that the two floor coverings have similar colors, but dissimilar patterns and textures.

Commonly available sheet linoleum is sold from as little as about $1.10 a square yard to $10 a square yard—and more. Again, the better versions are available in a greater number of patterns, they have embossed surfaces, they have no-wax, urethane finishes—and layers of cushioning. Most are backed with a non-slip, feltlike surface.

This type of linoleum usually comes in 9- and 12-foot widths and it's sold by the running foot. Thus, if you're covering a floor 9x6 feet, you buy six running feet at the 9-foot width. Again, check with your dealer for installation instructions.

POURABLE LIQUID

If you're not interested in a fancy wood or brick pattern, or if you don't care to have your kitchen floor look like the Alhambra, you can buy a pourable liquid floor that will give much the same effect as sheet linoleum.

This product, which is available at hardware and home center outlets and at flooring stores, is spread on the floor in several layers: a base coat, a coat of laminating plastic, chips of color, then a plastic sealant.

We find this kind of surface perfectly satisfactory for laundry rooms, basements, garages, etc., but not so nice for kitchens and bathrooms. Also, it's more work than putting down tile or sheet.

In addition, liquid linoleum sometimes has to be lightly sanded to remove surface roughness, and it requires one or two days to dry before the furniture can be moved back in.

Still, it does provide a seamless, easily cleaned surface that's a great improvement over concrete floors or plywood.

LINOLEUM "RUGS"

If all you want to do is temporarily cover up an ugly floor—of concrete, plywood, old linoleum, etc.—there's no simpler or cheaper way to do it than with a linoleum "rug."

This product is available in a few standard foot sizes—9x12, 6x9, 9x15 and 12x15—at many different outlets: discount stores, home centers, furniture stores, flooring stores, department stores, etc.

It's not fancy. You've seen the patterns a dozen times, perhaps beginning with Grandma's house. It's not exactly high-quality either. The sheeting is thin and hard. It can crack in cold weather.

But for covering up at small expense, there's nothing better. How much does it cost? You should be able to buy a 9x12 linoleum "rug" for about $12–$14.

You can take this stuff with you when you move, but you probably won't want to. It's just a way to make an ugly floor presentable without spending much money. And as long as you expect nothing more from it, it's perfect for that purpose.

Wood Floors

Chances are that your apartment has wood floors, even if they're covered by carpet, rug, linoleum, or tile. And, chances are, if you have something else—concrete, plywood, etc.—you won't want to take the trouble (and go to the expense) of putting down a wood floor yourself.

So we feel that this section should tell you how to take care of your wood floors, if you have them—not how to install them. Besides, installing a wood floor is a job for a very serious do-it-yourselfer—or a professional.

How you treat and care for your wood floor should be determined by its finish. Most older floors are varnished (ask the landlord or the previous tenant). But if that's impossible or they don't know, take a cotton swab dipped in rubbing alcohol and rub it lightly across an inconspicuous spot on the floor. If the finish comes up, you've got varnished floors.

To keep varnished floors looking nice, wax them twice a year with paste butcher's wax (it comes in a tin and you can buy it at the supermarket). Avoid using liquid waxes on wood. They don't take well and they can give wood floors a patchy, dull finish.

To wax your floor, put some wax on a rag and rub in circular motions, replenishing the rag as needed, until you've covered the whole floor. Now you have a choice—you can either get down on your hands and knees with a soft piece of flannel wrapped around a block of wood and buff until your knees are worn down—or rent a floor buffer.

If you choose the buffer—and that's what we recommend— plug it in and go over the floor, sweeping the machine from side to side. But watch out. These things have minds of their own and, if you get careless, they may get the upper hand and chase you into a corner.

To keep the shine looking good, wash occasionally with plain, lukewarm water. To remove old wax, use hot water and detergent.

Incidentally, one of our friends has come up with a unique way to wax a floor and make the room smell nice at the same time. He mixes a bit of lavender wax into the butcher's wax. It lasts for quite a while, and it's very pleasant indeed.

If you do the alcohol test and nothing comes up, you've probably got a floor with a urethane (plastic) finish. Lucky you. Don't wax it, because the gloss lasts nearly forever. (They use that stuff on ships' decks these days. No more holystoning.)

A urethane finish can be washed with a mild detergent, then rinsed with clear water. If you're the type who gives wild, drunken parties with lots of spilled vodka and assorted people passing out, urethane is what you need.

We once lived in an apartment previously occupied by a genuine swinging bachelor, who did a lot of floor-level bartending, as evidenced by the bottle-sized rings burned through the varnish in one corner of the livingroom.

We could even reconstruct certain events that had occurred at his parties. For example, there was a big splash stain almost three feet long near one window. Apparently, some dear woman had gotten miffed at her escort and thrown her whiskey sour in his face. The little dribbles near the front door were from the ones for the road. These scars in our varnish became conversation pieces when friends from the same building came down for supper. Of course, being sober, upright types, we never even spilled a little cooking sherry.

Maybe you live in such an apartment right now and you don't care for the alcohol stains. You'd like to cover them up, but the room would look silly with three area rugs set catty-corner, out of the traffic flow.

Well, if your floor has extensive alcohol stains, you'll have to refinish the entire floor if you want to get rid of them. But if it's just a case of one or two little drips, sand the stains lightly and apply several thin coats of fresh varnish with a brush, letting each coat dry thoroughly.

It's not easy to refinish a floor. But the results can make it worthwhile. If this is what you decide to do, first get your landlord's approval.

Then, wash the floor with hot water and detergent to get up

any old wax. Rinse and dry thoroughly. Next, rent a floor sander. After that, move all the furniture, pictures and drapes out of the room and shut the doors leading into the rest of the house.

After that, don a surgical mask and goggles, to protect yourself and your lungs. Then, start sanding, going in one direction only, never repeating yourself.

After the whole floor has been sanded, then vacuum, wet-mop, and let dry. If there are rough spots, sand them by hand, starting with medium-grade sandpaper, finishing with light-grade. Let the floor dry thoroughly—at least two days. And during that time, walk on it as little as possible.

At this point, you can stain the floor any color you want, or leave it natural, as long as your landlord agrees. Stain is rubbed in with a rag and left to dry for a day. But don't overstain or you'll get a much darker floor than you planned on. And remember that both varnish and urethane will darken the floor slightly. Furthermore, there may be some of the color from the old stain or varnish still left in the floor, soaked in so deeply that it will never come out.

Once the stain is dry, you're face-to-face with a big decision: to varnish or to urethane? Many people feel that varnish is more subtle, that its shine or gloss is deeper, more appealing, more traditional in feeling.

Others, who are fed up with waxing and worrying about alcohol and water stains, feel that the bright, impervious gleam of urethane suits them just fine.

If you decide on varnish, you must next decide how shiny you want your floor: There are three degrees: high-gloss, semi-gloss, and satin. High gloss shows every bit of dust, every footprint, every little scratch. But if you want to brighten up a room that doesn't get much traffic or light, it may be the right choice.

Semi-gloss also reflects and it's nice in livingrooms, where you may have a lot of brightly colored furniture. Satin isn't dull, but it has a pleasant sheen without a good deal of reflection. It's excellent for halls and for children's rooms. It also makes a too-big room a bit cozier. And it isn't blinding in a room that's already bright.

Okay. How do you go about varnishing the floors? Here's our method:

1. Pour out the varnish, a little at a time, and spread it thinly, using a sponge applicator (brushes leave streaks and hairs).
2. Do a small portion of the floor, then move on, trying not to overlap.
3. Sponge in one direction—and not in circles.
4. When the varnish is completely dry, buff it with a rented buffer.
5. Go over the rough spots with the finest grade (0000) steel wool.
6. Put down at least four coats of varnish—more in high traffic areas.

Here are some more varnishing hints:

- Don't varnish in wet weather—it will take two weeks to dry if water vapor gets into the varnish.
- Allow at least three days between coats.
- The thinner the coat, the less time it will take to dry.
- Don't varnish in extremely hot weather. This could cause the varnish to dry too quickly—and bubble.
- Don't apply varnish that's already bubbly. Let the can sit for a week or two, undisturbed, until the air bubbles disperse.
- Don't let anyone—or anything—walk across the floor until it's completely dry. We know one couple whose two-year-old daughter's footprints are immortalized in their livingroom floor.
- Once the floor is dry, wax it, buff it, and move your furniture back into place.

Unlike varnish, urethane is relatively easy to use. Apply it like varnish, but forget about buffing between coats. It's rarely necessary. Let each coat dry for two days. We recommend three coats. No waxing is needed.

Some authorities recommend a third finish for wooden floors: linseed oil. We don't think much of it. It's fine on furniture, but it's a fire hazard when used on something as big as a floor. Besides, it needs redoing every month or so.

Once waxed, a varnished floor needs only an occasional damp sponge mopping. Don't let the water sit, though, or it will stain. A mild detergent is all you need with urethane, if that. Most people we know who have urethane-finished floors just dust them from time to time.

Ceramic and Clay Tile, Bricks and Flagstone

It's highly unlikely that, as an apartment dweller, you'll want to install any one of these flooring surfaces, either by yourself or with professional help. They're expensive and they're permanent. They're probably too much trouble and too great an investment for the average apartment dweller.

Nonetheless, chances are your apartment already has some ceramic tile on its floors—in the bathroom, perhaps in the kitchen. It may also have a slate or brick entryway. These are becoming more and more common.

So here again, we'll tell you how to take care of what you already have. We also advise you to forgo installing these surfaces yourself, or having them installed, unless you're willing to spend a bundle and willing to say good-bye to them when your lease has expired.

CERAMIC AND CLAY TILE

Several things can go wrong with existing ceramic and clay tile: It can get stained, it can loosen, it can chip, the grout can crumble. But these problems have been covered in the chapter on bathrooms.

To briefly restate the solutions:

- If you've got stains (hard water, food, mildew, rust, etc.), dissolve three tablespoons of liquid bleach (the kind you put in with the white clothes) in a quart of warm water. Wash the tile with household detergent (dish soap, for instance, or a floor cleaner), and rinse.

  Then paint or spray the tile with the bleach solution and let it sit for about five minutes. Rinse and wash again. This should take out most stains without affecting the tile color.
- If your tile is chipped, fill in the hole with the tinted plastic or epoxy made for this purpose (it's available at hardware stores.) If you managed to rescue the chip, just glue it back into place. If a tile is broken, lift it out with a putty knife inserted near the edge, epoxy it back together, and put it back

into place, using the same epoxy. (You may then have to grout the tile, if it's that type. See the bathroom chapter.)

- If your bathroom or kitchen is missing some tiles, you should be able to get closely matching replacements at a tile store. If the tile isn't grouted, just glue in the new one. If you can't get a perfect match, paint it with matching epoxy paint. If the tiles are grouted, lay the new ones the same way, using grout that matches the original (but if you can't find any, use something similar and paint it after it's dry).

If the original builder of your apartment (or a subsequent remodeler) put down an unglazed, unsealed clay tile, he made a mistake—and you may wind up paying for it, at least aesthetically.

Unglazed tile looks naturally beautiful when it's put down, but it soon becomes pitted, stained, and scratched. Tiles like this must be treated a little more carefully than the hardier ceramic type. To clean, dilute your bleach solution by half, and test it in an inconspicuous place. And don't expect perfect results. Stains can soak deeply into unglazed tiles.

BRICKS AND FLAGSTONE

If you're lucky enough to have floors of these substances, about the only problem you're ever likely to have is dirt and stains, since both brick and flagstone are extraordinarily durable, at least in indoor applications.

You'll find that you can scour out most dirt and stains from either material with household cleansers. If these don't quite do the job, you can try the bleaching method, but test it first in that famous inconspicuous spot. And if that fails, try the commercial brick cleaners designed for smoke-blackened fireplaces. They're sold mainly at hardware stores.

If dirt and stains are a big problem in your household, you may want to seal your brick or flagstone floors. This can be done either with varnish or urethane. But check with your landlord first, to make sure it's okay with him.

Both sealers will change the appearance of your brick or flagstone floors, giving them a sheen or gloss, darkening them slightly. But their texture won't change and they'll be easy to clean.

Other Floor Coverings

Let's say you're the adventurous sort—the first kid to own a hula-hoop, the first one in your high school class to travel to Europe alone, the first to buy Scandinavian furniture.

You like things that are different, but not anything that will be outdated in a couple of months. Wall-to-wall carpeting is out —it's too bourgeois. You already own a Rya rug, which you have hanging on your wall. You're looking for something offbeat, something that might be a classic ten years from now.

Well, anything you like can become your own personal classic. For example, we have a much admired, seven-year-old Navaho-style throw rug made of plastic reeds. It's a little worn now, so we keep it in the back office, but in its time, it was a wall hanging, a bath mat, a beach mat, a bedroom rug, and a kitchen rug. It cost less than ten dollars—and we still love it.

Our friend Norman Mandele, who always seems to spot the right thing at the right time, was looking for cheap china in an import store about five years ago. What he found were some circular straw mats about eight feet in diameter. "They advertised them as something for the porch," Norm said. "I could see them under my diningroom table, in the bedroom, sewn together for my giant livingroom. So I bought six."

Of course, not all straw mats are round. They come in squares and rectangles, too, and in various sizes and designs. They're usually found in a natural color, but they may be dyed.

Norm, by the way, took one of the mats he bought and painted the concentric circles in a bright spectrum of colors. Sitting on a dark wood parquet floor, with a white, formica-topped diningroom table on top of it, the mat looked fabulous.

Rubber and plastic matting is another excellent "something different" floor covering. It usually comes as a runner—a long strip 30 inches wide or so. It's perfect for heavily traveled hallways. And the clear plastic kind is an excellent protection for expensive carpeting during the mud or snow season.

If you like the earthy tones of clay tile, but don't want to go to the expense or bother of installing a tile floor, you can still use tile in your apartment. How? By making a tile "rug."

Just get yourself a small linoleum remnant, a few dozen tiles and some epoxy glue. Then, make yourself a little tile "rug" to use as a welcome mat or as a livingroom decoration. But don't even consider making anything room-sized. You'll have trouble lifting it and putting it in place.

If you're the do-it-yourself type, you might consider making a painted canvas rug. They're not thick and luxurious, but they can be brightly colored and very attractive.

Just get yourself a piece of canvas the size you want at a fabric store. You can sew together a few strips, if you want—it won't harm the design. Or you can get a larger piece at a sailmaker's shop, if you happen to live near the coast. Then temporarily stretch the canvas on a sheet of plywood or a wooden frame, after hemming the edges. Prime it with artist's primer and paint your design on it with acrylics. Finish with two coats of shellac.

Needlepoint rugs can also be beautiful, if you're willing to make the initial investment and if you have the time and skill. You can either buy a rug kit or copy a design from books on this subject.

If you're not that skilled with needlepoint or if you want faster results, you can crochet a rug from heavy cord or twine, using a large crochet hook.

Crocheting is easy. If you can't find someone to show you how to do it, there are instructions in any needlework magazine. You can make a simple, single-crochet, square rug, a round rug, or even a rug assembled from granny squares.

If you like braided rugs, you can make one of those too. Ask your fabric shop or outlet mill for booklets on the subject. Also ask where in town you can buy the little gizmo that saves you the task of folding the cloth strips.

If you can, pick up lots of old wool clothing at garage sales, church rummage sales, thrift shops—or your mother's attic. Or try mill outlet stores or discount fabric shops. With a little work, you'll wind up with a most unusual handmade rug that you'll have for years—at much less than it would cost you to buy something nowhere nearly as good.

OFFBEAT FLOOR COVERINGS

If all of this is still too tame for you, we have a few somewhat more offbeat suggestions. You can't really call them rugs, though, and some of what we're going to suggest is better for looking at than walking on.

Fur. This can be pretty gauche as a floor covering—how many rabbits would you guess it takes to make 8 square feet of carpeting? Probably all the Easter bunnies in the egg-painting workshop.

On the other hand, if your otherwise bland room could use something exotic, you might look around for a skin—that's furrier's talk for a finished fur that hasn't been cut up for coats or upholstery. If you live in a major metropolitan area, call up a fur-manufacturing shop and ask for rejected skins.

Sheepskin. This is a somewhat more realistic floor covering. It's fluffy, warm, soft, and cozy. And you can be consoled that the animal it came from went to good use: mutton chops. Besides, sheep are raised for this purpose and if you buy a sheepskin, you'll be making some good herder a little richer.

Sheepskins are available through medical supply houses (they're used in hospitals to prevent bedsores and other circulatory problems) and automotive suppliers, where they're sold as car seat covers. On a bare floor or a dark rug, a sheepskin can be a nice place to snuggle.

We could go on all day about other exotic floor coverings, but it's really all a matter of imagination. Anything wide and long and flat can go on the floor.

The object is to think in terms of decoration, not practicality, in terms of beauty, not usefulness.

We're not saying, of course, that you should spread exotic floor coverings on every floor in your apartment. But here and there, in the livingroom or the den, something a little bit unusual can engage the eye and intrigue the mind. And that's very desirable—even on floors.

Chapter 6

WALLS AND
CEILINGS

Before you add furniture, drapes and curtains, carpeting, pictures, and plants, there's not much more to your apartment than four walls and a ceiling to each room.

But how these simple surfaces are decorated can mean the difference between feeling as though you're living in a box and feeling as though you're living in a comfortable home that expresses your personality and character.

The choices are many, ranging from simple paint jobs that take no more than an afternoon, to wallpaper of every imaginable variety, to many different types of paneling, to a wide range of fabric, to ceramic tiles, simulated brick or stone, mirrors, or cork.

In many buildings, especially in large cities, landlords repaint their apartments each time a new tenant takes occupancy. In this case, you'll probably be able to specify the colors you like, if you make your rental decision before he repaints.

In some cases, especially when you've signed a long-term lease, your landlord, as part of the agreement, will periodically repaint—once every two years, say, and you can specify the colors in each room.

In some instances, landlords are most unwilling to have tenants do anything to the walls except to live within them. If that's the case, of course, you're stuck with what you've got. But most landlords will listen to reason, especially when you're willing to pay for improving *their* property.

But don't do *anything* major to your walls or ceilings without discussing it first with your landlord. In one apartment we rented, our landlord told us that any wallpaper we put up must be removed at the end of our lease period (if we intended to move), at our expense. Another landlord practically clapped his

When are walls and ceilings one and the same? In designs like this one, of course. Here's a bookshelf idea that makes maximum use of the available space. It's an ideal technique in peaked-roof attic apartments.

hands in joy when we told him we wanted to put up some paneling to cover a plaster wall that had seen better days.

So it's an individual matter. The best rule to follow in such cases: Don't assume anything. Don't even assume that he'll repaint your apartment, no matter what he tells you. Make sure it's in your lease. And if you intend to undertake major decorative changes, get his approval in writing before proceeding. That could save you a great deal of grief—and money—when your lease is up.

When decorating both walls and ceilings, all the experts advise you to do the ceilings first, whether the decorative medium is paint or wallpaper. The main reason is that if you decorate the walls first, any spillage of paint or glue from the ceiling can ruin them.

But here we'll first discuss wall decorating, since we feel that most of you will find this of greater interest. Some of the concepts and techniques are essentially identical, anyhow.

Painting

Of all the means you might choose to decorate your walls, none is easier or less expensive than painting. But, sorry to say, even painting is likely to be more complicated and more expensive than you'd think.

TYPES OF PAINT

To begin with, paint is available in two basic types, each suitable for different surfaces and conditions:

Latex paints and stains (also called acrylic or vinyl paint). These are the easiest paints to use, since they're water soluble. That means that you can clean up with nothing more than water.

Latex paints are fast drying and, for the most part, odorless. They roll on more easily than other paints, they last longer, they hold their color and gloss better, they're nonflammable and they can be applied even to slightly damp surfaces. The available finishes range from flat to semi-gloss.

Latex paints are excellent on plaster or wallboard. And they're better than other types of paint in the case of concrete blocks, since they fill in the rough pores and adhere well to masonry surfaces.

The enamel versions of this paint are excellent for practically every wall use, even in bathrooms and kitchens. And they're better-looking on wood walls than standard latex paints.

Oil/alkyd paints and stains. These are generally slower drying than latex paints. They're also more difficult to clean up, since they require paint-thinner. On the other hand, they can't be beat for stain resistance, they're least affected by temperature extremes during painting, no paint adheres better, and they have the highest gloss finishes available.

Further, the gloss and semi-gloss finishes of these paints are extremely resistant to wear from rubbing, which makes them very useful in kitchen or bathroom applications where frequent cleaning is a necessity.

Both types are available in most finishes and colors and at varying quality levels—and prices. We recommend that you buy the best paint you can afford. You'll find it easier to take care of, easier to keep looking good. Since paint formulations change frequently, our advice is to ask the paint man at the hardware store or paint store which brand is best and why. (But if you're going to a Sherwin-Williams store, for instance, don't expect the salesman to recommend Dutch Boy or Kemtone.)

PAINT SHADES

Chances are, you won't have much trouble choosing the type and brand of paint you want. But you may go crazy when it comes to choosing a color.

To help you, the paint companies have provided enormous, three-tiered displays of paint chips, sample cards, etc. At first glance, all of this may be overwhelming. What do you choose when confronted, say, with fourteen different shades of what you would normally call "white."

The best advice we can give you: Don't panic. Look through the paint chips and sample cards and pull out what you truly like, with no other criteria. Don't ask yourself, at this point, whether the pale green you're fond of will go with the deep rose couch your Aunt Minnie gave you. If you're in doubt, if you're not sure whether or not you like a color, take the sample. Be generous.

Once you have all the samples at home, start looking them over, under both artificial light and daylight. Hold each sample up against the wall. Put it next to the furniture or rug that will be in the room you're thinking of painting. Begin the narrowing down process.

While you're narrowing down your color choice, keep these basic principles in mind:

Warm Colors. Rose and brown—two good examples—tend to create an intimate atmosphere. They make rooms seem slightly smaller, cozier.

Cool Colors. Blues and greens, for instance, and certain yellows make rooms look a bit larger than they actually are. They're also somewhat less "personal."

Bright Colors. Bright colors or very light colors can make a wall seem larger than it is. Dark colors produce the opposite effect.

So when you're choosing colors, you might begin by asking yourself what effect you want to achieve. Is your livingroom long and narrow? Then consider painting the shorter spans with a lighter color and the longer ones with a darker color, either contrasting or blending.

Or, is your bedroom so enormous that it makes you feel uncomfortably insignificant? Try painting it with medium rose or brown. That should simultaneously make the room appear smaller and more intimate.

Or, on the other hand, is your bedroom a little box, where the walls seem to be closing in on you? In that case, you may want to choose lighter colors, although perhaps in the same general shades.

Reflectivity is another important factor to consider when choosing paint colors. How bright do you want your room to be? Kitchens and bathrooms can hardly be too bright. But bright livingrooms or bedrooms can be harsh and a little overwhelming.

Different colors reflect different amounts of light. White, to name one, reflects 80 percent of the light that hits it. Ivory, however, reflects only 71 percent. And at the other end of the scale, deep rose has a reflectivity of 12 percent, while dark green reflects just 8 percent of the light that strikes it.

In general, as a rule of thumb, the richer and more saturated the color, the less light it reflects. The thinner the color, the greater the white component, the more light it reflects.

PAINT TEXTURES

Generally, paints are available in three textures: high gloss (usually enamels), semi-gloss, and satin (or matte) finish. Each has its proper application.

High gloss. This finish is usually used in kitchens or bathrooms, since it is extremely reflective. It's also good for woodwork.

Semi-gloss. This finish is popular in family rooms, small bedrooms, and powder rooms, or wherever you wish to enhance available lighting without creating glare.

Satin (or matte or flat). This finish is calming and quiet—suitable for bedrooms and livingrooms. It usually doesn't show fingermarks and dirt quite as quickly as higher-gloss finishes and it cleans easily in most cases.

In general, satin or semi-gloss finishes are best for large living areas, while higher-gloss finishes are best for decorative accents, window trim, woodwork, etc.

ESTIMATING YOUR NEEDS

Once you've selected your brand, color, type, and texture, your next task is to figure out how much paint you need. It's a snap.

First, figure out in square feet—perimeter times height—the total area to be covered. If you're using a different coating for trim, subtract from your total the area of the doors (about 21 square feet each) and windows (about 15 square feet each).

Second, divide your wall area total by 400 square feet, which is what a normal gallon of paint will cover. The result will be the number of gallons required for one coat.

If you've selected paint that's labeled with different coverage figures, of course use those. But never try to "stretch" paint. You'll only wind up with too thin a coat. Besides, it's always better to buy extra, for the inevitable touching up later. When you do this, be sure to label cans with the location where the paint has been used.

If your walls are some darker color and you've decided to paint them in a lighter shade, there's a very good chance you'll need two coats. If you're not sure, paint once and see—but be prepared to do it all over again.

Here's an interesting alternative to wallpaper. It's called "Guide A Wall-Cover." It works very much like a paint roller. Your local paint store, building supply, or hardware store stocks it, in several decorator patterns.

CHOOSING YOUR TOOLS

There are essentially three types of paint applicators: brushes, rollers, and pads. Like everything else, each has its advantages and disadvantages.

Brushes. Brushes ease the job of painting because they offer greater control, and minimize splattering. But if this is the route you choose, don't economize. Cheap brushes can ruin a job, leaving bristles in the wet paint, or worse, long brushmarks.

Good brushes are full, the bristles are springy and of varying lengths, they're flagged (with split ends) or tapered for smooth paint release, and they're firmly fastened to the handle.

Natural bristle brushes are made with hog hair. They're recommended for applying oil-base paints. Nylon brushes can also handle oil-based paints as well as latexes. The same can be said for polyester brushes, and both are easier to clean than natural bristle types.

A one- or two-inch brush will be needed for windows and smaller work, a three-inch brush for baseboards and doors, and a four-inch brush for the walls themselves.

Rollers. These are best for large areas. They apply paint much more quickly than paintbrushes, but still give a smooth, uniform surface. We recommend them for large rooms—the 7- or 9-inch size for walls, a 3-inch trim roller for woodwork, and a 3-inch (diameter) corner roller for, well, corners.

Roller frames either have a compression-type cage or the roller cover is held on with a wing nut. We like the compression frames, since they permit easier and faster roller removal and replacement.

Roller covers come in several different fibers and pile depths. For oil-based paints, the experts tell us that natural fibers (usually wool) are best, in quarter-inch piles for smooth walls, thicker piles for rougher surfaces. Synthetic fiber covers are best for latex paints.

Of course, if you're going to paint with rollers, you'll need a roller tray, to hold the paint and to apply it to the roller.

Pads. Pad applicators produce a smoother and more even paint surface than rollers. Also, they throw off very little spray, if any (unlike rollers). Some even come with little wheels which make it possible to use them for edging, allowing them to paint close to windows, baseboards, etc., eliminating the need for taping.

These are the latest forms of painting tools, and new versions are coming onto the market almost daily. As far as we're concerned, they combine the virtues of the roller and the paintbrush.

PREPARING YOUR WALLS

Once you've purchased your paint and gathered your tools, your next step is to prepare your walls. Paint must have a clean, solid, and dry surface if it's to "take." But each type of wall needs different preparation:

Bare wood. Fill nail holes, joints, and cracks with spackle, then sand and wipe off dust with a damp rag. Prime if paint requires it.

Plaster. New plaster must be given sixty to ninety days to dry. Fill holes and cracks with spackle, then sand and clean. Most paints require a primer before use on new plaster.

Wallboard. Spackle where necessary, sand, and clean. Check paint label to see if primer is required.

Wallpaper. It's best to remove it with a chemical wallpaper remover or a steamer (you can rent one). Then you should use a chemical remover to wash off remaining paste and sizing. Rinse and let dry. If you do paint over wallpaper, it must be firm, even, and pasted down in all corners and edges. You can't paint over foil papers without sealing first.

Painted surfaces. Scrape off loose or peeling paint. Sand, wash, rinse, dry, spackle, sand, clean off dust. Prime large, patched areas. Sand if you're painting over a glossy surface, so the new paint will stick.

PAINTING SEQUENCE

Paint your room in this order: ceiling; woodwork; edges near woodwork; and walls. Start in a corner diagonally across from the door.

PAINTING HINTS

While there's no teacher like experience, we can offer you a variety of painting hints, gathered from many different sources, over a long period.

- Use cloth or plastic drop cloths—otherwise, we can guarantee you that you'll splatter your furniture or the floor.

- If you're using a brush, dip it halfway into the paint. Tap gently to remove excess—don't wipe it across the lip of the can.
- Don't bear down heavily—just enough to make the bristles flex.
- If you're using a roller, roll it through the paint for about three revolutions. Each rollerfull of paint should cover about 4 square feet.
- To paint windows, raise the inside sash and lower the outside sash. Paint the inside one first, starting with the crossbars, then the frame. Don't paint the top edge of the inside sash— you'll be pushing it in a moment. Next, paint the outside sash, but not the bottom edge. Now, move both sashes back to about 1 inch of their closed positions, painting the formerly obstructed parts and the top edge of the inside sash. Next, paint the window casing and sill.

    After the paint is dry, move both sashes down as far as you can. Paint the upper part of the check rails. After the paint is completely dry, raise both sashes and paint the lower check rails.
- To paint doors, paint the top panels first, beginning with the molding edges. Then do the remaining panel area. When all the panels are painted, paint the remaining area, ending with the edges.

CLEANUP

Some people consider their painting tools expendable. Or they don't bother to clean them thoroughly—which amounts to the same thing. But it only takes a little while to clean up in most cases.

If you've been using latex paint, clean everything with soap and water. If you've been using oil-base paint, you'll need paint thinner. Either way, wipe all excess paint from the painting tool onto a newspaper.

After you've cleaned up, label the leftover paint and keep it for touch-ups.

Wallpapering

After painting, the most popular way to decorate wall surfaces is wallpaper—and this term applies to any type of flexible cover-

Chances are, the person who lives here calls this "the green room." And it is a cleverly coordinated symphony in that color. The wallpaper, white with a large-figured green geometric pattern, is reversed and, in a way, repeated by the linoleum. The plant theme is repeated in the chair. The floor cushions are also bright. Even the phone is green. It's a pleasant effect—and obviously the result of considerable thought.

ing that's pasted up on a wall: paper, vinyl, foil, flocked paper, burlap, cloth, grass cloth, cork-faced papers, etc.

There are also different categories, divided according to the way they're prepared for hanging, removal, cleanability, etc. For example, you can buy papers that are prepasted, papers that are strippable, papers that are scrubbable, papers that are scuff-resistant, papers that are pretrimmed—or any combination of the above.

Each type of paper and each category—sorry to say—has its own advantages and disadvantages, each has its pleasures and problems. And in many cases, each is hung differently—at least to some extent.

SOME DEFINITIONS

Before we talk about the various types of wallcoverings, let's first define our terms a bit:

Prepasted papers. These, of course, are coated with paste at the factory. That eliminates one of the most tedious and difficult steps in getting them ready to hang.

Strippable papers. As the name implies, these are papers printed on or made of material that's tough enough to strip off a wall by nothing more complicated than taking hold of a corner and tugging on it.

Scrubbable papers. These are super-tough wallpapers—often made of vinyl—that can be washed with soap and water.

Scuff-resistant papers. Again, super-tough papers, often made of vinyl.

Pretrimmed papers. Standard wallpapers come with a slight edging that must be trimmed before hanging. Pretrimmed papers don't have any edging of this sort. This eliminates one hanging step—but pretrimmed papers are also more subject to edge damage.

Any or all of these qualities can be found in almost any type of paper. These are the major types now on the market:

TYPES OF WALLPAPER

Vinyls. These include vinyl laminated to paper, vinyl laminated to cloth, or vinyl-impregnated cloth on a paper backing. In general, these are the most durable wallpapers made. Better yet, they're easy to clean. But the same cannot be said of vinyl-*coated* papers. These don't have the durability of their cousins.

Afraid of bold-patterned wallpaper? Don't be. It can be the basis for a striking
room, when combined with somewhat tamer carpeting, furniture, and drapes.

Vinyls can't be applied over old wallpaper. Because they're nonporous, they seal in adhesive moisture and cause the old wallpaper paste to mildew.

Further, they should be applied only over sizing, a mixture that's applied to bare walls to provide a good bonding surface (often a coating of wallpaper adhesive.) This makes it easier to align strips by sliding them around.

Two cautions concerning vinyls: Be careful not to stretch them when putting them up—it will cause hairline cracks. Also, use a squeegee rather than a smoothing brush to remove air bubbles.

Foils. There are two main types of foil paper—those made of aluminum laminated to paper and aluminum laminated to cloth. Both are nonporous, which means existing wallpapers must be removed before they can be applied.

One of the problems with foils is their bright, reflective surface. It magnifies any wall imperfections. For this reason, wallpaper authorities recommend that walls either be sanded or first papered with "blank stock."

We have two cautions about these papers, too: First, they crease if you look at them funny—and the creases don't come out. So be very careful about folding and bending. Second, they conduct electricity. That means you should cut off the power when trimming around electrical switches and outlets.

Grass cloth, hemp, burlap, cork. These "papers" don't resemble each other much once they're hung, but since they're all generally mounted on paper backings, they have more or less the same hanging qualities.

These papers also have in common a random pattern or texture, which means there's no worrying about matching patterns on the edges. None, by the way, are washable.

Textured wallpapers of this sort can be mounted over old wallpaper. In fact, that's often an advantage, since excess moisture in the adhesive can cause this paper to tear, stretch, or curl. But blank stock is even better—and either must be sized before the paper is applied.

Flocked papers. Flocking is a fuzzy nap of nylon or rayon. It's available on wallcoverings made of paper, vinyl, or foil. In general, it's handled and hung according to its backing.

Flocking presents a rich appearance, but it presents certain problems: it can easily be damaged—by rubbing, by allowing paste to get onto it, by using a seam roller to press down seams, edges, or ends (and thereby squashing the pile). For this reason, you must be careful with it.

Contact papers. These are papers or vinyls with self-sticking adhesive already applied to them. The adhesive is covered by a waxy brown paper that must be pulled off at the moment of application. Contact papers can be removed by peeling them off.

Generally, this type of wallpaper is too expensive for entire rooms. However, it's an excellent choice for trim, molding effects, splash guards, and graphic wall designs.

Paneling

Today, you can buy paneling that mimics (or is made of) practically every wood you can imagine. It's also available in many different textures, from barnsiding to basketweave. In addition, you can get it in a wide variety of plain colors, marblized finishes, "stones," and patterns.

Some wood paneling is just that—wood. And it has all the characteristics of wood. Other paneling, perhaps the majority, is made of laminated plastic. And many of the woods are protected with a plastic coating.

As far as we're concerned, paneling is more luxurious and richer-looking than all but the very best wallpapers. On the other hand, it's a good deal more expensive.

But, we're pleased to say, it's a lot easier to install paneling than you'd think. It comes in large sheets—usually 4 feet wide, by 8, 9, or 10 feet high—so it goes up fast.

In fact, the difficult part of putting up paneling is not the paneling, but the walls it must cover. Even if they're smooth and straight as a die, they require considerable preparation before the job can start. And if they're at all rough or uneven, there's a lot more work to be done.

But, once installed, paneling will give you a beautiful room that's easy to maintain. Of course, you should consult your landlord before you undertake such a major decorative alteration. Chances are, he'll be delighted, however, since you'll be substantially increasing the value of his property.

Wall paneling is one of the most effective ways to dress up a room, especially one with walls that aren't in very good condition. But it needn't be used in exactly the way the manufacturer intended, as this imaginative room demonstrates.

This room looks like it's paneled in expensive, custom-made barn board. But the walls are actually covered with sheet paneling, which is much less expensive and surprisingly easy to install. You can find it in a wide variety of colors and textures at your local lumberyard.

Specialty Materials

Painting, wallpapering, and paneling by no means exhaust your wallcovering options. You can use, for instance, a wide variety of fabrics, cork tile, mirror tile, simulated brick or stone, or even ceramic tile. Each has its advantages and its special cautions.

FABRICS

We've had good success covering our walls—at one time or another—with burlap, sheeting, unbleached muslin, and light colored cottons.

Other materials you might consider are glazed chintzes (for an English country house look, for instance), netting over painted walls (paint the molding covering the edges instead of covering it with fabric).

Sheets are also a possibility, but you may have trouble matching dye lots. Polyester/cotton blends can work out well, if you don't get one that's too light. But avoid loose woven wools, or blends, or anything that stretches.

CORK AND MIRROR TILE

You probably won't want to cover an entire room in either one of these—but that only makes it easier to put them up (and less expensive).

Both of these materials, of course, drastically change the appearance of any room, even installed on only one wall. A mirrored surface, for instance, makes rooms seem much larger. Cork surfaces, on the other hand, bring coziness. They also quiet rooms, which adds to that effect.

Cork tiles are a good choice if your walls are uneven or not quite smooth. But if you plan to put mirror tiles on anything but the smoothest walls, you'll want to put up furring strips, then cover the walls with hardboard or wallboard.

SIMULATED BRICK AND STONE

These come both in individual "bricks" and in sheets. The latter are far easier to install, in our experience. They can go up on furring strips or directly on wallboard, nailed to the studs.

The important thing about putting up sheets of simulated

What can you put on a wall? Anything that's reasonably flat and pretty. This straw mat does everything a picture can do and more, since, in addition to design, it also has a texture.

Here's a simple trick that can make your apartment look like a country farmhouse: wooden beams. Actually, these beams needn't be made of wood at all. The type made of plastic foam creates the same effect and at considerably less cost. They're lightweight, east to cut, easy to install.

brick or stone is to make sure the units are horizontally level—and laid out in advance, so they fit together properly once they're up. You can buy the panels already "grouted"—actually, it's a simulation, since the bricks are structurally joined anyway—or you can grout them yourself, with a caulking gun, smoothing the grout with a popsickle stick.

Ceilings

We've discussed wallcoverings first in this chapter, because most people are more interested in this than in refinishing their ceilings. But if you plan to do walls *and* ceilings, do your ceilings first. That way, you'll be less likely to mess up your new wallcoverings with paste or paint drippings from the ceiling.

PAINTING CEILINGS

Painting a ceiling may remind you of those early family sit-coms. You remember how they were described in the TV listings: "Steve Douglas and his three sons attempt to repaint the living-room ceiling, with help from crusty old Uncle Charlie, and Tramp, the lovable shaggy mutt."

Perhaps you can see yourself on the ladder now, dribbling paint on the rose carpet and Aunt Ethel's prize piano shawl. Meanwhile, your spouse is suggesting, "If you'll just do it like this . . . ," the baby is eating handfuls of yellow paint, and your own lovable shaggy mutt is painting the walls with his tail.

Well, banish this nightmare from your mind. You can paint a ceiling without ruining your marriage, your dog, or your baby's health.

First, get lots of plastic drop cloths and old newspapers, after moving all of the furniture out of the room. If you just can't move the furniture (if you have, for example, a Great Lakes Empire bed or a full-sized grand piano), use your largest, newest, and sturdiest dropcloths to cover these items.

You'll need something to stand on, and we recommend a scaffold. They can be rented for not very much money and, once up, they make ceiling work a pleasure.

But, for ordinary 8- to 10-foot ceilings, you can make do with a couple of sturdy stepladders and some strong, wide planking. Two sawhorses or two sturdy chairs will also work.

First, paint the edge where the ceiling meets the walls. Paint a 2-inch strip all the way around the room with a new brush, pad, or roller. Try not to slop paint onto the wall, even if it's the same color. Those little drips and dribbles wind up as bumps and ridges after they dry.

Now, move your ladders into a corner of the room and begin by marking off a 3-foot section and filling it in evenly and smoothly. Work your way across the room in these 3-foot sections, widthwise, feathering the edges into each other.

By the way, if your ceiling has complexion problems—cracks, peeling, stains, etc., you'd better talk to your landlord before painting. These flaws are usually indications of basic, deepset problems, such as broken beams or leaks. And if you paint before the underlying problem is fixed, it will soon show up again and all your work will be for naught.

When painting your ceiling, use a paint formulated for this purpose. This paint has a flat finish that minimizes lap marks and glare. It's made to be nonyellowing, to hide surface irregularities, to fill hairline cracks, and to minimize splatter.

Throughout this chapter, talking about walls and ceilings and the many different decorative approaches to each, we haven't discussed what patterns or colors to choose. Of course, final selection is entirely a matter of taste. But we can offer these guidelines:

- To make a room appear larger, use light, pale, or pastel colors.
- To make a room appear smaller, use dark colors.
- If you want to make one wall appear larger, decorate it with something that has a glossy surface.
- If you want to "raise" the ceiling, try wallpapers or paneling with a vertical pattern.
- If you want to "lower" the ceiling, decorate the walls with coverings that have a horizontal pattern.
- Don't forget to coordinate your wallpaper with your furnishings. Usually, decorators make sure both are from the same basic style family, but contrasts are nice, too. Just make sure that your walls and your furniture aren't engaged in a continual battle.

Chapter 7

WINDOWS

Webster's defines windows this way:

1. an opening in the wall of a building, the side of a vehicle, etc., for the admission of light or air or both, commonly fitted with a frame in which are set movable sashes containing panes of glass. 2. such an opening with the frame, sashes, and panes of glass, or any other device, by which it is closed. 3. the frame, sashes, and panes of glass, or the like, intended to fit such an opening.

Well, that describes windows, all right. But it leaves out practically everything about them that's important. When you're inside, windows are your connection with the rest of the world. They let you see what's out there, at the same time protecting you against wind and weather, allowing you to observe—but not participate.

Windows are the method we humans have devised to keep us and our dwellings constantly connected with the outside. They're openings which admit the beauties of nature. They're the way we can make contact with the world beyond our immediate surroundings. They're an essential part of our lives.

For those who live in apartments, windows are especially important. They're a substitute for lawns and gardens, for patios and decks, for the easy and convenient access homeowners have with nature and the outdoors.

Windows delight the eye, providing views—or, at least, light. And they promote good health, since they're the apartment dweller's chief source of fresh air. And the sunshine they admit can be the difference between life and death, so far as houseplants are concerned.

Windows are, for all practical purposes, an apartment's chief built-in decorative feature. They're so visually important to us, in fact, that we've invented paintings, posters, and pictures to imitate them and to supplement them—to catch our eyes and engage our minds where there are no windows to do the job.

But windows differ from wall decorations, not only in the sense that what we see through them is real and ever-changing, but also in the sense that, at least under some circumstances, they also provide others with a view of us—or at least of the place where we live.

In many cases, then, windows are an avenue of human communication, a way in which a glance can let us momentarily touch the life of someone else, giving us that sense of community we all feel when we glimpse in others a little bit of ourselves.

Windows are also unique in that we can alter their qualities from day to day and moment to moment. With drapes, curtains, blinds, shades, and shutters, we can increase—or decrease—the privacy they afford, and we can alter the view they provide.

In addition, windows offer us an excellent opportunity to be creative, to exercise our taste and our decorating abilities. We can use them to bring color to a room, we can frame them, we can unify them with the rest of the room's decor, we can even hide them.

Perhaps the only thing we can't do to a window—unless it's a tiny four-pane job that opens up to a solid brick wall less than a yard away—is leave them totally undecorated, ignoring them altogether.

All that said, what now? Well, your first step should be what we call the "window census."

The Window Census

To properly take a window census, you should first prepare yourself with the tools of the trade. You won't need anything fancy—just a pencil, a small notebook, and a ruler, tape measure,

When measuring your window for drapes or curtains, don't simply take inside measurements. Measure the total width and length you wish your curtains or drapes to cover.

or yardstick. (We recommend the kind that rolls up into its own case—at least 9 feet, preferable 12 or 15 feet long.)

Now, take a trip through your apartment, room by room, starting in your livingroom. First, make a floor-plan sketch of the room, showing the general location of all doors and windows. Number the windows on the sketch. Next, on succeeding pages of your notebook, sketch each window—roughly will do. Then, measure the window and indicate the measurements on the individual sketches.

There are two ways to measure each window, and you should use both of them, measuring to within ¼ inch.

Outside dimensions. Measure from the top of the window molding to the bottom of the lower window molding—starting where the wall ends, at the top, and continuing to where the wall begins again, at the bottom. Also measure on the width the same way —from the outside of the molding on one side to the outside of the molding on the other side.

Inside dimensions. Now, do the same thing all over again, but this time measure from the top of the sash (the movable part of the window) to the bottom of the sash. This measurement should omit only the window molding.

If you're thinking of hanging drapes, you might also want to take another measurement: the distance between the windows or between windows and doors. Also, you'll want to know the distance between molding and floor.

Incidentally, you can use this same notebook for all of your apartment dimensions and decorating information. We use a small, looseleaf notebook for this purpose and we carry it whenever we go shopping for drapes, carpeting, furniture, etc.

While you're taking your census, consider your window decoration possibilities. They are: drapes, simple curtains, fancy curtains, (store-bought or handmade), venetian blinds, vertical blinds, simple pull-down shades, fancy pull-down shades, shutters, window quilts, stained-glass windows, imitation stained glass, and full- or partial-window stick-ons. We'll take them one by one.

To Drape or Not to Drape

There's something enormously luxurious about drapes. They often look expensive even when they're not. They open easily and smoothly. They have a certain innate weight and value.

But all of that doesn't necessarily mean you should cover every window with drapes. In fact, there's a distinct possibility you shouldn't cover *any* window with drapes.

Drapes make particular sense in more formally decorated rooms, such as livingrooms or diningrooms, rooms in which you're likely to be doing some entertaining.

They're also especially useful when you have a window that admits too much sun, or that must be covered, at least from time to time, to assure privacy.

But drapes do have some serious disadvantages, even in those locations. They often must be custom-made, which means they'll be expensive and they'll probably have to be altered to fit your new windows when you move. They may need frequent cleanings, especially if they're hung on windows over forced hot-air registers—and cleaning drapes isn't a cheap proposition, either. Also, unless they're made from quality fabrics, they can fade in the sunlight, losing much of their beauty.

Let's say, however, that after weighing all the advantages and disadvantages, you've decided that nothing except drapes will do for that big sweep of windows in your livingroom—or for the windows on the bedroom's east wall, where sunlight wakes you up about an hour before your alarm clock goes off.

You will now find yourself confronted with an almost overwhelming array of choices—not just colors or patterns, which are largely a matter of taste, but also of fabrics, linings, and such decorative fininshing touches as valances and swags.

Of course, we can't tell you what to buy. Every alternative has its reasons for being on the market. But we can give you an idea of what's usually available.

FABRICS

Practically every fabric known to man can be—and has been —made into drapery, which is something to consider if you're thinking about making your own (more on that subject later).

But if you intend to buy either custom-made or ready-made draperies, you'll find that most are available in a relatively few proven fabrics:

Slubbed satin. This is a basically smooth surface that's broken up by an irregular texture consisting of short lines and occasional small lumps—they almost look like snags—of fabric, either in the same or contrasting colors.

These drapes cover an entire wall, leading the viewer to think they open to reveal a giant picture window. Actually, there may be only two small windows and a lot of wall behind them. It's a decorating trick that unifies a room, creating a very pleasing visual effect.

Like most drapery fabrics, slubbed satin can be made from many different fibers. We've seen some that are blends of polyester and cotton and others that are mainly rayon and acrylic.

But you don't have to worry much about fibers. Just find a fabric that hangs well, that retains its pleats, and that fits in with the rest of your decor.

Open weaves. These are fabrics that, to a greater or lesser extent, are very loosely woven. Even when closed, they'll let in some light, although they're usually woven closely enough to provide privacy. They're available in all sorts of solids and simple patterns.

Matte finish. Matte-finish fabrics are somewhat like slubbed satin, except the texture is far more subtle.

Nubby textures. This refers to a variety of weaves, all of them with patterns of visible texture, such as basketweaves or tweeds. In addition to the texture, they can have simple colors woven into the fabric.

Jacquard. This term refers to fabrics with small (usually) patterns woven right into the pattern—fleur-de-lis, for instance. Background and pattern can be the same color, or contrasting.

Sheers and semi-sheers. These are lightweight, usually translucent, and often woven in batiste, ninon, or voile.

Prints. Most commonly, these are patterns (of every imaginable variety) on practically any type of nontextured, closely woven fabric.

Velvet. Actual cut-cotton velvet is rarely used, except in theater drapes, but crushed velvet—velveteen, a much flatter fabric —is occasionally available in ready-mades and can be used in custom-mades, of course.

Damask. A reversible fabric of various fibers, heavily woven into patterns. Usually richly textured in dark colors.

LININGS

Most better drapes are lined. This helps to make them opaque, it retards fading, it aids "draping" qualities, and it can provide additional insulation against heat or cold. As with the drapes themselves, many different materials are used for this purpose.

Acrylic foam. This material, which has relatively recently arrived on the market, is usually cotton-flocked on the side not bonded or sewn to the drape itself, so that when you handle the drape, it doesn't feel like plastic sponge. It has excellent insulating qualities.

Cotton. This is a traditional drapery lining. It works well, although it isn't as good an insulator as acrylic foam.

Felted polyester. This material is translucent, so it's frequently used in combination with open-weave drapery fabrics. It reduces the amount of see-through and it has some insulation value.

Batiste sheers. This fabric is also used with open-weave drapery fabrics, for the reasons described above. It's not as good an insulator as felted polyester.

Cotton and polyester blends. These are similar to the traditional cotton linings.

Normally, linings are sewn or knitted to the drapery fabric. However, you may find drapery to which linings have been bound by a thermal process. We're not exactly thrilled by the idea, but it seems to work.

Incidentally, most lined drapes are not machine-washable. They must be dry cleaned. Just one more factor to consider.

DECORATIVE DEVICES

For most people, it's enough to hang some pinch-pleated drapes on a pull-cord drapery rod. But others find this arrangement unbearably plain. For these folk, the decorators have invented all sorts of gadgets and gimcracks to dress things up. Here's a small sampling:

Tiebacks. These are belts, usually made of the same fabric and color of the drapery, that hold it back in the middle, so it's fully parted only from the middle on down. Above the middle, the drapes gradually come closer and closer together, until they meet at the top. The effect is extremely theatrical.

Cornices. These are fabric-covered boxes that fit on top of the drapes, covering their top edge. They're normally covered with fabric, which, itself, can be pleated, tiered, or scalloped.

Valances. This arrangement creates a similar effect, but the fabric is attached not to a box or framework, but to a separate valance rod. It gives drapes an ultra-finished look.

Swags and cascades. These serve much the same purpose as cornices and valances, but are more elaborate and, some would say, more spectacular. The effect is of a short, miniature drape hanging above the main drape.

Lining drapes. These are usually sheer, pull drapes that fit inside the other drapes and are operated on a separate rod, with separate cords. They filter the light without totally blocking it.

PATTERNS AND COLORS

In addition to all the variations named above, there are the most important differences of all: fabric patterns and colors. There are literally millions of combinations.

To get some idea of what's available, check the decorating magazines and books. Or, better yet, drop into any large fabric store and browse. If this isn't enough to boggle your mind, ask to see the catalogs they carry. You'll be amazed.

How do you wade through this ocean of choices? Oddly enough, the best way to do it is through a series of logical decisions. Ask yourself the following questions:

- Do I want a solid color or a pattern? This depends mainly on the other decorative elements in your room, particularly your major pieces of furniture and your floor covering. If these are solid colors for the most part, or very large-figured designs, you'll probably want patterned or multi-color drapes, or drapes with geometrical designs.

    On the other hand, if you already have plenty of patterns, colors, and designs in the room, you'll probably be wide to choose a solid color for your drapes.
- If a solid color seems the best, which solid should I choose? Dress your room as though you were dressing yourself. The same color rules apply. Choose colors that either contrast or blend—colors that go well with each other—but also look for colors with similar intensitites. If you pick a color that's far brighter or richer than the rest of the colors in your room, your drapes will either be more dominant than they should be, or they'll disappear.
- If patterns seem the best choice, ask yourself if you should choose large-figured patterns, small-figured patterns, bold patterns, or subtle patterns.

    In general, the rule of opposites applies. Choose something that's very different from the other decorative elements in the room, so that each element sets off the other. This way, patterns can be mixed with patterns, without producing a too-busy visual effect.

For instance, if you have a large-patterned or geometric Rya rug, you may do well with small-patterned drapes. If your couch is covered in a fabric with white-on-white flowers, you might consider striped pastel drapes.

Of course, solids *can* be mixed with solids and patterns can be mixed with similar patterns. But this takes an instinctively good sense of design and color. If you're a little unsure of yourself, choose opposites.

- What texture should I choose? As they say in those college essay tests, compare and contrast. For instance, if you decorate your room with a shag carpet, a couch covered in wide-wale corduroy, and coarse, open-weave drapes, you're not really using the full potential of texture.

  Instead, try mixing heavy textures with smooth textures, thick fabrics with sheers, fine weaves with coarse weaves. If you can create a good mix, in which no single texture dominates so thoroughly as to "wipe out" the others, you'll have a room with a high level of textural interest.

- What additional decorative effects should I consider? Are cornices, swags, and the like for you? They may well be if you're decorating your room in a very formal manner, with fine furniture and carpeting.

  On the other hand, if you're creating a thoroughly contemporary room, or one that's basically informal, the fewer extras you have with your drapes, and the simpler effect you can create, the better.

  When you're making this decision, you should follow the "like likes like" rule. Otherwise, you may find yourself with some pretty bizarre combinations—combinations which give mixed messages to your psyche and to your guests.

The most important rule of all, in any decorator decision you're making, about drapes or anything else in your apartment, is "please yourself." After all, you're the one who'll be living here day in and day out, probably for a year or two, possibly for much longer.

Few window treatments are simpler than these café curtains. And, with the proper selection of fabric, color, and design, few are more effective—especially in kitchens or other informal rooms.

Opting for Curtains

Curtains are drapes' first cousins. The main differences, usually, are these: curtains are normally made of lighter weight fabrics, which means they're almost always translucent, admitting some light, while, to a substantial degree, providing privacy; curtains are normally hung on simple rods, without pull cords; curtains are used in less formal settings; unlike drapes, curtains rarely reach to the floor; curtains are used for "problem windows," such as the rows of window panes, and might be installed on either side of a front door; and curtains are almost never lined.

FABRICS

Curtains are available in a wide variety of fabrics. Among them are:

Ninon. A sturdy chiffon or voile constructed in either plain or novelty weaves.

Polyester knits. Usually structure designs or open-weave panels, with a lacy, lightweight, light-filtering effect.

Jacquard knits. These recapture the look of traditional lace better than most other modern fabrics. They're usually made of polyester.

Slubbed fabrics. Lightweight versions of the slubbed satins used for drapes.

Batiste. A fine, often sheer fabric constructed in either a plain or figured weave and made of cotton, nylon, or more commonly, polyester.

Seeded voile. A fabric of rayon, cotton, or polyester, mainly, with an open, canvaslike weave, plus light slubbing.

Smooth fabrics. Usually cotton/polyester blends of fairly tight weave. These are used to carry deeper, richer colors or patterns.

SHAPES

Curtains are also available in a wide variety of configurations. Among these are:

Priscillas. These are "draped" curtains, tied back with decorative rope or with matching fabric at about two-fifths of their length, open on the bottom and gradually closing at the top, beginning at the tie-back. The effect is rather theatrical, though not as heavy-looking in curtains as in drapes.

Panels. These usually consist of two rectangular drapes mounted top and bottom on traverse rods. They may be opened by pushing them aside. They're excellent for windows that don't open, but look better finished off. Simple curtains are usually composed of panels without bottom rods.

Tiers. These consist of two or three (or even more) sets of curtains, each slightly overlapping the other. Each tier requires a separate rod, and the arrangement allows you to uncover practically any part of a window—to admit sunlight, or to see a view.

Valances. As with drapes, these are strips of material that run across the top of a curtain rod, a sort of horizontal capstone to your curtains.

Swags. These are strips of curtain material that extend valances downward in a diagonal slant, veiling the curtains themselves.

All of these styles and configurations can be used in various combinations. Normally, however, a single curtain material is used, except for the occasional contrasting edging.

Buying Drapes and Curtains

Custom-made. If you have odd-sized windows, or if you're looking for something very special or very original, your best bets for custom-made draperies and curtains are fabric stores or professional upholstery/carpet shops that make curtains and draperies as a sideline.

These stores can show you a multitude of styles, color, and fabrics. You can choose a fabric they have in stock or order what you like. They may even send someone to measure your windows, just to make sure.

In most cases, however, they'll farm out the actual construction of the drapes or curtains to a local tailor. Ask his name and request a look at some samples of his work. If the store can't show you any, contact him directly. Don't sign any purchase agreements until you're sure he can do a satisfactory job.

If your heart is set on custom-made drapes or curtains, you'd better resign yourself to spending a fair amount of money. But don't let yourself be talked into extras, such as slipcovers or re-upholstery. Know exactly what you need and exactly what you intend to spend, maximum, before walking into the store.

By the way, you needn't feel that the money you spend on

custom-made drapes or curtains is money down the drain, should you move. Like skirts and pants, drapes and curtains can be altered—and by the same fellow, the tailor.

Just take the drapes or curtains back to him directly and give him your new measurements. That will save you the store's commission—plus the price of new fabric.

Another good place to get custom-made curtains and drapes: a large department store. Many have staff decorators you can consult if you're making a substantial purchase or if you're an established customer.

Ready-made. Department stores are also good sources of ready-made drapes and curtains. They often carry a wide range of sizes, styles, fabrics, and colors. And you can usually find all the hardware you'll need there, too. With luck, you'll get a salesperson who knows the merchandise well and can give you good advice.

Catalog department stores are also excellent places to find ready-made drapes and curtains. Their large outlets carry a variety that's usually the equal of a standard department store. Their catalogs sometimes offer much more. Prices are moderate, at most.

Our favorite catalog store offers such a variety of drape and curtain sizes that they refer to their selection as "made-to-measure." Now that's an exaggeration. But you'll have to have a might peculiar window not to find the size you need.

Other places to find ready-made drapes and curtains: bath and curtain shops, discount department stores, even dime stores. And if your budget is tight, don't forget to take a survey of your relatives. Anyone who's been married ten years or more is almost bound to have an extra set of drapes or curtains packed away somewhere.

And if your decorating budget hovers around the zero level, you should definitely consider visiting rummage or tag sales. What someone else can't use anymore might be perfect for you.

Making Your Own

Another way to economize, or to get exactly what you want, is to make your own drapes and/or curtains. If the mere thought of such a project is slightly terrifying, relax and take a deep breath. It isn't nearly as hard as you might think. Your local fabric store will have complete instructions. Or buy a good sewing book.

Installing Curtains and Drapes

Whether or not you make your own, unless you're buying custom-made drapes or curtains from a department store or custom shop, the chances are you'll be installing your own. If you're at all handy, you won't have much trouble doing it, however.

CURTAIN AND DRAPERY RODS

Curtain and drapery rods come in a variety of designs, suitable for every application. But these are the basics:

Sash rods. These are simple telescoping tubes, made for curtain panels. They're put up with simple brackets, one at each end, usually mounted on the window moldings.

Spring-tension rods. These are also simple telescoping tubes, but instead of being mounted with brackets, they're self-mounting, by means of their own spring tension. They're usually installed within the window molding or over windows in narrow hallways.

Standard curtain rods. These are squared-off metal tubes with extensions on either end (usually 2½–3 inches), which allow curtains or drapes to hang in front of windows. The extensions clip on metal plates installed immediately on the outside of the window molding.

Cafe rods. These are decorative, cylindrical rods, usually between ¾ inches and 2 inches, for curtains or drapes that have rings mounted at their upper edges. They rest on brackets attached either to the wall or to the window molding.

Decorative traverse rods. These look, at first glance, like cafe rods. But they have a concealed drawstring mechanism within.

Standard traverse rods. These are normally used for drapes with hooks. They're attached to the wall with brackets that also serve as extensions away from the wall. Longer spans are often reinforced with simple, midpoint brackets.

Electric traverse rods. These are essentially identical to the rods just described, except that they have electric motors, allowing you to open or close your drapes with the touch of a button. Are they expensive? Of course.

Putting any one of these rods in place isn't all that difficult. It's usually a matter of just putting in a few screws. If you're going into wood window molding, that's a cinch. It isn't too hard if you're going into wallboard or paneling. It can be more difficult if your walls are made of crumbly plaster. But even in this case, it should be well within your abilities. Just drill a hole (borrow or rent an electric drill, the simplest of power tools) and install a lead or plastic anchor of the proper size (ask the man at the hardware store).

The main problem in installing curtains and drapes is not how to get them up, but where to put them. We have a few hints on that score:

- Simple curtains can be mounted inside window moldings or on the window moldings themselves. The curtains should either come down to the sill or they should hang just below the bottom edge of the window molding.
- Drapes should be mounted so they completely cover the window molding. And, if you've covered the top and side moldings, don't let them end at the sill. It will look a little ridiculous.
- If you have two windows that are reasonably close together, consider covering them with a single drape. It will tie them together and unify the room. Alternately, you can mount a stationary drape on the wall between them and drape each window separately. This will allow you to open and close the drapes, yet keep the windows looking "finished." It will also give the illusion of a series of windows.
- If you're striving for a formal effect, let your drapes hang to the floor (with about 1 inch of clearance). But don't let them "break," as a man trouser's "break" on the instep of his shoe. This looks sloppy. Your friends and relatives will think you've miscalculated.
- If there are heating units directly beneath your windows, end your drapes just below the window sill. Otherwise, much of your heat will rise behind the drapes and it will be trapped between the drapes and the window, where it does you very little good at all—especially if you have insulating drapes.

Incidentally, in many cases you can combine several different types of curtain and drapery rods, to achieve a variety of effects.

Venetian blinds come in all shades today, not just white. But this apartment dweller decided to paint the blinds in stripes, as part of a super-graphics wall treatment. And all that was needed was a little paint.

Simple, yet sumptuous. What really makes this window treatment a winner is its coordination with the window-seat pillows. If you think in terms of coordinated fabrics, designs, and colors, you can achieve a decorator effect all by yourself.

This is a variation of venetian blinds. It consists of wooden slats mounted on a horizontal track. You can find this item in department stores or stores that carry venetian blinds and similar window coverings.

For instance, you can mount a sash rod or a conventional curtain rod behind a traverse rod, so that you can put sheer curtains up behind your heavier drapes, to set them off.

Or, if you like, you can mount a valance rod in front of your standard curtain rod or traverse drapery rod. This will allow you to install a valance in front of your main drape with the greatest of ease.

But enough of drapes, curtains, and their many variations. There are other ways to decorate your windows, some of them at least equally interesting.

Venetian Blinds

Venetian blinds have been with us for decades, although what their origins are, we don't really know (but we're fairly sure Venice had nothing to do with it). Anyway, whoever dreamed them up in the first place must have been a pretty clever fellow, since he discovered a relatively simple way to provide all kinds of window alternatives.

Tightly closed and slanted upward, venetian blinds provide complete privacy and fairly good darkness, without completely cutting off ventilation. With the blinds completely horizontal, they hardly impede your view at all, if you happen to have one, and air can enter freely if the window is open. Other adjustments allow you to fine-tune the amount of sunlight in your room. And if they're in the way, all you have to do is pull them up and they practically disappear at the top of the window molding.

Time was when the only venetian blinds on the market were the variety with wooden slates and cloth tape. They worked well enough, but they didn't last all that long. The wooden slats tended to warp and crack, especially if exposed to rain, which often happened. And the cloth tape rotted after a while, if it got wet.

But modern improvements have eliminated those two problems. Today, most venetian blinds on the market are made of enameled steel or aluminum (although you can get the wooden type from some decorator shops, if you insist). And the cloth tape has given way to fiberglass-reinforced vinyl. Unless you have kids who like to hang from the blinds, it should outlast practically anything else in your apartment.

There are two major styles on the market today:

Standard blinds. These are usually white, with 2-inch slats, two or three tapes (depending on width), two cords for adjusting pitch on one side and one cord for pulling up and down on the other. The better ones have dustcover tops, so that when the blinds are fully up, they're at least somewhat protected from dirt. The bottom rails, usually weighted so that the blinds will fall smoothly and stay down, now have plastic window ledge protectors.

Fashion blinds. These come in every color of the rainbow (and they're particularly attractive in pastels). They have 1-inch slats that practically disappear when they're exactly horizontal. And there are no tapes—just a latticework of polyester cords that match the color of the slats and are thereby all but invisible. Some have bottom rails that can be screwed down into the windowsill.

The more expensive fashion blinds have slats made of aluminum, with a baked-on finish for lasting color. And instead of cords, they have a plastic "wand" which can be twisted with one hand to open or close the louvers.

All three types do the same job, essentially, although the aluminum are prettiest. Unfortunately, they're also more expensive —in fact, considerably more expensive. In one catalog, for instance, standard blinds for a window 30x54 inches are $12.49, steel fashion blinds for that same window are $19.59, and aluminum fashion blinds are $48.00. You pays your money and you takes your choice.

For all their pleasures, venetian blinds also present some problems. These are two of the worst:

INSTALLATION It isn't easy. It's not that special skills are required. They're not. But you'd better be either strong or able to borrow a strong friend. They're not light and they have to be held up for quite a while before you can let go.

CLEANING Venetian blinds inevitably get dusty. And they're difficult to clean in place. You can face all the slats toward you, dust, then face all the slats away from you and dust again—and you still won't get everything. There are special dusting tools sold strictly for venetian blinds—they're essentially brushes with fingers—but they're only mediocre.

The best way to clean them, we've found, is to take them down and rinse them in the shower, or take them outside and use the garden hose on them. Then spread them in the sun to dry, after wiping off as much moisture as possible. Don't try to wash them in the bathtub—it's practically impossible, unless you have a very small set.

If you're lucky, venetian blinds have come with your apartment and they cover all of your windows. Should that be the case, you really don't need any further window decoration, unless you're the sort who isn't happy unless every window has curtains or drapes.

If you're buying them, measure the inside frame of the window and its length from top to bottom, also inside the frame. Don't get the blinds that are too short. They won't do. And try to avoid those that are too long. They're heavier to raise.

Vertical Blinds

A close cousin to the venetian blind is the vertical blind. The principle is the same, but the execution is different in several ways.

The first difference between the two is the most obvious. The slats in vertical blinds hang from floor to ceiling. In addition, the slats are far wider—usually about 3½ inches. And they have no tape of latticework strings to connect them—only slender, beaded chains at the bottom. Finally, vertical blinds, unlike standard venetian blinds, are available in textured finishes.

As of this writing, there are two main types of vertical blinds on the market:

The rigid type. These are usually made of vinyl. They can have plain plastic finishes in a variety of colors or they can have textured polyester inserts. (We've seen some that look like suede.) The rigid blinds are supposed to be able to darken a room. They do the job fairly well, but not as well as drapes or room-darkening window shades.

The nonrigid type. These are made of fabric (usually polyester) and weighted at their bottoms so they'll stay in place. They provide good light and privacy control, but they don't really darken a room. They're available in many different colors.

The slats on both types can be easily turned, in practically any direction, or they can be compressed to one side, where they will occupy about one fifth of their normal width.

There's no question that vertical blinds are beautiful and elegant. They're also somewhat easier to clean than venetian blinds, because the slats are so wide. But they're far more expensive. To cover a window 30 feet by 54 inches, for example, you'd have to buy blinds costing more than $100.

For this reason, the stores that sell them recommend them mainly for wall-to-wall windows and patio doors.

Are vertical blinds for you? If you can afford them, sure. But beware that they'll probably remain in the apartment after you've left, since their installation is a little on the permanent side. But perhaps you can get your landlord (or the next tenant) to buy them from you.

Roman Shades

The next most elaborate window treatment we can imagine is the "Roman shade."

Roman shades are, in essence, hundreds of long, narrow, wooden or plastic slats, tightly woven together with cord and fabric into sheets of practically opaque material, that can be hung in front of windows.

Let down, Roman shades cover a window and its molding. Raised up by pulling on a cord, they more or less disappear behind a valence of the same material.

Roman shades serve the same general function as ordinary window shades, but they're much heavier and more decorative. Windows with ordinary shades, for instance, look unfinished. Not so, windows with Roman shades.

Like practically everything else in this world, they're available in a variety of qualities—and prices. The simpler the weave, the plainer the design, the less expensive the shade. The fancier, the more expensive.

Some examples: A ready-made Roman shade with simple slats and only enough weaving to hold them firmly together costs about twenty dollars for a window 29x48 inches. A heavily woven one of the same size costs $35. And there are many gradations in between.

If you like the Roman shade idea, but need something less expensive (after all, you have plenty of windows to cover), you might consider a similar but less complex shade usually called a roll-up.

Roll-ups look very much like Roman shades when they're down, except that they have a pair of strings visible along their entire length. But it's when they're rolled up that the differences become obvious. While the body of a Roman shade automatically disappears behind its built-in valance, the roll-up does just that: It rolls up, leaving you with a large cylinder of material at the top of your window. This sounds worse than it actually is.

At any rate, the decreased complexity also means a lower price. You can get good-looking roll-up shades for about one half the price of Roman shades. And inexpensive vinyls are available for about five dollars for our 29x48 inches comparison size. That's one fourth the price of an inexpensive Roman shade. On the other hand, they're a lot less attractive.

Window Shades

The least expensive way to cover your windows, of course, is the old familiar window shade, the kind that rolls up on a roller and pulls down.

But even here, there are many alternatives, mainly in the quality of the shade but also, to some degree, in style and design.

The simplest of these is made of single-ply, 4-mill-gauge vinyl and it comes only in white. You can buy any size from 18 inches through 37¼ inches (and 6 feet long) for around two dollars. But, aside from limited durability, this shade doesn't provide much more than privacy, since it only filters the light, illuminating rooms with diffused, filtered sunlight. That could be ideal, however, in a small bathroom or in the kitchen, where you have no reason to darken a room. It might not do in a bedroom, though.

A room-darkening shade of the same size runs about six dollars. And for that money, you can get something a little better—usually 6-mil-gauge vinyl, with a heavy ribcord texture. But you won't have much of a color selection. In fact, you'll probably have to make do with white.

If you're willing to spend somewhat more, you can get shades of better quality, more interesting design, and a greater range of colors. For instance, for about eight dollars, you can get shades made out of 8-mil-gauge vinyl, which is a quite durable weight.

These shades not only hang straighter and provide some insulation, but they also resist tearing quite well. And they're available in four or five different colors—yellows, greens, browns, usually.

More money yet, of course, will buy you still better shades. For about twelve dollars for our sample comparison size (18 to 37¼ inches wide, 6 feet long), you can get shades made of five-ply, 12-mil-gauge vinyl that has a fiberglass core, for strength. Shades of this weight resist tearing, hang straighter, and their edges curl less than the cheaper variety. They also insulate better, keeping heat in during the winter and heat out during the summer. For another four dollars or so, you can get this shade with a scalloped and fringed bottom.

Beyond this are shades intended as much for insulation as for decoration or room darkening. For instance, for twenty-five dollars, you can get a light-filtering shade with a bronze-tinted film on the street side which greatly reduces heat loss in winter and somewhat reduces heat gain in the summer.

The same price will also buy you a room-darkening shade that's even better at reducing heat loss. This shade has mirror-like, silver-color plastic film on the street side.

Incidentally, if you decide to buy shades mainly for their insulating value—which may be wise if you're paying for utilities, especially in these days of high energy costs—be sure to hang them on the outside of the molding. That's when they're at their most efficient.

If you're dissatisfied with the varieties of window shades available at your local department, discount, or dime store, you can always decorate the basic shades yourself, with fabric, paint, stick-ons and transfers, or trim.

But wherever you buy them, just bring your measurements and the salesperson will cut them to size in no time at all. As for hanging them, that could hardly be simpler. All you need do is put the two little metal holders (they're usually sold separately) up on the molding with tiny nails, then put the shade in place. It shouldn't take more than ten minutes.

Window Alternatives

Let's just say, for the sake of argument, that none of these traditional solutions to "the window problem" appeals to you. Or let's say they just won't work in your situation. What else can you do, other than tack up bedsheets over the windows?

Well, actually, there are many alternatives. Among them: shutters, window quilts, stained-glass windows, imitation stained glass, decorative transfers, and plastic film. Let's take them one at a time:

SHUTTERS

These are usually wooden frames with movable wooden louvers within. They're often made in two or more hinged sections, so they can be fully or partially opened, depending on your desires. You can buy them unfinished, stained, or painted. Some even come with fabric inserts replacing the movable louvers.

Depending on how you finish them and what room you put them in, shutters can be folksy or sophisticated. You can stain them a natural wood shade for a bedroom or a casual livingroom, paint them black to contrast with white stucco walls, or paint them the same color as your walls, so your windows seem to disappear when the shutters are closed.

If shutters appeal to you, our advice is to buy them at a discount lumberyard. You can get them to cover the top or bottom half of a window, or both halves (with two tiers), or the complete window.

Mounting shutters isn't very difficult. Just nail the hinges they usually come with into the back side of the shutters, making sure they're straight and plumb. Then line up the shutter on the inside of the window frame and lightly nail the rest of the hinge into the wood frame. Now line up the parts of the hinge on the shutter with the parts on the inside of the window frame, making sure they're level and even. Then replace the nails one by one with wood screws.

If you're willing to spend a little more money, you can get shutters that are even easier to hang. These have "hanging strips" with half-hinges already in place. These strips are pre-drilled and hardware is included. Just screw them into your window casing and slip the shutters on—or off, for cleaning. It's a cinch. And it's a necessity for out-of-square windows.

Alternately, you can use outdoor shutters. These can look refreshing when used as a window accent in a large, airy room. Usually, they're nailed to the wall and aren't intended to be opened or closed. But they can be attached with outdoor shutter hinges.

If you want to install outdoor shutters in this manner, do it just as you would the smaller, indoor shutters. One caution, though: Since these shutters are much heavier, they'll require some helping hands and some longer and heavier wood screws.

To prevent them from banging into the window molding and damaging it, put little plastic door stops at the middle of the top and the bottom of the window frame. And to make sure they stay closed when you want them to, install hook and eye or hook and button closures on the room side of the shutters.

WINDOW QUILTS

The energy crisis has spawned its own window treatment—the window quilt. These are a self-sealing, space-age insulated type of roll-up blind. The side facing the inside of the room is usually fabric or fabric-textured and is available in many different colors.

If your apartment is pretty well insulated except for the windows, you might save a lot of money on your fuel bill by installing window quilts—assuming you're billed for fuel separately and that you live in a four-season climate.

If you live in an area with cold winters, but you're *not* billed separately for fuel, window quilts are mainly a comfort item, preventing drafts and heat leakage, perhaps near the couch where you usually sit.

But there is a rub: Window quilts are expensive, and they must be fitted to the window by someone who knows what he's doing—usually a professional installer. Since they're cut to size, taking them with you won't make much sense, unless you're moving to an apartment with windows the same size as your present one.

STAINED-GLASS WINDOWS

Your apartment is a two-minute walk from the subway. It's Victorian, with beautiful little fireplaces, big brass handles on the doors, and a stained glass window in the livingroom.

Unfortunately, the only thing you can see from your bedrrom is the delicatessen across the street. And from your kitchen window, right over the sink, you see the man across the alley shaving twice a day (7:15 A.M., while you're filling the teakettle, and 5:45 P.M., while you're scrubbing the asparagus for dinner).

If you have a large window that seems to let the cold air in no matter how tightly you close it, try a "Window Quilt," an insulating shade. This type of shade is attractive and effecient—and a good substitute for an ordinary window shade, although considerably more expensive.

You know he has a blonde girl friend who visits on weekends and combs her hair a lot. He wears a gold terry bathrobe, which she borrows when she stays overnight. The whole situation is embarrassing—so much so that you're reluctant to wash the dishes until they've gone out for the evening.

Of course you can't tell a total stranger that he could get shutters or a shade for his bathroom. But you can do something yourself: Hang a stained-glass window in your kitchen.

A stained-glass window will cut out the view across the alley, without blotting out the little light you get. Besides, it will continue the theme developed in your livingroom.

Of course, your landlord might or might not appreciate it if you removed the existing glass and replaced it with a stained-glass window. And such an alteration can be very expensive. But there's a better way.

You can go to a stained-glass shop and purchase a lightweight decorative panel to suspend inside your existing window frame. It's easy to hang it—all you need are hooks and eyes. And you *can* take it with you.

Alternately, you can check a housewrecker's lot. Many have Victorian stained-glass windows removed from older homes. The prices are usually less than totally outrageous and the effect can be splendid. In fact, we can't think of a better way to give an apartment some character.

IMITATION STAINED-GLASS WINDOWS

If you don't think the woodwork will hold a glass panel, or the frame is too shallow, or you don't want to spend the money, you can create a stained-glass effect with something called "glass stain." You can buy it in a department or discount store. It goes on easily and can be removed without much trouble.

Or, you can use diluted tempura or acrylic paints to create a similar effect. Apply them with a small sponge. When and if you want to remove them, wash with warm, soapy water. To simulate leading, put down some gray or black tape in long, narrow strips.

Another way to create what looks like stained-glass windows is by using pieces of cellophane, cut out into an attractive shapes, and taped into place with strips of grey or black tape.

PLASTIC FILMS

Let's say you have a situation where drapes and curtains are too expensive, and blinds, shades, and shutters simply can't be put up, because of the window's construction. What then?

No matter what your situation, you always have the glass itself to work with. And that gives you several possibilities.

Many lumberyards sell a variety of plastic films that can be attached directly to your windows. These come mainly in two types: transparent mirror-finishes and translucent, textured patterns.

The mirror-finishes are available in silver and bronze tones. Some come preglued, either with adhesive that must be dampened before application or with self-sticking adhesive. All you have to do is cut them to size with a scissors or razor blade and put them in place (but make sure your window is clean first).

The mirror-finishes are ideal for filtering strong sunlight. Some darker ones are just like putting sunglasses on your windows. And one-way mirror-finishes are also available. They let you look out, but prevent anyone from seeing inside. They work especially well if there's no illumination from within the room.

The textured patterns, usually small-figured geometrics, are ideal for bathroom or even bedroom situations, where you are anxious to get as much light as possible into the room at all times, but are equally anxious to achieve total privacy.

Of course, once you put up the plastic films, they're there until you peel them off and throw them away. You'll never be able to reuse them. But they're not all that expensive and they're sometimes the answer to a window problem that seems to have no solution at all.

TRANSFERS AND STICK-UPS

The simplest, least expensive window decorations of all are plastic, transparent transfers and stick-ups. You've seen them—they're miniature rainbows, brightly colored peacocks, and other designs. Recently, we've seen a stunning new line that's based on Chinese paper cut-outs.

Transfers and stick-ups are a splendid way to turn an otherwise drab window, one with hardly any view at all, into something pretty and decorative. They let light in, yet increase privacy.

If you decide on this course, just make sure that the transfers blend with your room decor. And don't overuse them. A transfer or sticker on every window (or, worse yet, on every pane) is a bit much, no matter how beautiful they are. On the other hand, they're the least expensive way to beautify a plain white window shade.

We think that there's a place for at least one transfer in every apartment, regardless of the age or gender of the tenant. You can buy them in gift or card shops for two or three dollars each.

These, then, are the major ways to decorate your windows. But there are many others, for this is a decorative area where your only limitation is your own imagination.

Decorate your windows and set them off properly, add light-filtering or room-darkening shades—and they'll pay you back by offering lovely views, fresh air and sunshine, and excellent, decorative focal points for your room.

So, if you're going to be living in your apartment for a year or two—or more—give your windows some thought and spend some money on decorating. You'll be pleased with the result.

Chapter 8

THE KITCHEN

What's the most important room in an apartment? Well, you can certainly make an excellent case for the bathroom, the bedroom, even the livingroom. But without a kitchen of some sort, an apartment isn't really an apartment. It's just a set of rented rooms.

Kitchens are what free you from having to find a restaurant every morning and every night. They're what save you from mooching off Aunt Sophie all the time. They give you the freedom to have guests, invite people over for dinner, throw parties, etc.

In some families, kitchens are the focal point of most communal activities. They're where Mom and Dad see the kids every day. They're where family conferences—and arguments—are held. They're the homemaker's office.

Even for those whose cooking is limited to opening cans and heating contents, kitchens have a psychological significance that can't be dismissed. They're the source of sustenance, the provider of food. And, except for the air we breathe, there's nothing more important to us.

And so when you go apartment hunting or even after your search has ended, you'll probably spend a lot of time figuring out how to maximize your kitchen's capabilities.

There are many issues to deal with here—more than meet the eye, certainly.

Size. Can you make do with a too-small kitchen? What about those that look large, but aren't? Can a kitchen be too big? How can you increase usable kitchen space without breaking into your neighbor's apartment?

213

An inexpensive table-and-chair set, a plastic étagère, a few simple decorations—and what do you have? A perfectly pleasant kitchen eating nook, just right for breakfast for two.

Appliances. Should you stick with the ones that the landlord provides? Should you buy some of your own? How can you test out old appliances? What about getting them repaired? How about the fancy new appliances—should your apartment have them?

Cookware. What will you need? When should you buy it? Where should you buy it?

Dishes and glasses. What are your basic needs? How about optional extras? Where should you buy them? Mix and match, or just mix?

Kitchen utensils. Buying the basics. Luxury fill-ins. Selecting knives—and keeping them sharp. Table cutlery—silver or stainless? The minor necessities.

Kitchen linens. The difference between what you need and what you want. What to buy and where.

Consumables. Learning how to navigate through the soap-and-Brillo-pad section of your supermarket. Which cleaner for which job?

Food staples. What do you need to start—quality, quantity? What should you resist?

Storage space. The pitfalls and the pleasures of the refrigerator. Arranging your nonrefrigerated edibles. Ordering your dishware. Showing the under-the-sink area who's boss. Taming your broom closet.

The ugly appliance—and what to do about it. How to beautify the old, the ugly, and the decrepit. Simple ways to restore appliance efficiency. Putting a little light on your subject.

Little livestock. Strategies and tactics for eliminating unwanted kitchen wildlife. When to do-it-yourself and when to call the landlord.

Routines. How to keep things humming. Making your kitchen into an information center.

As you can see, then, there's more to kitchens than you might think, without considering the matter. Let's take up these matters one at a time, starting with . . .

The Question of Size

All too often, an apartment kitchen is little more than an open, walk-in closet, with a small stove, a small refrigerator and a few hanging cabinets.

Can you make do with such a kitchen? That depends mainly on you—on your lifestyle, your needs, your tastes, your inclinations.

For people to whom cooking is an alien task, to be attempted only when starvation is approaching, tiny kitchens are really quite acceptable—especially if one is single.

For such folk, kitchens are more than adequate if they're large enough to store a jar or two of peanut butter, a selection of single-serving cereals, and some canned soups.

These people can live quite satisfactorily if their refrigerators are large enough to hold only a quart of milk, a few bottles of soda, and possibly some eggs, and if the freezer sections are capable of making a tray of ice cubes every few days and of holding three or four TV dinners and a quart of ice cream.

For such culinary minimalists, counter space is adequate if there's room for a toaster oven, cabinet space is sufficient if a place setting of dishes can be hidden within, and drawer space is enough if there's room for a few knives, forks, and spoons, and a can opener.

If this description fits you, you're going to have a hard time finding an inadequate apartment kitchen. Chances are, you'll find yourself with more kitchen than you need. But, if—as is more likely—you expect to cook *meals* in your kitchen, perhaps not only for yourself, but also for others, the glorified walk-in closet won't do.

But let's say you're the sort who needs a working kitchen and you're shown an otherwise perfect apartment with the walk-in closet type of kitchen. What do you do?

You will ask yourself some questions, and you answer them honestly. Am I willing to eat out most of the time? Will my spouse or children accept this situation? Will I be frustrated by the impossibility of making a real meal at home? Are the apartment's other features worth the extra expense of frequent restaurant meals?

Some people can compromise on the kitchen issue. But for most of us, an adequate working kitchen is essential. Whatever else an apartment may have, if it doesn't have that, it isn't for us.

But sometimes, it can be hard to find an apartment with a real kitchen. You may have to look around for a while until you find a kitchen that suits you.

Got yourself a big kitchen with a lot of extra floor space? Why not consider building yourself an "island," a self-contained structure with either a butcher-block or plastic top, with a "kneehole" so it can be used in combination with stools for snacks, parties, etc. This island also has drawers with shelves for added storage space.

If you're really hurting for kitchen storage space, put some shelves on the inside of a closet door. You won't be diminishing the usefulness of the closet, but you will be providing yourself with a place for kitchen staples.

One good place to start: Victorian homes that have been made into apartments. The first-floor apartments in such buildings usually have the house's original kitchen. It may not be modern. It may not have much storage space. But it will probably be large enough that you can make it into what you want.

But large kitchens aren't always as large as they look at first glance. We lived in one apartment that had a kitchen with more floor space than our bedroom. But only one corner was usable. The rest of the room was taken up with five doors (!) and two very large windows. Even a small kitchen table broke up the traffic flow.

We did the best we could, under the circumstances. We put a chopping block island near the stove and a fold-out table against a wall. It wasn't any great pleasure, but short of a major remodeling job, it was all we could do.

But we learned our lesson—and we're passing it on to you: When you're looking at an apartment kitchen, especially an empty one, don't be snowed by floor space alone. Figure out how it can be used. Sometimes, what looks like a large kitchen is actually quite modest. And the reverse is also true. Some small kitchens actually have tremendous potential, if they're intelligently organized and arranged.

Making More Space

Unfortunately, you can't add on to an apartment by knocking out a wall and putting up another room. And your upstairs neighbors might object if you raised the ceiling to install a loft. Still, there are almost always ways to make a kitchen "larger," to add storage space and work room. It's all a matter of ingenuity.

Take the cupboards, for instance. Quite often, kitchen cupboards have shelves so widely spaced that you can get another one between them. If you're lucky enough to have this situation, here's how to add your extra shelf:

1. Take out one of the existing shelves and measure it. (If you can't remove it, measure it in place.)
2. Get a duplicate cut at your local lumberyard, and get two braces to fit under the shelf and hold it up. Usually, 1x2 lum-

ber is ideal for this purpose. Get two pieces, each one as long as the shelf is deep.

3. Nail the braces halfway between the existing shelves, using a level to get them into position. Paint them the same color as the inside of the cupboard, or something close.

4. Now paint your plank and let it dry. Then slide it in on top of the braces. You can nail it down if you like, but that's not necessary.

Even if you existing shelves aren't widely separated, you can still add shelf space. If you need a small shelf for spices and the like, you can make it half the width of the existing shelves and install it between them. You can follow the steps above, with one addition: You'll need a vertical dividing board between the shelves. One end of your new half-shelf will terminate there.

Shallow half-shelves like these really do add convenience to your kitchen. They make your spices easy to see and reach. And they still leave room for those extra tall vinegar, oil, or wine bottles.

Incidentally, this needn't be a do-it-yourself project if you don't want it to be. Your local dime store or kitchen gadget shop has all kinds of racks and shelves that are made to hang from existing shelves, taking advantage of the unused air space within your cupboards. These require no carpentry and you can take them with you when you move. But the cost more than the do-it-yourself variety.

You can also increase cupboard space by buying stacking shelves for your dishware. These let you use all (or almost all) of the space between your shelves, without forcing you to stack your dessert plates on your dinner plates.

Another useful, if old-fashioned, way to increase cupboard space: cup hooks. These keep your mugs and cups off the shelves, leaving more room for saucers and plates. You can either mount them on the bottoms of shelves inside your cupboard or, if you have a beautiful set of mugs you'd like to display, you can mount them on the underside of the cupboard itself.

But what if you're short of cupboard space altogether? Well, if you have some empty wall space in the kitchen, the diningroom, or a nearby hallway, you're not out of luck. In fact, you have three options:

First, you can install kitchen cabinets (but are you sure you want to put in anything that you won't be able to or won't want to take with you?).

Second, you can buy a white metal kitchen cabinet. These look something like your old high-school locker or the bandage cabinet in the doctor's office. They're available through the mail-order department stores or at large discount stores or furniture stores.

Metal kitchen cabinets aren't terribly expensive, but they aren't terribly elegant, either. On the other hand, they're usually fairly sturdy and, painted in basic white enamel, they usually blend with kitchen appliances.

If you decide that one of these is the best solution to your cupboard space problem, don't hesitate to redecorate it to suit your taste. Tape up a poster or two. Better yet, glue on some cork panels to use as a bulletin board. Might as well make 'em serve two purposes.

Third, you can buy a semi-antique "Hoosier" cabinet, with a pullout sideboard and perhaps a large, built-in flour sifter. But if this is your choice, don't go to an antique store and pay top-dollar for a refinished version. Go to an auction house or secondhand shop. What you'll find there may be painted dull green, but it will cost much less, and you can paint it or refinish it to fit your decor.

Some close friends of ours—we'll call them George and Sue, to avoid embarrassing them—once bought one of these cabinets for their kitchen. They measured everything, so they thought, to make sure it would fit. But when they got it home, they found that they couldn't pull out the sideboard and still stand in front of it. Moral of the story: Measure first, then buy. Don't buy, then measure.

If you decide that one of these cabinets is just what the doctor ordered, and you buy one, you can often save money by offering to cart it home yourself. It's easier than you think. The top section usually separates from the bottom section, to make moving easier.

One caution about moving this sort of furniture, however: Remove all of the drawers and tape all the doors shut. Otherwise you'll have parts falling out, or off, at the worst possible moment.

But what if you have no space for metal cabinets or "Hoosier" cupboards. What if your wall clearance is just too close for such items? Well, all is not lost even then. You can still use your walls to increase storage space, through the magic of pegboard.

Put up pegboard on those otherwise useless walls and install hooks on the pegboard. Then hang up your pots, pans, egg beaters, ladles, mugs—whatever has a hook or a handle. You'll find yourself with an interesting wall design, more accessible cookware, and cupboard space you can put to better use.

Incidentally, pegboard isn't the only way to accomplish this particular feat. You can buy wire racks at your local gadget store that will achieve much the same purpose. So will the semi-circular, wrought-iron racks made specifically to hang cookware. Both can be mounted on the wall.

And if you have no wall space whatsoever, there are even some racks that can be hung from the ceiling, such as the traditional circular rack for hanging pots and pans. When it comes to increasing space, where there's a will, there's a way.

But let's say you have a fair amount of counter space but very little cupboard or cabinet space. What then? At least a partial answer to your problem may be a decorative cannister set, or even several of them.

You can put just about every foodstuff in cannisters—flour, sugar, tea, coffee, spices, nuts, oatmeal, raisins, cereals, etc. And the more you put into cannisters, the less you'll have to find room for in your limited cabinet space.

One modern cannister set we like doesn't use cannisters at all, but a variety of plastic bins and containers, all housed in an attractive, rectangular, wooden box, usually painted white. This box can be put on a countertop or even hung from the wall.

But you don't have to invest in expensive, decorator cannister sets or accent pieces such as the one described above. Just go to a restaurant or bakery and ask for the large jars that usually contain mayonnaise, prepared relishes, crunchy toppings, or prepared frostings. Wash them, dry them, and you have large, attractive, clear glass "cannisters."

For smaller items, you can buy a case of canning jars. These come in pressed-glass designs or colors. Spice racks are also useful ways to transfer items out of cabinets onto counter tops. Look for those with good labels and easy-to-open tops.

If you like, by the way, you can make your own spice rack,

Don't have room to put everything away? No problem. Just get yourself some pegboard, paint it in pretty colors, and let it all hang out. Notice that in this kitchen, the table folds right up into the wall and its underside is also a storage area.

If there's one word that should be your kitchen byword, it's "Organize!" It will save you time, money, and aggravation. And no area needs organization more than the under-sink area, the most disreputable spot in most apartment kitchens.

with baby food jars and a compartmented wooden box. Just paint the covers of the jars and get some pregummed labels to note the contents. Hang the box on the wall, or set it on the back of the stove, and your spice storage problem is solved.

You can also convert counter space into cupboard-type storage by using double-tiered lazy susans or racks that hold wax paper, foil, and plastic wrap. Just go to your local kitchen gadget store or the kitchen department of your local department store and give your imagination free reign.

Another frequently overlooked source of additional space is in the under-sink area. Almost certainly, this is the place you should store cleaning items. It's also the best spot for the garbage pail. But there's almost certainly more space here than you think.

Do you have shelves under the sink? Racks for foil and plastic wraps? Hooks for dishcloths, brushes, and the like? Or do you just stash everything on the floor, like most people? If so, you're missing some opportunities to increase your storage space.

Our advice: Organize that under-sink area. Put in shelves, or at least two-tiered lazy Susans. Install racks on the doors. And wherever you can't put anything else, screw in hooks.

Of course, you won't want to store any foodstuffs down here, especially if you've decided to make this garbage and cleaning headquarters. But it's a perfectly acceptable place for pots, pans, and cooking crockery.

If you're short on counter space but have plenty of cupboards, you can set aside one or two convenient cupboard shelves and make them your cannister and condiment area, reducing the burden on your limited counter space. But there are other ways to increase it.

If, for instance, you have a double sink, consider buying a sink-top cutting board to cover half of it. This will give you several square feet of "counter" space exactly where you're most likely to need it. And if you find you need both parts of the sink, converting back will take only a moment or two.

Another way to increase counter space, at least on a temporary basis, is to install a folding shelf against an otherwise unused wall. If there's plenty of width to your kitchen, you can make the shelf permanent and even put another one beneath it, for storage purposes. If, on the other hand, yours is one of those long, nar-

Here's another version of the fold-up kitchen table, mounted on an otherwise useless wall. The base, in this case, is made of kitchen stools, which have been made into storage shelves.

row kitchens, you can install a collapsible shelf, keeping it up while preparing meals and down while serving them.

If you're not only short of counter space, but also have no space for a kitchen table, you can use the same general idea to fill both needs, building a dining table that can serve as a countertop during meal preparation and seat two people comfortably at breakfast, lunch, or dinner.

You'll find yourself using this simple piece of furniture not only for meals, but also while chopping onions or tomatoes for supper, while watching the news (or soap operas, if you prefer) on your portable TV.

This combination countertop and dining table can also serve as an island in a large kitchen, or as a divider in a large doorway between kitchen and living room. It could even be placed in a hallway next to kitchen.

One last kitchen space-saving hint before we go on to other matters: When buying utensils, dishes, cups, cookware, etc., etc., etc., buy the type that stack, nest, collapse, come on their own rack, fit into corners, etc. This will give you less to store—which is, in the end, the best way we know of stretching the space you have.

Appliances—Yours or Theirs

Some apartments come totally bereft of appliances of any kind, although local statutes usually require that a landlord provide, at minimum, a stove and a refrigerator.

Other apartments come with a set of brand-new appliances (usually in brand-new buildings or those that have been recently remodeled or recently turned into rental units).

Still others are equipped with appliances that, to look at them, seem old enough to have been used by your great-grandmother's great-grandmother.

If you find yourself moving into an apartment totally without appliances, don't panic. You needn't sell your soul to General Electric, at least not immediately.

Instead, get yourself a hotplate and an ice chest. They'll take care of your immediate needs, for a few days anyway. Then you can shop for what you need in leisure.

If you're on a tight budget, consider used appliances. You can usually find good used appliances for 20 to 30 percent of the price of comparable new ones.

There are two main places to look for used appliances: newspaper want ads (or the want-ad newspapers that can be found in some major metropolitan areas), and appliance and/or furniture stores.

You can very often find good buys through newspaper want ads—relatively young appliances at good prices. These are sometimes advertised by families moving to another part of the country. They may have bought the appliances five to seven years ago and are pricing them not according to today's inflated pricetags, but according to their original cost.

Used appliances found at retail outlets are another matter altogether. Usually, they've come into the store as trade-ins on new appliances. Now people don't get rid of their appliances and buy new ones simply because styles have changed. They have another reason—usually that their old appliances have been giving them trouble.

Most retail outlets understand this and they have the appliances put back into good working order. But some don't. Therefore, if you choose to buy this way, you'd better be careful.

The best way to protect yourself in this situation is to have the appliance demonstrated to you. See it work with your own eyes. Then, in addition, get a money-back guarantee.

You won't be able to get a guarantee, of course, if you buy from a private individual, especially one who's leaving the state. But if you see the appliance working properly—the stove cooking, the refrigerator refrigerating, you're fairly safe.

You can also sometimes find good used appliances at auctions or estate sales. But your risk goes up here, since it's often difficult to test the items before you purchase them. If you can't test them, but still want them, get yourself a *written* guarantee and pay by personal check. That way you still have a chance of getting your money back if the appliance turns out to be a dud.

If you buy used appliances, or if your apartment comes with a set that looks as though it's seen better days, you owe it to yourself to put everything into good working order. Stoves, in particular, can be dangerous if they don't work properly. And a faulty refrigerator can ruin a lot of expensive food.

If you find yourself with an electric stove that's more than five years old, check the burners carefully to be sure they don't spark or crackle. If they do, have them replaced. This is a relatively simple and inexpensive job (although if the appliance belongs to your landlord, he's the one who should pay).

If you wind up with a gas stove, find out if the jets have been cleaned recently. If not, contact a competent repairman and have worn parts replaced and the jets reassembled properly.

You should also check out oven temperatures, using the gauges you can find in dime stores or hardware stores. If there are any serious discrepancies, have a serviceman reregulate the temperature dial.

Once everything is in working order, give your stove a good general cleaning, to remove the dirt and grease that has accumulated over the years, and you'll have an appliance that—for all practical purposes—is just as good as new.

Refrigerators are an even simpler matter than stoves. In general, those made in the last fifteen years or so are among the most reliable appliances ever made by human hands. So your chances of getting one that's in excellent working order are very good indeed.

But there is one good reason to buy the newest refrigerator you can afford. In the last five years or so, refrigerator insulation and energy use has been improved dramatically. So if you buy yourself a newer refrigerator, you may be saving money in the long run. (Even if you don't pay for utilities now, you probably will in the next place you live.)

What about "luxury" appliances—dishwashers, microwave ovens, convection ovens, trash compactors, electric grills, and the like? Well, in our experience, the more of these an apartment comes with, the higher your rent will be. You're not simply renting space, after all—you're also renting its contents, and in particular, the appliances it comes with.

If you have a choice then, it may be wiser to buy the "luxury" appliances you need and move them from place to place, rather than pay for the privilege of using them.

If you buy, you'll get the ones you want, you'll always know what condition they're in, and you'll own something tangible when you move.

By the way, don't underestimate the value of getting the specific appliances you want—model, brand name, features, etc. Your landlord is likely to buy what costs him least, whereas you're likely to want the highest quality you can afford. Even in the short run, there's a lot of difference between those two approaches.

If you end up buying your own new appliances—refrigerator, stove, or any of the others—spend your money as wisely as possible. Check the consumer magazines to find out what brand and features suit you best. Then do some comparison shopping at local stores.

When buying major appliances, there's no substitute for knowing what you're looking for. And that may be more difficult than you think. For instance, two types of unconventional ovens are now on the market and there's been plenty of confusion between them: microwave ovens and convection ovens.

Just to clear up the confusion, here's a brief explanation of each:

Convection ovens. These work exactly like any ordinary oven, except that they circulate the hot air within them, which helps foods cook more quickly and brown more evenly. Faster cooking, of course, means less energy usage.

Microwave ovens. These work on an entirely different principle. They irradiate food with radio waves. This makes the water molecules inside the food expand quickly. Thus, food cooks from the inside out.

For frozen foods and leftovers, microwaves are hard to beat. But they're not as good at baking cakes or making biscuits. And unless they have conventional heating elements in addition to everything else, they're not good at browning foods, so even those that are thoroughly cooked often don't look quite right. On the other hand, they're much faster than any other kind of oven and they're energy savers.

Our point: Either one or both might be right for you, depending on your lifestyle and your cooking habits. But you can't be sure until you know what both will do.

The different types of dishwashers on the market can also create confusion, when it comes time to buy one. When you eliminate all the knobs and dials, you'll find that there are just two basic types: built-ins and portables.

The built-ins are those that are permanetly—and we do mean permanently—installed beneath a kitchen counter. They're connected to water and sewer lines and wired into electric outlets. Then countertops are laid down on top of them and nailed in.

Portables are essentially the same machines mounted on casters. You plug them and unplug them into a wall outlet and you connect them and unconnect them to your faucet by means of a rubber hose. They come complete with their own counter-tops and they can be stored in any part of the kitchen that's convenient.

We've had experience with both types of dishwashers and we can assure you that they're equally good at cleaning dishes. And despite the hookups, portables aren't really much less convenient than built-ins.

Which should you buy? Unless you're building a house, we recommend the portable variety. It can travel with you from apartment to apartment. Or you can sell it if you find yourself moving into a place that's already dishwasher-equipped.

As for brands and features, you'll have to choose those yourself. But one feature is worth mentioning, if you're an apartment dweller. Some apartments have "cool" hot water—water heated to about 110 degrees or so. This isn't really hot enough to sterilize dishes. If this is your situation, get yourself a dishwasher that has a built-in water heating element. That way, you'll never have to worry.

By the way, trash compactors are also available in portable models. And they're a real joy if you have a large family. What they do is simple enough: They take all of your papers, rubbish, and garbage and compress it into relatively small blocks. In practical terms, this means many fewer trips to the garbage cans outside. If you live in a third-floor walkup in a cold climate, you'll congratulate yourself again and again if you buy one.

Most people buy their appliances when they need them. But if you're able to choose your time of purchase, wait until late fall or early spring. That's when most major department stores hold their appliance sales. The fall sales are intended for Christmas giving and the spring sales for Mother's Day. But don't let that stop you.

Cookware

If you're lucky enough to own a full set of cookware, or if— and this is very unlikely—your landlord has provided you with a set, you can skip this section and go directly to the next one.

But the chances are you're going to have to buy the cookware you need. Just what should you get?

Well, for one thing, if you have a typical, apartment-sized kitchen, there are some items you can cross off your list right away, because they simply won't fit. For example, you're unlikely to have an oven big enough for a roaster or a large cookie sheet.

We first discovered this particular fact four Thanksgivings ago, when one of our friends, a woman named Marsha, invited us to her first Thanksgiving dinner.

Marsha is the traditional sort when it comes to holidays, so we weren't surprised when she brought out a large turkey. But when we asked her how in the world she'd managed to cook it in her little oven, we learned a lesson we can now pass on to you.

To get the turkey into her oven, Marsha had to bend the handles of her roasting pan upward at a 90-degree angle. This got the turkey done all right, but it pretty much wrecked the roasting pan.

What should she have done instead? She should have invested in some large-sized foil pans. These can be bent to fit into practically any oven, then thrown out when the cooking is done.

In our opinion, the best cookware you can get yourself are those convertible dishes that can serve as a casserole, for serving, or, with the addition of a snap-on handle, work as saucepans.

You'll find ceramic, enameled, aluminum, and glass cooking dishes that not only do this, but also can go from freezer to oven to table—then into the refrigerator, for storing leftovers. They're ideal.

We recommend that you buy the circular variety of this cookware. That way, you'll also be able to use it as a mixing bowl (and you'll find it far superior to the usual pressed aluminum or plastic mixing bowls, because it will be heavier and sturdier).

Three medium-sized, all-purpose casseroles will serve most kitchen and diningroom needs. We prefer the ceramic variety. You can buy them in plain white, which goes with any decor, or in any one of the downright beautiful patterns now on the market. We've even seen a set in jet black, which goes with any decor and provides an appetizing background for food.

If you're willing to time your purchase, by the way, you can save from 20 to 30 percent if you buy a month before Christmas or right afterward. That's when these items usually go on sale. But don't buy at Christmas, or in the late spring when the brides are out shopping. Prices are highest then.

You can probably find exactly what you want in your local department store or at your kitchen gadget shop, if you're lucky enough to have one nearby. Discount china shops are another good place to look as are discount department stores and dime stores, which often carry name brands at cut rates.

These items, plus a teakettle, should take care of your basic needs. But after a while, you'll probably discover that you need additional pieces of cookware—egg poachers, boilers, muffin sheets, skillets, etc. Our advice: Wait until you know that you need an item before you buy it. And always look for items that do double duty. They save you money and space and they're often more convenient to use.

Dishes and Glassware

If your hope chest happens to be equipped with a full set of dishes and glassware, or if your landlord is providing all you need (which actually does happen occasionally, in some sublet situations), this is another section you can skip. Otherwise, read on.

Although it's possible to fix many a meal—and serve it—from a single pot, most people find this arrangement gets pretty boring after a while. Besides, it lacks a certain gentility. What to do? Buy dishes, even if you're anything but the domestic type.

Of course, you can start out with paper plates. They're certainly better than nothing at all (unless you're serving beef stew). Some of them have plastic coatings and they're fairly sturdy as a result. Some are even passably attractive. And it's tempting to use them, secure in the knowledge that you'll never have to wash a dish. But don't try to fool yourself into thinking you're saving money. With the money you spend on a few weeks worth of paper plates, you can have a set of dishes all your own.

The next step up from paper plates—and it's a giant step—is Melmac. Melmac is a hard and very durable plastic. You can drop Melmac plates from tall buildings and they'll bounce. You can put them through a thousand dishwashing cycles and all they'll do is fade a little. They're practically indestructible (and about the only way to get rid of them, should you ever want to, is to throw them away).

Melmac dishes come in a wide variety of patterns and styles, some of them quite pretty. They're also quite inexpensive—thirty dollars or so for a service for eight. You can buy them at your local department store or through one of the large catalog stores.

The next step up from Melmac is something called Corelle, a ceramic developed by Corning Glass. Like Melmac, Corelle is inexpensive and practically indestructible. But it's obviously not plastic. The main problem with this type of dishware is that it isn't available in many patterns or colors. But for pure practicality, it's hard to beat.

If you want something a bit more elegant, but no more expensive, you might consider ironstone. Ironstone is that thick, sturdy, heavily-patterned dishware usually sold in sets (as opposed to open stock) in department stores, discount stores, kitchenware shops. You can usually buy a set for less than forty dollars.

Of course, you don't have to buy dishes in sets—or in regular retail outlets. Dishes are frequently sold by the boxful at auctions. They're also sold by the piece at tag sales and garage sales, sometimes for as little as a dime a plate.

If you buy your dishes at tag sales, of course, you're unlikely to find matching sets. But if you stick with the same general size and color, you can usually assemble an acceptable grouping. If you intend to buy your dishes this way, our advice is to stick with white. This is the color in the greatest supply, and the easiest to match.

We learned this trick from an antique-loving couple we met in Toronto, Ontario. While visiting in the Maritime provinces, they went to a number of antique shops, asking for plain white Victorian china at each place.

By the time they were ready to head back home, they'd put together a service for twelve. The plates didn't match exactly, of course, but the differences were more interesting than disturbing.

Of course, if you're basically rebellious, you needn't seek out any particular pattern or color. Just buy whatever you happen to find, regardless of color or style, until you have as many settings as you need. That way, you'll have a guaranteed conversation starter when you have guests for dinner. But beware: Some of them may think you're a little looney.

If budget buying isn't your main concern, by all means go down to your local department store or china shop and pick out something that pleases you. Contrary to what some people think, you needn't wait to get married to own fine china. Anyhow, who knows what the future will bring—if you have the money, why wait?

We do have some cautions abut buying fine china, however. If this is your choice, don't look for closeouts, odd lots, or similar bargains. Instead, buy china made by reputable, well-established manufacturers, in open-stock patterns. That way, you'll always be able to fill in if you break something.

Also, don't limit yourself to just a few place settings. Buy the standard eight—or twelve, if you can afford it. Although patterns are continued in open stock—and that's the way to fill in broken pieces—dye lots and manufacturing standards can and do change as the years pass. So if you buy, say, four place settings, with the thought of buying four more after a couple of years, you may find yourself with a set that doesn't quite match. And when you're spending a fair amount of money, that's something you don't want to happen.

Glassware offers many of the same problems as dishware— and the solutions are similar too. Assuming your trousseau didn't include a set of crystal glasses and your landlord hasn't provided a set with the apartment, you have a whole range of choices in front of you.

If budget is your watchword, take a trip to your local dime store or discount store, where you can pick up odd glasses for fifty cents to one dollar apiece. Or stop in at the local secondhand store, where they're even cheaper. Or visit an auction or a tag sale.

Of course, you can always accumulate or make your own glasses, from jelly jars or wine bottles (there's a gadget in the stores these days that lets you cut bottles down to size, but it requires patience). But you'll have to do a lot of wine drinking or make a lot of peanut butter and jelly sandwiches to come up with any sizeable number of glasses.

In our experience, we've found that the best way to acquire a set of glassware quickly and at minimal cost is to buy a packaged set at your local department or discount store. You shouldn't have any trouble finding a set of twenty-eight (in three different sizes, no less) for about twenty dollars. They're not pretty enough to make it at the Museum of Modern Art, but they're not ugly, either.

If, for some reason, you need a large number of glasses, or you're seeking very sturdy glasses (maybe you have a house full of five-year-olds), try a restaurant supply house. They offer several simple styles that are attractive, break-resistant, and easily matched.

On the other hand, if keeping costs down isn't one of your guiding principles, you can find some really beautiful crystal stemware at one of the better department stores in town, or at fine jewelry and gift shops.

Years ago, when we moved into our first apartment, we bought ourselves a cheap set of glasses for everyday use, but we went to the best store in town and got two beautiful crystal wine glasses in an open stock pattern. As the years went buy, we occasionally added more. Today we have twelve (and that's after breaking a few) truly lovely wine glasses.

Even if your budget is tight, you owe it to yourself to have a little luxury, a little beauty, and a little elegance at hand—and we don't know of any better way than the one we've just described.

By the way, don't buy your glassware—or dishes, for that matter—until you've moved into your new apartment. Otherwise, you'll be putting them through the risks of moving. And when you move again—perhaps we should say "if"—be sure to insure any expensive china or crystal. Breakage is practically inevitable.

Gadgets, Utensils, and Other Cooking Gear

Remember that drawer in the kitchen at Mama's? You opened it up and there lay some of the oddest contraptions you ever set eyes on. No matter how closely you examined them, no matter how much imagination you used, you couldn't figure out what their purpose was.

Well, those were the gadgets, utensils, and other cooking gear we're about to discuss. Such stuff comes in practically every imaginable shape and variety. Some items are quite useful, others just curiosities—or objects suitable only for expert use.

Which do you need—really *need*—to set up housekeeping in your new apartment?

Let's start with the obvious—cooking utensils, such as large spoons, spatulas, forks, etc. There are essentially three types to choose from: plastic (usually nylon), wood, and metal. Each has pluses and minuses.

Plastic. You can buy these by the set or by the piece. Advantages: They don't scratch ceramic or non-stick pan coatings; they don't burn or melt; it takes quite a while before they get uncomfortably hot. Disadvantages: Mainly looks—they aren't very stylish. Also, while they're fairly durable, they do break or wear out after a while.

Wood. These are usually purchased by the piece, but you certainly can put a set together if you want. Advantages: They don't cost much; they don't get hot; they wear reasonably well. Disadvantages: They quickly discolor or pick up food odors; they're sometimes difficult to clean; they burn if you leave them on the wrong place on your stove.

Metal. Again, available by the set or individually. Advantages: They wear practically forever; they're often nicely designed. Disadvantages: They're usually more expensive than the other two types; they'll scratch some pan and pot finishes; even those with wooden handles occasionally get too hot to hold (and if they have plastic handles, those can sometimes melt).

Our choice: plastic. In the long run, they're the most versatile, least expensive, and easiest to care for.

The next most vital cookware item: knives. You can't cook without 'em. But what knives do you need, at a minimum?

We'd advise buying at least two knives—a paring knife and an eight-inch, all-purpose blade. If you're at all clever, there's hardly anything you can't accomplish with this pair.

We've bought bargain knives and high-priced knives in our time and, to be honest, there's no substitute for quality. So we strongly recommend that you buy good quality cutlery. It will last forever, if properly cared for and sharpened, and it will consistently do a better job—with fewer nicks and cuts—than its less expensive relatives.

You can usually spot good-quality cutlery by its handles and rivets. The rivets will extend all the way through both pieces of the wooden handle and the wood will be well-finished. The price will be another giveaway.

You'll probably find yourself with a choice of stainless steel blades or carbon steel blades. Which is best? That depends on your needs. Stainless steel is definitely easier to keep clean. On the other hand, carbon steel keeps its edges longer.

Incidentally, when you buy your first good knives, buy a knife sharpener at the same time and learn how to use it properly. Poorly sharpened knives *will* cut, but they require much more effort on your part and they can massacre the food. They can also massacre you, if they slip off a tough tomato and slice your finger. So keep your knives sharp.

On the other hand, keep in mind that you can ruin a knife's edge by improper sharpening. If that happens to you, take your knife to a professional and have it reground.

When you can afford it, consider adding more knives to the basic pair above: serrated-edged bread knives, cleavers, steak knives, etc. But don't rush. Figure out what you really need and buy your knives one at a time if you need to, but buy quality.

Table cutlery, however, is another matter altogether. We've identified the following quality levels here:

Stamped steel. Short of plastic, this is the cheapest you can get. Buy it by the fork, spoon, or knife in your local discount store. Or, if you need quantity, try a restaurant supply shop. But unless you're sure you'll be doing dishes daily, buy at least four place settings so you'll have clean tableware on hand when you come home after a long, hard day at work.

Stainless steel. There is stainless steel and there is *Stainless Steel.* The former, you can find at your local department or discount store for less than fifty dollars for a service for eight, in patterns ranging from the unadorned to the horrendous. (We've found the simplest designs are easiest to take, year after year, but perhaps that's a matter of taste.)

The latter, *Stainless Steel,* can cost whatever you'd like to spend—and more. Silverware is now so outrageously expensive that manufacturers have greatly upgraded the design and finish of stainless—and also the price.

Brand-name stainless steel, for want of a better term, can be truly beautiful and well-balanced—a pleasure to look at and to use. But it's a pleasure you'll pay for. You'll find it at better china or gift shops.

By the way, some companies make stainless in the same patterns as their silverware. The idea, as the proprietor of a fine china shop explained it to us, is to start out with stainless and gradually replace it with silver.

Silver. This is the Cadillac—no, the Rolls Royce—no, the Ferrari of tableware. It's beautiful, it's heavy, it's costly, it's valuable, it's difficult to keep clean, it's easily stolen (and easily disposed of), it's easily sold, it's easily damaged.

Should you buy silver? Not in our opinion, unless you're a Rockefeller or a Mellon. Should you accept it as a gift? Of course. It's not only useful, it's an asset.

But just a minute, you say. What about silver plate? The way we see it, that's a poor compromise. Give it any real wear and the silver will begin to disappear very quickly. This is particularly true, by the way, for serving pieces.

If you have your heart set on silver, buy (or get someone to give you) a few silver serving pieces. Or if that's impossible, splurge a little on silver plated candlesticks, candy dishes, or napkin rings, depending on your budget. They'll make you feel a little wealthier, perhaps, than you actually are.

So much for the obvious kitchen and cooking gear. Now what about those odd-shaped gadgets we mentioned earlier?

Well, depending on how much you like to cook, and how much you have to spend, you can buy practically anything you can imagine, from thirty-nine-cent plastic lemon juicers to food preparation centers that cost hundreds of dollars.

But what do you really need, to start with?

We recommend the following:

Balloon whisks (perfect for making scrambled eggs), tongs (great for pulling the bacon out of the skillet), and rubber spatulas (for mixing anything or spreading butter on pans, etc.)

What about the rest? We advise buying the gizmos that have something in common with your style of cooking. For instance, if you're an onion-oriented chef, you might like an onion comb to hold down those slippery roots while you slice them, or a self-contained chopper for quick mincing. Or if you're a wine cook, you'll need a decent corkscrew and an all-purpose cork replacement.

There's lots more, of course—garlic presses, cheese cutters, jar openers, and containers of every style and variety. If you love this sort of stuff, it's easy to get carried away. Fortunately, most of it isn't all that expensive.

But if you find your drawers are bulging with what-is-its, we know a good way to cut the accumulation down to size: Have a gizmo contest at your next party (or hold a party for that purpose, if the situation has become really critical).

Hold up each gizmo and ask your guests to write down what it's used for. The loser gets the gizmo, since the winner obviously has it already.

You can dispose of all kinds of silly gadgets this way—gadgets you purchased during a weak moment or gadgets you were given by someone who didn't know better. And you can have fun at the same time.

Tablecloths and Napkins

Were you lucky enough to inherit some old Irish linen tablecloths and linens? Did your great-grandmother bring a lace tablecloth with her when she came from Belgium years ago?

If so, the chances are you have such heirlooms packed away in a drawer or a box, wrapped in tissue paper or maybe even plastic. Well, unpack them now. They're at least part of the answer to your tablecloth problem.

What, you ask—use these precious possessions as tablecloths? Yes. That's what we're suggesting. Use them as often as you can. If you don't, no one will ever see them and you'll wind up passing them on, still wrapped and folded, to the next generation—which won't use them either.

If you keep your fancy tablecloths shut away, they'll get yellow and musty. Should you ever find an occasion important enough to exhume them, they may disappoint you.

But if you use them, the stains and wrinkles that come from ordinary usage can be easily handled by a good cleaning shop. In fact your cleaner (or local seamstress) should also be able to repair them, to almost invisibly mend the little rips and tears sometimes caused by sharp utensils. Very often, if you're a good customer, they won't even charge for this service.

But let's say that there isn't a tablecloth in your hope chest, that your family was perfectly content to dine on a bare table. Should you invest in tablecloths for yourself? We think so. They're a necessity when it comes to entertaining. And they can lift your spirits when you dine alone.

If you'd like to buy the heirloom you never inherited, try garage sales and second hand shops. Who knows, you might even find a set of napkins embroidered with your monogram. You have one chance in twenty-six, you know.

Of course, your local department store is also a good place to buy table linens, whether you're looking for an instant heirloom or something far more casual. And you can find some real bargains at secondhand shops and tag sales, if you're not too particular.

If all you want are placemats and casual table napkins, check out the five-and-dime or the nearby discount store. Quilted and woven placemats can be found there, along with the vinyl type. For casual napkins, we recommend the extra large size bandanas. They're colorful, easy to match or replace, and easy to wash and iron.

Kitchen Consumables

Now that you have a basic supply of permanent kitchen goods, it's time to start thinking about consumables.

What we're talking about now, mainly, are cleaners and cleaning aids. If you've ever wandered down the household goods aisle of the local supermarket by accident, you'll know what a bewildering selection is available, thanks to the fine folks at Procter & Gamble and their fellow soap wizards.

But you don't have to be a cleanser-hardened hausfrau to banish the bewilderment and choose exactly the items you need. Just follow these guidelines:

1. Buy a name-brand dish detergent. In our experience, they really do go further than Brand X. It's one of those pleasantly surprising instances in which commercials happen to tell the truth.
2. Avoid the soap-filled, steel-wool pads. They rust under the sink or in the soap dish, they leave irritating splinters in your fingers and hands, and they rarely last through more than four grungy pans.
3. Buy instead nylon net scrubbers for nonstick finishes and enamels (they'll last for weeks), and copper netting for aluminum and stainless steel. We also like the net-covered sponges

and textured nylon pads backed by large, thick sponges. Long-handled, nylon bristle brushes are also useful.

4. Buy some name-brand bleaching, abrasive, powdered cleaner and keep it next to the soap dish, at the corner of the sink. It's a necessity with a white enamel sink and it's about the only stuff we know that can get grape juice off a plastic countertop. But don't use it on a stainless steel sink. It can scratch.

   While we're on the subject of washing dishes, you can save your sink, your dishes, and yourself a lot of grief by buying a plastic dishpan and a dishdrainer with a mat underneath, or a rubber sink mat at the minimum. These items promote cleaning, neaten the workspace, and protect fragile dishware and glasses when your fingers get slippery.

5. Buy the following items as your situation requires: floor cleaners, floor waxes (or some combination thereof, depending on the types of floors you have); upholstery cleaners, an all-purpose spot remover; rug cleaner; all-purpose cleaning liquids (like Mr. Clean or Fantastik); room deodorizers—solid or spray; glass cleaner, Drāno (or some such), oven cleaner, washing machine soap and fabric softeners, silver or metal polish, furniture polish, and Endust.

6. Unless you're familiar with the brand, buy a small size at first. Once you know you like the stuff and it works well for you, buy the biggest size you can carry. Not only will it be cheaper in the long run, you'll spend less time in the supermarket.

7. Buy the following "paper goods": paper luncheon napkins, paper dinner napkins, one set of paper plates, cups, and spoons (you never know when the urge to picnic will strike), two boxes of plastic wrap (one in medium width, one in wide), two boxes of aluminum foil (one in each width), a roll of wax paper, some paper towels (the roll variety), a package of fiber wiping cloths, a couple of packages of plastic sandwich bags (the zip-loc variety are excellent for storing leftovers), and some garbage bags. You may need several sizes of these, one for your wastebaskets (if that's the way you've been raised), one for your under-sink garbage can, and one for carrying out to the outside garbage cans. We recommend the heavy-weight variety for this last task. The others, whatever they might claim on TV, have a tendency to split open.

8. Also buy a broom (we like the plastic type—it doesn't shed and it lasts longer), a dustpan, an assortment of sponges, a

long-handled sponge mop (for kitchen floors and bathrooms), a long-handled dust mop (for wood or parquet floors), a long-handled toilet brush, a pail (the metal ones last longer), a garbage can (the largest size you can comfortably fit under your sink), a plumber's helper—a plunger, that is, with a medium-sized "bell" (the smaller sizes being practically useless), a selection of 100-, 75-, 60-, and 40-watt bulbs, a package of dustcloths (unless you have some old clothing that will do the job).

Some of this stuff will last pretty much forever. Other items will be quickly consumed. But this is what you'll need to run your apartment efficiently and to take care of the small-scale emergencies that happen every day.

Food Staples

Now let's see. By now you should have a completely equipped kitchen. You should be ready to begin operations, providing meals for yourself and your family, if any. There's really only one thing we haven't discussed: food.

If you're an experienced cook, you won't need to be told what you should have on hand in the way of food staples. Nothing prepares you better for food buying than food preparation.

But we expect that many people reading this book will be occupying an apartment for the first time, perhaps even living away from their families for the first time. And the others may not have lived alone for years and may be a little rusty.

For these reasons, we think it's appropriate to provide a brief list of basic food staples, items you'll want to have in your apartment if you have even the slightest intention of putting your kitchen to the use for which it was designed.

These are the basics, then:

- Five pounds of flour (for gravies, stews, biscuits, bread, chocolate chip cookies, etc.);
- Five pounds of white sugar (for coffee, bread-making, sprinkling on grapefruit, sweets of all sorts);
- Two pounds of brown sugar (for all of the above except gravies and stews). You might want to supplement this with a box of powdered sugar, a jar of honey and a jar of molasses, if you're into that. But don't be fooled by the raw sugar pro-

paganda. It's chemically identical to the refined stuff, and it's just as good or bad for you.

- A box or two of sugar cubes (you may not use them, but how about guests?);
- A bottle of ketchup. (Can you defy tradition and buy a wide-mouthed bottle? If you do, you'll find it's a lot more convenient);
- Dried parsley, garlic cloves (or powder), onion salt (or powder), oregano, bay leaves, any other spices you like (these items are for seasoning whatever you happen to cook);
- A bottle of Worcestershire sauce;
- A box of salt (iodized is better for you);
- A box of pepper;
- Two boxes of toothpicks—one containing the round type, the other the flat type;
- One large jar of spaghetti sauce;
- A pound of spaghetti (buy the enriched, high-protein variety —it's more nutritious, and as far as we're concerned it even tastes better);
- A box of tea bags (or some fancy teas, if you like them);
- A jar of instant coffee (not sure which brand you like? Buy three small jars and do some sampling);
- Half a gallon of milk;
- A six-pack of your favorite soft drink, plus large bottles of gingerale, diet soda, 7-Up, or whatever else you think your guests might prefer (incidentally, be sure to get club soda— it's an excellent spot remover);
- A pound of butter and/or margarine;
- A bottle of cooking oil;
- A can of shortening;
- A bottle of vinegar;
- Two jars of mustard, one yellow, one brown;
- A Box of Sweet n' Low or other low calorie sweetener (even if you're not a dieter, one of your guests surely will be);
- A box of Ritz-type crackers;
- A box of saltines;
- A selection of hot and cold breakfast cereals, if you're that sort;
- A few cans of tuna fish;
- A container of cottage cheese;

- A container of cocoa powder;
- A jar of peanut butter;
- A box of raisins;
- A box of pancake mix;
- A box of cake mix;
- Some ice cream;
- A few frozen dinners (we don't love them either, but they're an easy way to get your belly filled at the end of a long hard day);
- A selection of canned soup;
- A few boxes of Jell-O;
- A bag of potato chips;
- A bag of corn chips or pretzels (so you'll have something to put out if an unexpected guest drops in);
- A couple of bottles of salad dressing;
- A container of grated cheese;
- A bottle of grape jelly;
- A bottle of preserves (we like raspberry, but you choose);
- A pack of sliced American cheese;
- A loaf of white bread and a loaf of something else—whole wheat, rye, pumpernickel, etc.;
- A dozen eggs;
- A pack of bacon;
- A can or two of baked beans;
- A box of frozen chicken;
- A carton of orange juice (or two containers of frozen juice);
- A bottle of cooking wine;
- A bottle of white wine for drinking;
- A bottle of red wine, likewise;
- A box of baking soda;
- A box of powdered milk (you never know when you'll run out of the fresh kind);
- A container of book matches and a couple of boxes of kitchen matches;
- A selection of canned veggies;
- A selection of canned fruits;
- A quart of canned pineapple juice;
- A quart of canned tomato juice;
- A box or two of cookies;
- Some bouillon (we recommend onion, beef, and chicken);

- A healthy supply of toilet paper and facial tissue;
- A can of grapefruit juice;
- A large jar of mayonnaise;
- A jar of non-dairy creamer;
- A three-pound bag of onions;
- A can of Spam (or some packets of other prepared luncheon meats;
- A selection of frozen vegetables (broccoli, green beans, peas, corn, etc.);
- a ten-pound bag of potatoes;
- a head of lettuce, a bunch of celery and a bunch of carrots;
- Some apples, pears, peaches, plums, and whatever else you might like that happens to be in season.

What? you say—you've left off X or Y. Or conversely, you say, why do I have to buy that? I never eat it. Well, this list is meant to be a reasonably inclusive list for the average person, assuming he or she has at least a speaking acquaintance with the stove, refrigerator, etc. You may, of course, add or delete what you wish.

And the list includes no main course items—no meat, chicken or fish. What you want, and how much of it, is strictly up to you and your specific needs.

But we feel fairly confident that if you buy everything on this list, and replace it when you run out, you'll usually have the food staples you need, whether you're confronted with breakfast, lunch, dinner, or just snacktime.

Incidentally, if you buy all of this in one trip to the supermarket, prepare to part with a substantial chunk of your hard-earned cash. As of this writing, all of these items could total up to between $125 and $175, depending on quantity.

On the other hand, that's money you won't be spending every time you go to the supermarket. Many of these supplies will last for months. And we do have some hints on how to keep costs down:

1. Shop the supermarket sales. They really do reduce prices. But don't buy what you don't need, regardless of price. And you should generally avoid the no-name brands. They're rarely as good as their better-known counterparts. On the other hand, save and use discount coupons.

2. Buy in quantity. As with soaps, detergents, etc., buy the largest size you can carry. It will normally cost less than a comparable amount of the stuff in several smaller containers. And you won't run out as quickly. The large-size philosophy is the best way we know to avoid frequent, hour-long trips to the supermarket.

3. Check weight (or volume) and price. The manufacturers of processed foods are absolute geniuses at creating confusion in the minds of consumers. They market boxes of 16.7 ounces of whatever at 73¢ and defy you to figure out if that is cheaper or more expensive per ounce than 28.6 ounces at $1.26.

   But two developments have robbed such manufacturers of their ability to sow doubt and confusion: unit pricing and pocket calculators. Unit pricing refers to a law in many states in which the supermarkets must calculate the per-ounce price and post it immediately above or below the item. If yours is one of these states, your comparison shopping has been considerably simplified. All you need do is pick out the three or four top brands you like and buy the container with the lowest per-ounce price.

   If your state doesn't have unit pricing, you can do it yourself—in your head if you have a good head for numbers, or with your handy-dandy pocket calculator. Just take the price in cents and divide it by the ounces. It only takes a moment to save yourself a little money and have the satisfaction that you've outwitted the packaging wizards.

4. Use coupons. You've undoubtedly noticed those coupons that sometimes come in the Sunday newspaper or the monthly magazines or in the newspapers or a dozen other places (we got a packet recently in a Publishers Clearing House Mailing) They're not a rip-off. They actually save you money.

   Many people think that coupons, even if they're genuine money-savers, only save you a few cents and are more trouble than they're worth. Not true. Some people make a career out of clipping such coupons, and save 20–30–40 even 50 percent of their grocery money!

But there are a few tricks to it:

• Clip every coupon you see, unless it's for a product you're not interested in and know you never will be.

- Use your coupons as soon as you can. Some of them are dated.
- Keep them near your shopping list. You won't be happy with yourself if you go shopping, then find coupons at home that could have saved you a few dollars if you'd had them at the checkout counter.

To do all of this smoothly and efficiently—and not spend half your life shopping—you need a system, and not necessarily a complicated one. Here's ours, for what it's worth.

We tack up a pad on the kitchen bulletin board. (No bulletin board? Use little novelty magnets to put up a piece of paper on the refrigerator). This pad is our shopping list pad. We use it for nothing else. And woe betide the person who removes it.

Whenever we throw out a cereal box or any other empty food container, we jot down the item on the pad. It's an iron-clad rule. Even our teen-age daughter follows it—and why shouldn't she, since it's in her best interest. If she uses up the Cinnamon Life and doesn't jot it down, there won't be any in the pantry the next time she looks.

As for the coupons, we have a little box for these on top of the refrigerator. It's an old recipe box, but a plastic 3x5 file box would do as well. Inside the box, we have a set of paperboard dividers, with tabs. The tabs are labeled with product categories: canned vegetables, laundry products, pharmaceuticals, cereals, etc.

We each take the responsibility of clipping (actually tearing out) the coupons we come across in our reading or whatever, putting them into the box, behind the appropriate divider. Occasionally large coupons need to be folded, but no matter.

Then, once a week we shop, list and coupon box in hand. It's simple, it's automatic, it's quite convenient. Best of all, it works, saving us time and money.

Making the Best Use of Your Kitchen Space

All right, there you are, back from your first expedition to the nearby supermarket with eight or ten bags of groceries. What now? Well, as the bullfighters say in Spain, you have arrived at your moment of truth. Can you accommodate all this stuff? If not, what do you do?

We've already given you an idea of the major surgery that can turn a cramped, spaceless kitchen into one with as much space as ingenuity and Rubbermaid can devise. Now we're going to talk about how to *use* the space you have, how not to squander the square inches.

Once upon a time, back during great-grandmother's day, as she's certainly told you, houses were built with walk-in pantries. These were lined with shelves, to hold all the canned goods needed for the coming month. The large pots were also stored here, and perhaps the everyday linens had a little cupboard all to themselves. Some pantries even had pass-throughs into the dining room, for quick serving and cleanup.

One house we visited often when we were very young not only had a kitchen with a pass-through, but also a pantry, a walk-in closet, a "wash room" off the kitchen, and out in the shed between the house and the barn, a "cold room" for meats and fresh vegetables. In later years, the cold room gained a freezer.

After the children were grown, the wife reluctantly gave up the large pantry so her husband could have his own office. She put more shelves into the "cold room" and "wash room" and stored more of her homemade jams and pickles in the root cellar (another idea well-loved but long gone).

Like many large, older homes, this one was oriented toward feeding a large family and several servants or farm hands. The wife's job was to supervise and help with the food preparation and her wing of the house was geared entirely to this all-important matter.

But times have changed, even in this home. Things have gotten easier for the homemaker, and not just because the children have found homes of their own. Refrigerators, freezers, microwave ovens, and Campbell's soup have changed the character of her duties.

This transformation has been repeated all over the country. And, as a result, the Victorian pantries have almost entirely disappeared, turned into powder rooms or clothes closets, or removed entirely to expand a kitchen blessed with a score of electric appliances.

Also gone is that English innovation, the butler's pantry. This is where the servants sat, keeping the next course warm while the man of the house and his family had dinner.

Many of the big houses that once had butler's pantries have

long since been subdivided into apartments. And sometimes, the butler's pantry has become a much-too-small kitchen (yours, perhaps). More's the pity,

In a way, all modern apartment kitchens seem derived from the butler's pantry, since they provide minimal service and minimal convenience in minimal space.

As for the storage pantries, they're gone, replaced by prefabricated kitchen cabinets either too high or too deep or too low to be completely practical. This is the price, we suppose, of progress.

But enough complaining and daydreaming about the good old days. What can be done to make life easier today, especially when it comes to putting those ten bags of groceries away?

Well, there isn't much you can do to achieve the utility of the long-lost pantry. But you can make life easier if you group your edibles in one place.

Don't choose the cabinet right next to or over the sink. You'll want to put your glasses there. Don't choose the cabinet on the other side of the sink either, or the one next closest. That's where you'll want to keep the dishes.

But take the next closest cabinet, hopefully one that's fairly large and well lighted (if you can't see inside you'll have trouble telling the canned beans from the canned peaches.)

Next, divide your cans by category: soups, beans, fruit, vegetables. Put each one in its designated place. And maintain the pattern. It will save you a lot of time when you're preparing meals. You'll also know immediately if you're run out of something (if you haven't been keeping your list up to date.)

It's also wise to set aside a special section for opened jars that don't need refrigeration—peanut butter and large spice jars, for instance. These are best put on a high shelf next to or near the stove, where you're most likely to use them.

Dry goods—flour, sugar, crackers, even bread—should be put in airtight containers, to keep out moisture. You can store these items in your pantry/cupboard or you can put them in cannisters or other containers on your countertop.

Now, what about the goods that need to be refrigerated?

If you're short of refrigerator space, there are two possible causes: your refrigerator is simply too small or you've been saving too many leftovers and not organizing your food.

Unless you have a family of six living with you in your apartment, the chances are your refrigerator really isn't too small, if you use its space wisely and well. So let's concentrate on the other problems: the disorganized refrigerator and the one with an overload of leftovers.

Both problems, it seems to us, are either a matter of habit or a matter of upbringing. Many people, for instance, can hardly bring themselves to throw out anything that's still edible. You can almost hear their mothers telling them, "Think of the starving children in India . . ."

One friend of ours delights in describing how his ex-wife used to run their refrigerator. "It was populated almost entirely with little bundles wrapped in Saran wrap or aluminum foil, or Tupperware containers half filled with something or other. I never had any idea what. So our actual refrigerator space consisted of about six inches in front of all the leftovers. That's where we put the fresh edibles. When we finally broke up—and this wasn't the reason—I found some leftovers in the back that were more than two years old."

How can you avoid falling prey to this malady yourself, especially after your mother has spent seventeen years telling you it's a sin to throw food away? Well, if you follow two reasonable rules, you'll be able to keep your leftovers down to a useful minimum:

1. Label your leftovers with the type of food and the date prepared. That way, you won't have to unwrap everything in aluminum foil to find the piece of cold chicken you were planning to have for lunch. You'll also be able to follow Rule 2.
2. Throw out anything you've kept longer than a week. It may not be spoiled, but you're certain to have lost interest by then. Even worse, there'll be more recent leftovers to discourage you still more from using the older ones.

Rule 2 has a corollary, by the way: throw out or consolidate any jar or bottle that's less than half full.

In our home, this is one of our worst refrigerator problems. She's forever opening new soft drink bottles, even though there are several in the refrigerator already opened. So he's forever trying to pour the contents of one quarter-full bottle into the another, to save refrigerator space. He says she's wasteful. She says he's fussy. The issue remains unresolved at press time.

If you're starting with a new refrigerator, your job is a simple one, all you have to do is put the tall bottles where the tall bottles go and the short, flat packages on the short shelves. Everything to its place. Then, keep it that way. You'll always be maximizing your refrigerator space. Everything will be easy to find. Ain't logic grand?

If, on the other hand, you're starting with a used—but empty —refrigerator, give it a good cleaning before you start loading your groceries into it. If you don't, your food may smell for weeks of the last tenant's onion dip.

If this information has gotten to you too late—that is, after you've already started using your refrigerator—don't worry. Just empty out your refrigerator, apply Rule 1 and Rule 2 (and, he insists, the corollary), wash it out and start over.

Here are some more hints to make your refrigerator even more convenient:

- Put all the condiments—ketchup, mustard, mayonnaise, etc. —in the door shelves, assuming your refrigerator has them.
- Put paper toweling—one layer is enough—in the bottom of the crisper drawers, then drop in your fruits and vegetables. This will absorb excess moisture and help protect these items from wilting.
- Buy some stick-on labels and keep a soft pencil in the butter compartment for labeling leftovers with ID and date.
- Put meats in their own special drawer or on the bottom shelf. It's usually the coldest place in the refrigerator. Heat rises, remember?
- Put eggs and "future leftovers" on the second shelf, unless you have a built-in egg bin in the door.
- Keep milk and other bottles on the top shelf.
- If you're taking any medication that must be refrigerated, put it on as high a shelf as possible if you have children. As far as they're concerned, anything in the refrigerator is edible—unless it's out of reach.
- Get little plastic shelves for the freezer section, to hold the ice cube trays. They'll let you stack the trays so they won't occupy too much space or stick together.

- Consider buying the no-spill ice trays. They're not very expensive and they work well. Otherwise, be prepared to towel up some spills every time you fill up your ice cube trays.
- Keep frozen fruit juices and ice cream in the freezer door.
- Organize frozen vegetables by meals—that's the way you'll be using them.
- Label frozen leftovers. Nothing is less likely to be used than a frozen, foil-covered lump of indeterminate content.

Still not enough space? Take a trip to your local department or discount store and wander through the kitchen section. There you'll find a variety of add-on racks and shelves that will help you take advantage of every square inch of refrigerator space.

For instance, there are racks than hang below a shelf where you can store two six-packs of beer or soft drinks in very little space indeed. Best of all, these racks dispense one can at a time.

Also available: clip-on wire shelves to add space for egg cartons and such.

While you're in this section, buy yourself some of those plastic containers made for refrigerator use. These come in several sizes and shapes (square, round, rectangular, even pie-shaped). For us, the most useful are the ones about 3½ inches square. They hold quite a bit and they can be stacked two or three high within a refrigerator.

Now you've gotten all that food put away. But what about the rest of your kitchen goods. Dishes, for example, seem particularly hard to put away. If you stand 'em on edge, you're in continual danger of playing dishware dominos, a game of falling crockery. If you stack 'em, the one you want is always on the bottom.

Even worse, dishes and glassware seem to have a habit of getting jumbled together. This means that whenever you reach for a plate, you're in danger of bringing down the wine glasses —or vice versa.

The solution to this problem is fairly simple: put the items you use everyday—two plates, two glasses, napkins, etc.—on one shelf together and store the rest of the stuff further up, out of harm's way.

Your least-used pieces, which are often also your most valuable, should be stored in your least reachable cupboard. You may need a stepstool to get them, but you won't be knocking them down every time you want to get a drink of water.

Of course, arranging your dishes and glassware this way will force you to wash the dishes after each meal. But that isn't such a bad idea, especially if your apartment is subject to ants and other creepie-crawlies.

Speaking of creepie-crawlies and other kitchen uglies, consider now your under-the-sink area. If a refrigerator is a kitchen's high-rent district, then the under-the-sink area must surely be its slum.

In most kitchens, the under-the-sink area seems the natural place to store cleansers, chemicals, brushes, rags, and similar kitchen riff-raff. It's also where the garbage can resides. And unless you're luckier than most, it's home to the leakiest pipes in the entire apartment.

If you live with children or pets, you may want to defy tradition and store your cleansers and chemicals elsewhere. Why? It's simply too accessible to exploring fingers and/or paws. And some of those chemicals are deadly.

Even if yours is an all-adult household, you should exercise some caution. If cleansers and other chemicals get wet and leach into each other, the result could be anything from stripped paint to minor explosions to clouds of chlorine gas (the stuff used in gas chambers). No, we're not exaggerating. Mix chlorine bleach and ammonia and that's what you get.

Unless you're confident that you can keep everything safe and separate—and away from two or four-legged curiosity seekers—you should seriously consider storing these items up high, in a dry place.

As for the rags, etc., this is the place for them—unless they're covered with shoe polish, furniture oil, or grease. Throw these rags out. They're candidates for spontaneous combustion. But, by all means, keep your dishcloths here, on hooks inside the door or on a small towel rack mounted in the same place. Store brushes and pot scrubbers in a plastic bucket. That way, they won't get everything else wet.

Do all this and that disreputable under-the-sink space will be transformed into a truly useful storage area.

If you have an older apartment, you may have been blessed with a broom closet—a tall, narrow cubbyhole designed specifically for mops and brooms. But once you put in the mop and broom, then try to take them out again, you may feel cursed, not blessed.

All too often, you simply can't take out *one* broom. Any effort in that direction brings out everything in the closet. The solution: broom clips. These are little metal pincers. You can find them at drug, grocery, dime, and hardware stores.

Buy yourself a handful of broom clips and nail them across the back of your broom closet. Then push the mop and broom handles into them. And the next time you reach for a broom, you'll get a broom—nothing else.

Some people use broom closets to store many things other than brooms and mops. We've seen them stuffed with umbrellas, ice skates, snow shovels, garden tools, even odd bits of lumber. Our advice: Don't do it. It only makes a mess, and you'll never remember what you put where.

Keeping Things Humming

Now that you've put everything in its place, take a good look at your kitchen. Is it a pleasant place to work? Are the appliances attractive? Is it bright and cheery?

Unless you're moving into a brand-new apartment, chances are you haven't answered all of these questions with a confident "yes." But you can improve your kitchen's looks with relatively little effort and expense.

APPLIANCES

Maybe you can't restore them to their youthful grace, but you can clean them until they gleam. This will not only make them look better, it will give you the feeling that they're yours—which they are until another tenant takes possession.

Incidentally, cleaning does more than beautify kitchen appliances, it also makes them work better. This is particularly true in the case of refrigerators. Dirty condenser coils in back cut their efficiency dramatically. Vacuum them for best results.

If a thorough cleaning doesn't sufficiently beautify your appliances, you can always consider painting them with heat-resistant enamel paint (but get your landlord's approval first). You can beautify your refrigerator even more easily, with magnetic appliques or by taping posters to them. But don't try the same thing with your stove. Even well-insulated stoves get too hot for that.

FLOORS

Is the linoleum old and ugly? Try a good thorough cleaning. You may be surprised how bright and cheerful that pattern really is, under all of that old ground-in dirt and wax. But even if you get it clean as a whistle and find it's horrendous, you still have an alternative: Many large furniture stores or carpet stores carry linoleum by the roll. This stuff isn't very expensive (and it isn't very permanent either), but it can be cut to size and tacked down with gratifying results, if you choose a nice pattern.

WALLS

Most kitchens don't have an awful lot of wallspace. They have cabinets and cupboards and refrigerators. But all too often, the wallspace they have is dingy and dull. Try the cleaning routine. Usually, kitchens are painted with enamel, which cleans up very well. But if yours doesn't, you can do some inexpensive redecorating with a roll of contact paper. Try your discount store.

LIGHTING

Nothing is more depressing than a poorly lit kitchen. Well, almost nothing. And many apartment kitchens have only a single ceiling fixture for lighting, with a socket for a single bulb.

Resist the temptation to install the largest wattage bulb you can find. Chances are the electrical circuit is already slightly overloaded, what with refrigerator, stove, toaster, radio, etc.

Instead, consider replacing that incandescent bulb with a fluorescent one. The fluorescents are brighter, they last longer, and they burn less electricity.

Alternately, buy yourself some clip-on photographer's reflectors and install 60-watt bulbs. Put them on cabinets or door frames so that they illuminate your most important workplaces: the stove or the sink. Or point them upward, if you have a light colored ceiling.

Another quick solution is the fluorescent fixtures—GE calls them "lightsticks"—that install under the cupboard with just two screws. All you need is an outlet nearby.

Combating the Creepie-Crawlies

What's the worst kitchen problem you can have, short of a bonfire? you guessed it: bugs. Ants, roaches, silverfish, and other nameless but obviously despicable creatures.

If you have a serious infestation problem, have a serious talk with your landlord. Ask him to send in an exterminator. If he won't cooperate, get one on your own. They're usually not all that expensive. We've done kitchens for less than twenty dollars.

If you can't afford professional help, however, you may be able to do it yourself. Figure out what bugs you have and get an aerosol bugkiller that promises to kill them. Then cover or put away all food or preparation utensils, farm out the kids or the dog or cat for a night, and spray every crevice in your kitchen. Might as well include your bathroom, while you're at it.

If you do this once a week for a month, your pests will probably throw in the towel and slip away in search of more hospitable terrain. But keep spraying once a month for another four or five months to be sure.

For really bad household infestations, get yourself a "bomb"-type insecticide at your local hardware store. Put all food (even the dry stuff in boxes) into the refrigerator. Be prepared to wash all of your china, cookware, tableware, and utensils.

Then set off the bomb, which will spray the room with a penetrating gas, and leave the house for the recommended length of time, taking your children and your pets with you (even fish and birds).

When you return, wash off everything. Actually, rinsing is enough. Your kitchen may smell like the hospital, but the bugs will like it even less than you do.

For minor problems, there are traps, sprays, powders, tapes, and a variety of other products, including little electric devices that electrocute bugs that happen to wander too close. Just keep them away from your kids and pets.

If you've tried everything and your bugs won't take no for an answer, that probably means the whole building is infested. This is a matter for your landlord. Sit down and have a serious talk with him. He won't be delighted, not only because no one wants to own or manage a building full of bugs, but also because it costs a fair amount for building-wide extermination.

If your landlord resists—and he might—be prepared to fight. Get other tenants on your side. Threaten, then make, if necessary, a call to the board of health.

But don't let up until all of the apartments and common areas are decontaminated. It's downright unhealthy otherwise.

But let's say your problem is on a smaller scale. You can do the job yourself. But how do you keep the pests away after you've decontaminated? Follow these basic rules:

1. Don't leave food out. Someone will find it, someone tiny and nasty.
2. Wash the dishes right away, instead of letting them accumulate in the sink or dishwasher. Your leftovers are tiny livestock's feasts.
3. Keep the garbage in a tightly covered pail, otherwise you'll be establishing a food distribution center for bugs.
4. Wipe grease from stove, walls, and floor as soon as you can after cooking. Many insects love the stuff.
5. Keep your bathroom clean.
6. Tell your landlord that you want halls, basements, and laundry rooms swept daily and washed at least weekly. Tell him why. He may find it a reasonable preventive measure.
7. Insist that outdoor garbage containers be emptied at least twice a week—daily if possible. Outdoor garbage attracts not only creepie-crawlies, but also mice, rats, squirrels, dogs, and other uninvited guests.
8. Get together with the other tenants and agree never to leave trash or garbage bags in the hallways or on the stairs. Also check with them occasionally to see if they have problems with insects.

Follow all of these rules and you'll have a good chance of banishing kitchen bugs forever.

As you can see, there's a lot to say about apartment kitchens. They're an important part of apartment living. And if your new apartment is going to give you all the convenience and pleasure it can, your kitchen will require considerable attention and care. But in our view, it's worth the effort, since, as we said at the beginning of this chapter, the kitchen is probably the most important room in your apartment.

Chapter 9

THE BATHROOM

What is a bathroom?

Now that's a dumb question, isn't it? Everyone knows what a bathroom is, save a few Australian aborigines living in the bush and an Eskimo or two who've never traveled more than ten miles from their igloo.

A bathroom is a small, lockable chamber with a sink, a toilet, a tub, and/or a shower. Right?

Well, that definition is correct as far as it goes. It's hard to call anything a bathroom that doesn't have at least these basic appliances. Not in this day and age, anyhow.

But bathrooms can be so much more . . .

They can be quiet, private retreats, where you go to immerse yourself in warm water and soap bubbles and soak away your troubles or your aches and pains.

They can be beauty parlors, into which you go, haggard and timeworn and from which you emerge, as the butterfly from the chrysalis, young and beautiful and ready to face the world.

They can be centers of creative and meditative activity where, while shaving, showering, or brushing your teeth, you come up with your most inspired ideas.

They can send you off in the morning smiling and ready to go and welcome you back in the evening, willing and able to tend to the day's minor wounds and injuries.

They can be the most private place in your life or they can be your apartment's version of Grand Central Station, where the door is no sooner closed than there's a knock on it.

If your apartment is typical, chances are your bathroom is your smallest, barest, and ugliest room. But, while you probably won't be able to make it any larger, there's no reason you can't fill it up with attractive bathroom goodies and make it into a room that's a pleasure to enter and use, not a horror.

There are two basic aspects to every bathroom and we've divided this chapter in half, likewise. The basic aspects: 1) practical matters; 2) decoration and beautification. Of the two, of course, what comes first is:

Practical Matters

On the practical level, all bathrooms are more or less the same. There's cleaning, problems with the fixtures, mildew and bugs, safety, and storage space. We'll take them in that order:

THE INITIAL CLEANING

Are you your building's (or apartment's) first tenant? Are the bathroom fixtures, floors, and walls brand-new? Lucky you—you don't have to worry about rouge stains in the sink, rust stains in the toilet bowl, and who-knows-what on the walls. All you have to think about is keeping your bathroom reasonably pristine. But read on, anyway—because this is how you do it, whether your bathroom was born yesterday or whether it antedates recorded history.

For cleaning your fixtures, you'll need six items:

- Scouring powder with chlorine bleach in it;
- A nylon scouring pad;
- A long-handled toilet brush;
- A quart of warm water, to which you've added a quarter of a cup of liquid bleach;
- A plastic spray bottle (it needn't be new, but it must be clean);
- A large, thick sponge.

Now, let's tackle those stains.

First, flush your toilet. Then sprinkle the scouring powder above the waterline, while the bowl is still wet. Next, scrub up under the rim with the brush. In fact, scrub out the whole bowl. Now flush.

Stains still there? Okay, now pour in half a cup of liquid bleach, let it stand for about fifteen minutes, then scrub again. If you must let the bleach stand longer, open the door and window or leave the room and work someplace else. Most bleaches shouldn't be breathed for any length of time.)

Making progress? Fine. Just repeat the process a few times. That should do it. But if it doesn't, if you still have stains, get to know them and make friends with them. They'll probably be with you for the duration of your lease, and the tenants who follow you won't be able to get rid of them either.

Incidentally, you may be tempted at this point to use steel wool or some other abrasive cleaner. Don't. These strip off the glazing, the shiny surface that covers the vitreous china from which the toilet is made. The purpose of glazing is to seal the china, making it less likely to absorb stains and mildew. So you'll only be defeating your purpose or making more work for yourself if you use an abrasive cleaner.

Besides, even if you have stains remaining at this point, you can be reasonably sure that you've rid yourself of most of the germs, fungus, and mildew that might have been clinging to your toilet.

Now, take a look at your sink. Does it have the same problems? If so, soak your sponge with the bleach solution and sponge it on. Doesn't work? Okay, try this:

Wet your sink, sponge on some scouring powder, then wipe vigorously with the nylon pad. Usually, this will lift any makeup or grease stains quickly. If not, repeat the process. Do the same with rust stains. If the stains remain after all this, they're there to stay.

Bathtubs are also subject to staining—usually rust or stains from the constant dripping of hard water, near the drain. Try the technique recommended for sinks. It will usually do the job.

But what if all of your cleaning efforts have no effect and your toilet, your sink, and your tub are a compendium of unsightly blotches and discolorations? Well, they *can* successfully be painted. But it's far more difficult than painting wallboard. We'll deal with this subject later, in the section on decoration and beautification.

Sometimes, you'll find hairline cracks in the china. Toilets and sinks are particularly subject to them, but they're not unknown in bathtubs, either. Unfortunately, these tend to become discolored with rust and/or dirt. What do you do?

Start by scrubbing them out with a brush, then try cleansing powder. Rinse thoroughly and try bleach, if necessary. Get the cracks as clean as you can. Then coat them with enamel cleaner (your hardware store has it) to keep out moisture and prevent further discoloration. Do the same thing for chipped areas.

Bathroom walls and floors are almost always made of stain-resistant and moisture-proof materials, such as plastic sheet (walls only) or ceramic tile (walls and floors). But they still get dirty.

To clean them, take that spray bottle, fill it with bleach, and coat your walls with the solution. Don't forget the walls of the shower stall.

Let the solution stand for ten minutes, then rinse with clear, warm water. This will brighten tile and plastic paneling and it will kill most germs and fungus.

If you've got stubborn stains, try the scouring powder, first with the sponge, then with the nylon pad. If that doesn't take it off—well, maybe it's part of the design.

If you're particularly nervous about germs, fungus, and other such creatures, or if the last tenants were a tribe of champion swimmers who had bright red feet and showered four times a day, get an anti-fungal disinfectant cleaner, liquid or spray, and apply it to the shower and the bathroom floors. Do the same to the toilet seat. Then wash with all-purpose cleaner. That should eliminate any problems—and your worries about them.

Now, to keep your bathroom gleaming, all you have to do is clean with an all-purpose liquid cleaner once a week, or even once very two weeks. If you wait much longer than that, however, you're going to have a major cleaning job on your hands.

THOSE LEAKY FIXTURES

From the practical standpoint, leaky fixtures are a much more worrisome problem than fixtures that are stained., However, they're usually more easily fixed. It's kind of like the difference between getting a cold and getting pneumonia. You have to suffer through a cold, but it isn't serious. Pneumonia is more serious, but it can be cured.

If your bathroom fixtures leak, that can mean one of two things: loose connections or broken seals. The latter is far more common.

If tub or sink faucet handles leak, for instance, this is a "broken seal" problem. It means that a little washer within the faucet is worn out.

What to do? Well, you can always call your superintendent. And he may even fix the leak, if he's like Schneider in *One Day At a Time*. Or you can call the plumber, if you've just come into a large inheritance. Or, find a plumbing how-to book and fix it yourself.

If your appliances are leaking not through the faucets or faucet handles but in the pipes leading up to the sink or bathtub, you'll definitely need help, unless you happen to have a closet full of plumber's tools.

Ask your superintendent for help. If he's reticent, remind him that leaking pipes mean rotten wood and rotten wood means a major repair job—all in a couple of months.

If he doesn't respond, talk to your landlord directly. He doesn't want major problems, so he's likely to have yours fixed.

If your toilet is leaking between the fixture and the floor, the probable cause is a dried-out seal. This repair should be handled by a plumber or a very experienced amateur, since it involves removing the toilet in order to put in a new wax or plastic gasket.

Incidentally, don't confuse sweating with leaking. Your water puddle may be from condensation on a cold toilet tank dripping to the floor. We've found one trick that usually cures this problem: turning up the bathroom heat, or putting a small electric heater close to the toilet (but away from the sink, the bathtub, and any towels or drapes you may have).

If that fails, and sometimes it does, the only answer is better bathroom ventilation, to equalize moisture throughout the house.

THE WAR AGAINST MILDEW

Speaking of moisture, can you guess what a bathroom's biggest problem is? No fair. You cheated. But you're right, it's moisture—and the mildew that often accompanies it.

Mildew, according to our Webster's Unabridged, is "a coating or discoloration caused by fungi which appears on cotton and linen fabrics, paper, leather, etc, when exposed to moisture."

According to us, it's one of the most stubborn household problems you can confront. Even when you get rid of every visible patch of it, all you have to do is wait a week or two and it will return.

What to do?

Well, if it occurs in the bathroom crockery, scrub it with bleach or ammonia (but never use the two together—the mixture produces deadly chlorine gas). Even if this treatment doesn't cure your mildew problem, it will take the steam out of the nasty stuff.

If your plastic shower curtain contracts this particular disease, put it into the washing machine, along with a heaping dose of bleach. Fabric curtains can also be washed, then sprayed with a water repellant, which will inhibit moisture retention—and mildew.

You can also try the commercial mildew sprays and aerosols available at your local discount store or the hardware store, but don't put too much faith in them.

As far as we're concerned, there is no permanent cure for mildew. But its unsightly discoloration can be kept down by frequent treatments of the affected areas, as above.

Fortunately, the stuff is harmless.

MAKING YOUR BATHROOM SAFE

Nine out of ten household accidents occur at home. Where the tenth occurs, no one has ever discovered. But those mishaps that do occur inside your apartment happen mainly in the bathroom and the kitchen.

Kitchen safety is mainly a matter of using knives and other sharp implements wisely and of being careful with stoves, ovens, and the hot stuff they produce.

Bathroom safety is a bit more complicated. There are two main sources of danger: water—and the slippery surfaces it causes; and electricity.

Bathtubs (and shower floors) have a deserved reputation for causing accidents. The slip of a foot on a glazed surface and wham! down you go, with bruises, scrapes, possibly even broken bones. Even if you don't live alone, the consequences could be serious.

The solution to this problem, however, is simple enough. The next time you're visiting your local department, discount, or hardware store, ask for "bathtub appliques." These are pebbly plastic stick-ons about the size of your palm. They come in a variety of colors, shapes, and patterns.

All you have to do is peel them off their protective backing

Many an apartment bathroom has minimal storage space. But that's nothing to worry about anymore. Wall units like these are available at your local bathroom store in a wide variety of shapes, colors, and designs.

and stick them on the tub or shower floor, as directed. They won't interfere very much with your bathing comfort and they'll provide the traction you need for a safe exit.

Electricity in the bathroom is inherently dangerous. Wet bodies are notoriously good conductors of the stuff. That's why many an unknowing bather has been electrocuted. Dangerous as the problem is, however, it's fairly simple to eliminate it.

First, make sure there's no exposed wiring in the bathroom, especially wiring that could get wet or touch metal (towel racks and the like). If you spot any, go over it with electrician's tape. Be generous. And turn off the current on any wire you may be working on.

Second, don't bring *any* electrical appliances into the bathroom (well, a battery-operated radio is okay, so long as you don't attempt to plug it in.)

We've heard too many horror stories of radios, heaters, even tiny TV sets somehow falling into the bathtub and killing their owners. And it isn't always a matter of the owners' carelessness. The swipe of a dog's tail or a cat's paw can send small electric appliances tumbling.

The only time we're willing to see this rule bent is if the bathroom is gigantic, the tub is at one side, and the appliance is clear across the room. Even so, if you get out of your bathtub, soaking wet, and go to adjust the radio, TV, or heater, you could get yourself fried.

By the way, it's not that the plastic knob you'd be touching is inherently dangerous. It isn't. In fact, most appliances don't present shock hazards. They have to be faulty in design or broken somehow. But are you willing to take the risk? We're not.

MAKING MORE SPACE

If you're living in an apartment, chances are you have to make do with a single bathroom—and a tiny one at that. But if you're clever at using shelves and medicine cabinets, you can put those hard-to-reach corners and the space over toilets to good use. And vanities can give you gobs of space exactly where you need it.

Shelves. The easiest way to add storage space to almost any bathroom is shelving, either the do-it-yourself variety or the ready-made kind. There are several places to put them: above the level of the tile (usually about eye height), above the toilet, on the back of the door.

Yes, of course you can use the medicine cabinet that comes with your bathroom. But if it's small, ugly, and cramped, or if it has inadequate lighting, you can always get your own—something like this beautiful, commodious unit. Try your local bathroom store.

There are some ready-made units that can be suspended on floor-to-ceiling poles on either side of the toilet. These provide either two or three shelves or a shelf and a cabinet, which is perfect for private items. We've also seen a ready-made set of shelves designed to fit against the back of the door. The shelves are no deeper than those you'd find in a medicine chest, but there are about ten of them and they hold plenty.

If you're looking for ready-mades, try the dime store or the discount store. They come in enameled metal in several colors and are passably attractive. Of course, you can easily build your own, out of wood. All they are is miniature bookcases. If you decide to go this route, however, we have a hint for you: Use a level to get the shelves straight. And use it again when you're mounting the unit on your wall. Crooked shelves are a continual annoyance.

In some apartments, there's a window over the toilet. Instead of putting in curtains, how about installing a little set of shelves? You can put a few plants on them, plus your large aerosol cans —hairspray, etc. That way you'll have added space, no less privacy, and no curtains to wash.

If your bathroom has a mirror but no medicine chest, you've been presented with an easy way to increase existing space. Just install your own medicine chest. They aren't that expensive and they're the ideal place for, well, medicine: prescriptions, salves, aspirins, Band-Aids, etc.

These days, you can get medicine chests with hinged doors or sliding doors. You can get single, double, or even triple units. The triple units usually have folding outside mirror panels that will give you a look at the side of your head, if that's what you're interested in seeing.

Many medicine cabinets now come equipped with built-in lighting—fluorescent, incandescents, even combination. Some can be recessed into the wall, others hung directly on the wall. And if you have an existing small, recessed unit, your landlord may give you permission to remove it, enlarge the opening, and install a larger one.

Incidentally, there's no reason why you have to limit yourself to a single medicine cabinet. If you have the space, by all means put up a second one. If there are two in your family, the pair of medicine cabinets will give you some separate space. And even if you're a single, the extra room won't hurt.

You might also consider replacing your current sink unit with a combination sink and vanity. This may cost a fair amount, however, and it will require your landlord's permission. On the other hand, if you have the right sort of landlord, he might be willing to install one for you. We'll talk more about vanities when we discuss decorating and beautifying your bathroom.

Oddly enough, your bathroom and shower enclosures also provide opportunities for increasing bathroom storage space. We've recently seen a plastic shower curtain, for example, with pockets on the inside—for shampoo, a razor, bubble bath, conditioner, etc.

Also on the market: several types of shelves that hang on the shower head and a tray that fits across the tub, to hold sundries while you bathe. We've also seen stick-on corner units that can be mounted in the tub area. All of these devices serve useful storage purposes. And if you need to, you can buy them all.

Many toilet brushes, by the way, store themselves, in pleasant-looking plastic containers that sit on the floor beside the toilet tank. Put one there and you won't have to worry about finding some other place to put it.

Chests. If there's substantial room in your bathroom, but few storage facilities, you might want to buy or consider building a larger cabinet or chest in which to store extra toilet paper, Kleenex, soap bars, towels and washcloths, perhaps even your bed linens. We've seen some nice unfinished chests with sliding, louvered doors that are perfect for this purpose. They can be purchased at unfinished furniture stores for fifty or sixty dollars—and you can take them with you when you move.

Racks. Practically every bathroom—even every apartment bathroom—comes with some towels racks: one or two by the sink, perhaps even attached to the sink; one on the tub wall, at the end opposite the faucets; perhaps one or two on the door.

But if there are more than two of you living in the apartment, standard issue is rarely enough. The solution: Install more. You can buy everything you might be able to imagine at department stores, discount stores, bath shops, or mail-order catalogs.

Most of these racks screw onto the wall, so you'll have to mount them above the tile level. Don't worry about putting screws into the wall—just follow the directions in the picture section of this book. When the times comes to move, you can leave the racks in place (they don't cost much) or you can take them with you and easily repair the screw hole.

There are some racks that you can put on the back of your bathroom door, but in our experience, you'll be happier if you install hooks in this spot. Hooks allow you to hang large bath towels instantly without folding them or even thinking twice about them.

Finally, if you have no wall (or even door) space, you can buy free-standing racks, usually small chrome affairs about waist-high. They'll do the job and you can take them with you when you move.

Decoration and Beautification

On the decorative level, every bathroom is quite individual, requiring the particular application of taste, color sense, design, etc. Nonetheless, the subject breaks down into the following categories: the colors on the bathroom walls; towels and other furnishings; to carpet or not to carpet; those ugly pipes; let there be light; curtains and drapes.

Of course, we're not familiar with your taste, and we're not interested in imposing our own. But, as usual, we have some guidelines to offer, ideas that will help you decide what's right for you.

And, naturally, the beautiful and the decorative are also often the practical or the impractical. We'll try to point that out, too, so you'll end up with a bathroom that not only looks good but also makes sense.

THE COLORS ON THE BATHROOM WALLS

We think that tiny bathrooms practically beg for bright wall treatments. If you agree, you'll find that there are a number of ways to accomplish this: paint, wallpaper, wall hangings, contact paper, and other wall coverings such as burlap, plastic paneling, etc.

The cheapest and simplest of these is paint—washable enamel or semi-gloss. Flat paints just don't have enough pizzazz for bathrooms, in most colors, and those that aren't washable are sure to be instantly disfigured by muddy, greasy, or dusty hands fumbling for the light switch.

When the owner of this apartment moved in, he found that his bathroom contained an old-fashioned bathtub, its legs exposed, and a free-standing prefabricated shower stall. The room was anything but attractive. But a little carpentry and some wood transformed the old-fashioned bathroom into a modern beauty, complete with towel racks and storage cabinets where none existed before.

As for colors, certain shades have become traditional for bathrooms over the years: light blue, aqua, pink, or lavender. You're safe with any one of these. But if you want to be a little more daring you might try instead lemon yellow, peach, or fire-engine red, for instance.

Of course, the safest color of all is stark white. But that's more than a little boring these days, unless highlighted by chrome or clear plastic accessories or brightly colored towels.

But if you're decorating a bathroom you'll have to use every day, choose a color *you're* comfortable with. After all, you'll be seeing a lot of it.

On the other hand, if you're decorating a children's bathroom, remember that kids love really bright colors—the primary reds, blues, and greens, for instance. These can easily be dressed up with stick-on numbers and letters made out of contact paper, or with posters.

If you're decorating the kids' bathroom, by the way, don't forget to mount towel racks within reach and mirrors within view. And provide a stepstool so the little tykes can use the sink easily.

If you'd rather paper than paint, you'll need a vinyl (plastic-coated) or other water-resistant paper. Otherwise, if you put it up on Monday, it will be peeling by Friday. And even if, by some miracle, it doesn't peel, it's sure to pick up water stains from condensation or splashes. Mildew will also like it.

We once met a couple in a small New England village who were in the process of vacating an apartment on the Cape from the Revolutionary War era. They'd had conflicts with the landlady, a wallpaper fiend who'd even put the stuff in their closet-sized bathroom, which was without a window or fan.

Although most of the wallpaper in the apartment was peeling, because the bathroom moisture vented into the living areas, the landlady refused to redecorate.

The worst room of all, of course, was the bathroom. Not only had mildew gotten a stranglehold on every one of the walls, the wallpaper—a repeating pattern of ladies in tubs—was hanging in festoons.

The couple had offered to pay for decorating themselves, but the landlady was adamant. She liked the wallpaper and had spent a lot of money on it only the year before. So our friends reluctantly departed.

We heard from them not very long ago, as a matter of fact. They're now living in a high-rise apartment building where every room is painted white, including the bathroom. But they've spread a selection of posters throughout, coating those in the bathroom with plastic floor varnish—and they're happy as clams.

Our friends had confronted not one villain, but two—the other being humidity. Humidity is the enemy of all wallpapers, even the vinyl type. If it doesn't attack the paper itself, it tends to loosen the glue. The solution is a fan in the window or in an outside wall. Fans vent the humidity outside, where it can't hurt anything.

If you put up wallpaper, see if you can get your landlord to install a fan (assuming the apartment doesn't have one to begin with, which few do). Point out to him that they're inexpensive and easy to install and that they'll make the apartment more attractive to the next tenant someday.

If he refuses, get his permission and do it yourself, if you can afford it. You'll find what you're looking for in your local hardware or home improvement store. And once you put it in, you'll wonder how you did without it.

Fans not only protect the decor, they also make bathrooms more habitable. You'll be able to take you shower or bath, for instance, then switch on your fan, and your spouse will be able to come in and shave or apply cosmetics without sweating or staring into a fogged-over mirror.

Wall hangings and fabrics generally don't do well in bathrooms. They wilt, they retain moisture, they mildew, they rot. You can probably get away with a set of curtains, but don't cover your walls with fabric. Even textured wallpapers, such as grasscloth, can be a problem.

Contact paper, on the other hand, is a reasonable choice, assuming you don't have a very large area to cover (perhaps most of the room is tiled). On a square-foot basis, this stuff is quite expensive, when compared to wallpaper. On the other hand, it is very easy to put up.

Plastic paneling isn't really decoration. It's major surgery. Most people put the stuff up to hide something, such as stained, ugly, or cracked walls, or cheap tile that's deteriorating. If your apartment is in an old building that doesn't have ceramic tile, plastic paneling is probably the cheapest way to make the bathroom reasonably water-resistant. But there are problems.

For one, no matter how nice a pattern you choose—and there are some fairly nice ones available today—it will never be anything more than plastic paneling. It will be, at best, utilitarian. It won't be elegant.

For another, it's expensive.

For a third, it's a major alteration. You'll need your landlord's permission, and he may not be delighted.

Obviously, we're a little leery of the stuff.

There's one more subject to be covered in this category: changing the color of your tiled bathroom walls. Stuck with plain white, when you want something snazzier? Dismayed by a collection of stains or blotches that even a third-rate museum of modern art would reject? Well, you can alter your fate with something called epoxy paint.

Epoxy paint (it's a mixture of glue and paint) is the only product that we know of that will successfully change the color of pre-existing tile walls—even floors, if you like. It comes in a reasonably wide selection of colors and, if carefully applied, leaves a shiny enamel finish that, although it's obviously painted on, can look quite presentable.

But we have a couple of cautions about this material. First, it's very difficult and very unpleasant to apply. When wet, it has an odor you'll remember for years. And it's an odor you'll have to breathe for hours while your crawl around on your hands and knees, painting underneath the sink, behind the pipes, and in back of the toilet. It's an arduous task, although you may feel the results are worth the trouble.

Second caution: This comes under the heading of major alterations. You'll need your landlord's permission. Perhaps he'll see your point, if the walls and/or the floor is really horrendous. But perhaps he won't. Ask before you buy the materials.

TO CARPET—OR NOT TO CARPET

For those of us who live in northern climes, there's no debate about bathroom carpeting. All you have to do is stand in front of the sink on a January morning in your bare feet and you're automatically in favor of carpet.

There's no doubt that a carpeted bathroom is more comfortable than one with bare tile floors. But that isn't the only reason to carpet your bathroom. The other major reason is that carpets can be a major decorative element in any bathroom, bringing color to drabness, coordinating with colored fixtures, towels, bathmats, or walls.

If you intend to carpet your bathroom, you have three basic choices, each with advantages and disadvantages:

Area rugs. Made especially for bathrooms, these come in basic popular bathroom colors. The pile is usually a high, but lightweight, nylon shag. The back is usually rubber coated, to prevent slipping.

Rugs like these are practically indestructible and they resist practically every bathroom hazard—heat, humidity, mildew, etc. Furthermore, when they get dirty, all you have to do is throw them into the washing machine. And when you want to mop the bathroom floor, it's simple to pick them up and move them out of the way.

On the other hand, despite their nonslip backing, they wrinkle and they get out of position, letting your tootsies touch the bare tile, which, as we all know, can be quite a shock to the system in certain seasons.

But they're inexpensive and you can get them practically everywhere (though we'd shop discount stores for the best prices). Take a swatch of your paint or wallpaper or a washcloth with you if you want to match colors. Also, get a matching toilet seat cover.

Wall-to-wall carpeting. This can be purchased in rolls or rectangular pieces sized to fit most bathrooms. It's made of the same material described above. It's so lightweight that you can easily cut it with a good shears.

You don't have to be a particularly skilled or even patient workman to make a paper template (we use 8½x11 paper, taped together) duplicating every zig and zag in your bathroom, including the curve of your toilet base and any pipes that may run up through the floor.

Then it's no great trick to take this template into the livingroom, lay it on top of the rectangle of wall-to-wall bathroom carpeting, and cut and shape it to size with a shears.

Just make sure you have your template and carpet right side up. Otherwise, you could wind up with a bathroom carpet that fits perfectly, but only if the nonslip rubber back is facing upward.

The main advantage of this type of carpeting over the area rug is that every square inch of your bathroom floor is covered. This not only protects cold feet, it also gives a unified look to the room.

But the disadvantage is that you'll have to pull up the carpet every time you clean the floor or get a spill. Fortunately, this isn't very difficult, since the carpet is just lying on the tile, not tacked or pasted down.

Other types of carpeting, such as standard house carpeting or indoor-outdoor carpeting. If you have a remnant from the wall-to-wall carpet installed in your livingroom, it can be quite tempting to use it in the bathroom. Our advice: Don't. Most standard house carpeting isn't suitable for this purpose. It doesn't have a non-skid back, it absorbs moisture, it can't be cleaned easily—and its jute back may rot in the high humidity.

Indoor-outdoor carpeting might also be tempting, since it's available in more colors than standard bathroom carpet usually is. But it, too, isn't really suitable for bathrooms. It's stiff and hard and unpleasant to walk on. Also, it retains moisture. In addition, it's far more difficult to clean.

TOWELS AND OTHER FURNISHINGS

Nowadays, you can achieve practically any decorating effect you want in your bathroom, regardless of its size. By selecting the appropriate towels and other furnishings, you can make it into a gentle, feminine room, a boldly masculine room, a cheerful children's room, or a sexy hideaway.

Which of these paths, or their many variations, you decide to follow is your choice, of course. It's all a matter of taste—although we'd advise against extremes, which may be smashing at first look, but boring or abrasive before their first week is out.

So the color scheme is up to you. We can tell you, however, just what you'll need to establish a convenient, well-equipped bathroom.

Towels. These are a major decorative feature, and also a major comfort item. For this reason, they should be selected with some care. You'll need four hand towels, four wash cloths, and two bath towels if there are two of you in the apartment. Add one towel in every category for each additional person.

There's quite a difference, by the way, between good towels

and inexpensive towels. The cheaper variety are smaller, thinner and, because they have a higher proportion of polyester to cotton, less absorbent.

If you're trying to keep costs down, we recommend that you stay away from low-priced towels (and discount stores and even catalog stores don't really sell anything else) and wait until your local department store puts some good towels on sale because of irregularities. You'll usually be hard-put to spot the irregularities. The price won't be much above what you'd pay for lower-quality goods—and the comfort, colors, and durability will be much higher.

The best towels you can buy are the all-cotton variety—thick, luxurious, woven into loops on one side and cut like velvet on the other. They're a joy. What's more, they really dry you off.

Also, don't scrimp on size. There are lots of so-called bath towels, many of which are scarcely bigger than hand towels. Ask for "bath sheets" instead. These are toga-sized towels that not only dry you but cover you up almost completely, which is just what you want when you step out of the shower.

Bathmats. Bathmats are those thick, towel-like rectangles you put down outside the bathtub or shower and step on when you get out. You'll need two, one for keeping in place, one for cleaning (although you don't have to wash them after every shower or bath.) Buy a pair that match your towels.

Tub mats. These are rectangular rubber mats intended for bathtub bottoms or shower floors. The best kind are smooth on top, with tiny suction cups on the bottom. Their purpose: to prevent you from slipping when you get out of the bathtub or shower.

These are useful items, especially if you're not terribly sure-footed. They provide considerable more traction than the paste-on appliques. But they attract mildew like magnets attract metal filings. If you buy one, clean it at least once a week. Otherwise you'll need another within a couple of months.

Soap dishes. For some reason, humanity has spent an inordinate amount of creative energy trying to devise a soap dish that allows water to drain away from the soap so it won't melt. And for some reason, no one has succeeded in coming up with the ideal design.

There are, to be sure, devices that do the job. One comes to mind immediately—a gadget that hangs from the wall and holds the soap magnetically. But this requires you to install a metal plug in your soap bar, which is not only a nuisance, but it's downright difficult, especially with a fresh bar of soap.

Our advice: Avoid the more ingenious products of this type. Instead, get yourself one of the little circular pads that has tiny suction cups on both sides. True, your soap will eventually melt on one of these things, and it will need cleaning from time to time, but we think it's the best compromise on the market.

Shower curtains. These come in two major varieties: the simple plastic sheet, which hangs from plastic rings from the metal bar that runs across the front of your tub, near the ceiling, and the fabric shower curtain, which uses a plastic sheet as a liner. Of the two, the second is consideralby more expensive.

Of the two, we recommend the plastic sheet. These days, they're available in a wide variety of patterns and colors—everything from clear plastic imprinted with barroom scenes to imitation bamboo. You shouldn't have much trouble finding one you like. Your discount store will have the best prices.

We're not against the two-piece shower curtains, but that outside fabric layer is nothing more than decoration. Furthermore, unless the manufacturer has choosen the right kind of fabric or treated it with the proper chemicals, it could attract and retain mildew. Finally, it's more expensive.

Cup dispensers. Most bathrooms have a toothbrush holder that also has room for a glass. Unless you're living alone, however, you should not put a glass in the space provided. We know of no better way of passing colds, flu, and other virus diseases from family member to family member. What to do instead: Put up a little plastic paper-cup dispenser. Use the paper cup once, then toss it out. It costs about 1¼ cents, and we can't think of a cheaper or more effective cold preventative. Another good thing about paper cups: They don't break on the floor or the sink if you should drop them.

Paper goods. Maybe we're stretching a point here, including paper goods in this section. But every bathroom has to have them and we have a few things to say about them that might be helpful.

Over the years, we've tried practically every brand (including no-name and Brand X) of toilet tissue and cleansing tissue. And we've discovered something we'd like to pass on now: There's no substitute for quality.

The good stuff—name brands—is softer, stronger, and more reliable (that is, the quality is the same from box to box or roll to roll). It costs a bit more, to be sure, but we feel that this isn't the place to economize.

Besides, you can get the best for less than you think. Watch for sales, particularly at discount stores. These items are frequently cheaper there than at supermarkets. If you keep your eyes open, you'll sometimes find substantial reductions. And when you do, buy in quantity.

While we're at it, we might as well mention some other bathroom items you're sure to need—over-the-counter medicines and first-aid supplies. These are the basics:

- A bottle of aspirin (a big bottle, if you're subject to frequent headaches). We like the buffered variety, but that's one argument we're not going to get into;
- A large box or can of assorted bandages;
- A bottle of antiseptic solution. Merthiolate doesn't sting, but we prefer the spray-on stuff;
- A package of antacids, such as Alka-Seltzer;
- A thermometer;
- A jar of petroleum jelly;
- A bottle of baby lotion;
- A container of baby powder;
- A bottle of Pepto-Bismol or something similar;
- A bottle of cough syrup;
- A box of throat lozenges;
- A package of cotton-tipped swabs;
- A package of extra razor blades (we assume you already own a razor);
- A package of dental floss;
- A tube of toothpaste;
- A tube of first-aid ointment (we like A & D ointment);
- A roll of adhesive first-aid tape;
- A bottle of milk of magnesia;
- Some bath soap;
- Your favorite shampoo and hair conditioner;
- A bottle of nail polish remover;

- A container of hair spray;
- A shower cap.

With these supplies, you should be able to deal with most minor physical emergencies. And you'll thank yourself for having them on hand if you ever need them in a hurry. (If you think you have the flu, for instance, the very last thing you'll want to do is go out and buy a thermometer.)

THOSE UGLY PIPES

Unless you're into High Tech in a really big way, you'll find those exposed pipes under the bathroom sink are one of your decorating challenges. But this particular ugliness can be easily vanquished, and there are two ways to do it.

One way is to build a three-sided box from 1x2s—just an open frame, with no filled-in sides. Make it exactly the right size to slide underneath the sink and in front of the pipes.

Then visit your local fabric store and pick out something you like in nylon, polyester, or polyolefin—all of which resist the effects of moisture and mildew. Get enough to cover all three sides, plus a few inches for hemming.

When you get home, hem the top and bottom, turn the edges under ¼ inch, and sew. Then install the fabric on the frame-box with upholstery tacks (your hardware store will have them)—and say good-bye to your pipes.

Incidentally, this simple device can be used for more than just decoration. You can easily store paper goods, bottles, and other items behind it.

Another method is to buy a ready-made vanity. These are consideraly more expensive, but they're also a lot nicer than the decorative device suggested above. There are two basic parts to a vanity: the base cabinet and the sink top. Usually they're purchased separately, at discount stores, large hardware stores, and bathroom or plumbing-supply shops.

Vanity bases are usually made of hardwood, plywood, and/or composition board. The backs are open to accommodate the sink pipes. They're usually painted or covered with plastic sheet. Doors may be made out of hardwoods or plastic, depending on how much the unit costs. The units are available in various styles —contemporary, traditional, French or Italian Provincial, and Co-

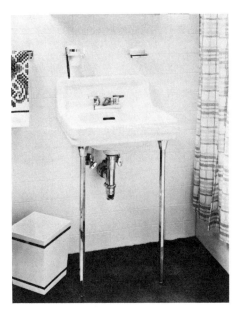

Here you see the ordinary apartment sink. Not very beautiful, is it? A lot of wasted space underneath, right? Well, you can eliminate both problems with an undersink unit like that in the second picture. It's less expensive than you'd think. Do-it-yourself shops, lumberyards, building supply houses, and department stores carry these units.

lonial. Some have one or two doors that swing outward, others have doors plus drawers. It's all a matter of how much room you have and how much you want to spend.

Countertops come in four basic materials—plastic laminate, ceramic tile, cultured marble (mixtures of marble dust and epoxy glue), and synthetic marble. The most expensive: ceramic tile. The least: plastic laminates. The sinks themselves are dropped into an oval opening in the counter top.

If you decide to go this route, be prepared to spend quite a bit —probably $100 minimum, possibly $300–$400. Also be prepared to stay in your apartment for a long time, since you probably won't be able to take your vanity with you. And since this is a major alteration, you'll probably need your landlord's permission. He's unlikely to refuse, however, since you'll be substantially improving his property.

LET THERE BE LIGHT

Bathroom lighting is both a decorative and a practical matter. But many an apartment's bathroom lighting is limited to a single, dim fixture. This can be downright spooky. It can also make you hesitant to shave or to apply mascara, fearing that your aim might be off.

You can brighten things up a bit, usually, simply by changing to a light bulb with a slightly higher wattage, upgrading the landlord's 40-watt bulb to a 60-watter, or the 75-watt to a 100-watt. This will shed a little more light on the subject. But don't exceed the fixture's suggested wattage, if it has any. The last thing you need is an electrical fire in your bathroom.

If this doesn't add enough additional light, try cleaning out the fixture's globe. Globes have a habit of collecting dust and dead flies inside. And if that doesn't work, the next-to-least-expensive alternative is to buy a clear globe at the hardware store. In most cases, they only cost a couple of dollars.

The next-to-most-costly alternative is to get a multi-bulb fixture. Even these aren't all that expensive—we've seen them for ten or fifteen dollars—and they really do the job.

Another idea is to put the light where you really need it, which is usually at the mirror. Some medicine chests have fluorescent fixtures attached, and they're fine if you can get used to looking a little on the green side.

For natural lighting, however, you can install strips of incandescent bulbs. And five to seven bulbs, each of 25 or 40 watts, will brighten up your bathroom in a hurry, without hurting your eyes.

You can buy these fixtures preassembled, or you can make your own, with painted scrap lumber and ceramic sockets. Wire them in series, not parallel, so that if you blow a bulb, you'll know which one to replace. This fixture works well if you have nearby wall outlets for plugging it in. If not, you may have to get professional help from an electrician.

Perhaps the most poorly illuminated place in your bathroom is your enclosed tub/shower. If you're the sort who likes to read in the bathtub, or shave your legs there, you'll need a decent amount of light to see what you're doing.

The solution: a ceiling light. You can make one yourself, with a square piece of 1x4 lumber, a ceramic socket, an extra-long cord with a plug on the end, and a small glass shade or globe.

Mount the socket on the piece of wood, install a bulb, attach the globe or shade, and connect the cord. Then staple the cord down across the wood (or feed it through a hole drilled next to the socket before connecting it).

Then attach the entire contraption to the ceiling with an anchoring bolt or two, the type used to hang pictures on wallboard. If you have a thick plaster ceiling, use a plaster bolt in all four corners. Staple the cord to the ceiling and down the wall outside the tub. Or, if you have a suspended ceiling, run it over the panels, then staple it down the wall to the outlet. Paint the cord and the wood to blend with your ceiling and wall.

If this is too much work, or your ceiling is too low, consider buying a stickup, battery-operated lamp. These work quite well, as long as they're securely fastened.

CURTAINS AND DRAPES, ETC.

When it comes to decor, there's no substitute for curtains or drapes. They soften a room. They frame it in color. They set off a window—and provide privacy. And that goes for every room, even bathrooms.

So if you're lucky enough to have windows in your bathroom, you'll want to finish them off with curtains or drapes—or blinds or shades of some kind.

Just what you choose, of course, is a matter of taste. But we have a word of warning: Remember what room you're decorating. Bathrooms have an environment different than any other room in your apartment. They're extraordinarily high in heat and humidity. And both elements can be destructive to whatever sort of window dressing you choose.

If you're interested in making your own curtains or drapes, for instance, be sure to choose a fabric that's water- and mildew-resistant. Likewise if you buy ready-mades.

Most window shades are made of water-resistant material to start with, so you won't have to worry much on this score. And metal venetian blinds are also immune to heat and humidity.

Wooden materials, on the other hand, are very vulnerable to both. So if you're considering the "Roman" shades that roll up at the top of the window and release with a cord—the type made of many slender wooden slats woven together—don't put them in the bathroom. They'll warp, peel, and eventually rot.

If your bathroom is to be more than just a cubicle in which to perform some of life's less interesting necessities, if it's to add substantially to your comfort and pleasure, if it's to help make your apartment a better place to live, you'll have to devote some time, energy, and money to it. But in our view, there's nothing that can more dramatically improve the quality of your life.

Chapter 10

FINISHING
TOUCHES

Okay, you've done it.

You've moved in, lock, stock, and barrel. Your floors are beautiful, your walls are neat. Your window treatments are just right and your ceiling is the envy of all who happen to notice it.

What's more, your furniture fits, your kitchen is a marvel of efficiency, and your bathroom—well, whatever a bathroom should be, yours is.

But something's seriously wrong.

For all the work you've put into it, your apartment seems lifeless. There's no discernable pulse. What's wrong? And what can you do about it?

Well, if you've noticed the title of this chapter, you already have an idea. What your apartment needs is "finishing touches," the little extras that transform moribund space into a living entity, that make the difference between an apartment and a home.

Everyone has his own idea of what finishing touches really are. For some they consist mainly of a healthy dose of disorder —a pile of magazines and newspapers on the table, an open book on the easy chair, some children's toys under the couch.

We're all in favor of imperfections like these. They give an apartment character. They make it seem lived in. They're a signal that you've finished installing yourself in your new digs and you're starting to relax. But they're not what we mean when we talk about "finishing touches."

What then?

For us, finishing touches consist mainly of two sorts of items: pictures and plants. These are the objects that give you the chance to impose your personality on what otherwise might be a

This efficiency apartment has been decorated at minimal expense. Yet it's quite charming and colorful. The finishing touches—plants and pictures—have a great deal to do with the final effect. Without plants, the room would look cold and sterile. Without—well, not the picture, but the guitar—it would be rather ordinary.

Here's a simple finishing touch that can add dimension to a crowded apartment—a simple folding screen. Before the screen was purchased, this was one room, in which only one activity could take place (comfortably, at least) at one time. Now, it's practically as good as two rooms.

standard apartment layout. They give you the opportunity to endow your flat with character and individuality. Best of all, they give you the chance to express yourself, to demonstrate your good taste.

Pictures and plants are an enormous softening influence in any apartment. Pictures relieve the tedium of bare walls, entertaining your eye and engaging your mind. Plants put you in touch with nature. And when you're alone, they can even keep you company, in a way, since they're also living things.

Picking Out Pictures

Take a look around. What do you see? Walls, that's what. Four of them in every room, unadorned but for paint or wallpaper. Keep looking. Exhausting, isn't it? Boring. There's nothing there to stimulate you (or any guests who might visit, for that matter).

If you're going to make your apartment your home, you'll have to do something to make those walls interesting, attractive, and varied. You'll have to hang something on them. What we're talking about is art.

What do we mean by art? We mean anything from card shop posters to Picasso etchings. We mean photographs, tapestries, prints, signs, collages, charcoals—expensively custom-framed, mounted in dime store do-it-yourself frames, pasted on posterboard, or even tacked up.

BARGAIN BASEMENT ART

You don't have to be Rockefeller to have art—even fine art— on your walls. All you need is a few dollars and a little imagination.

If you're an art seeker with a tight budget, your best bet is the local greetingcard or poster shop. If you've never looked at their poster selections, you're in for a pleasant surprise. The larger shops have a wide variety of art works—colorful modern posters, movie poster reproductions, posters of current celebrities, abstracts and scenics, photo reproductions, etc.

The best of these shops also carry other items that look fine on walls: paper rainbows, mirrors in ceramic frames, enormous greeting cards, wire or metal "sculptures," and many other imaginatively conceived novelty items. Very few cost more than ten dollars each.

If you're looking for something more classic, or if you'd rather hang prints of some of your favorite famous paintings, try a good framing shop. Most not only mount pictures, but also sell reproductions of both well-known and not-so-well-known art works.

Usually, framing shops have a fairly large selection of reproductions in stock, stored in easy-viewing bins. But in addition, they usually have catalogs from art-reproduction houses. Some of these are book-size, with thousands of different reproductions illustrated.

These catalogs offer a wide selection of famous paintings and photographs, plus landscapes, cityscapes, coastal scenes, boating scenes, mountains, etc. Here, indeed, is something for every taste. And most items are less than twenty dollars—not a bad price for the Picasso you've always liked. The framing shops will order what you want.

ORIGINAL ART

Wait a minute. Tempted to skip this category? Scared off by the thought that original art is only for those in the fifty percent tax bracket? Well, stick with us for a moment and be surprised.

The truth is, you—and we do mean *you*—can buy and hang original art on your apartment walls. For not much more than you would spend at a poster shop or framing establishment, you can purchase original prints.

Original *prints?* Unless you know the lingo, that seems a contradiction. There's original art and there are prints, you say. How can anything be both?

Well, original prints are, essentially, limited-edition, artist-supervised artworks that were designed specifically as prints. They're not reproductions of anything, any more than your 1978 Volkswagen Rabbit is a reproduction of a Volkswagen hanging in a museum somewhere.

Original prints are usually signed, dated, and numbered by the artist. And after a set number are printed, the plates are usually destroyed. So, if you find a print entitled, say "Winter Moon," by Jane Smith, you'll probably find a pencil notation on the bottom or on the back saying "Winter Moon, 1975, 16/50, Jane Smith."

Two finishing touches are in evidence here. The first is the interesting wooden wall piece. It lends an attractive texture and color to the room—and isn't likely to be found elsewhere. The second is the mobile/room divider. With sun colors at the top and grass colors at the bottom, it's meant to reflect nature's color balance. And, though you can easily see through it, it does have the psychological effect of separating the livingroom from the entryway.

This notation gives you the title, the year of execution, the number of your specific print, the number of prints in the edition, and the name of the artist.

Prints vary in price according to several criteria: the printing process used, the artist's fame, the number of prints in the run (the fewer the prints, the more each one will cost), the size of the print, the number of middlemen between you and the artist (remember, everyone takes a cut.)

Prints are made by any one of four different processes:

Intaglio. This refers to acid-etched block. Intaglio prints are usually made on thick paper. They're characterized by deep, depressed areas.

Relief. This refers to prints made by the wood or linoleum block method, where the design is raised on the block.

Silkscreen. This is a process in which several colors are laid over each other, one by one, through a layer of silk.

Lithograph. This process involves blocking out areas on a flat surface with ink-resistant material, such as a grease pencil.

Any good print, no matter how it's produced, should have clearly defined areas of color, sharp lines, and little or no bleeding of one color into another. The paper should be of good quality and it should be mounted on a high-rag-content mounting board.

You can buy original prints in several different price ranges.

In the $10–$50 range, you can get good small prints by artists of substantial ability, but without any special reputation.

In the $100–$200 range, you can buy larger works of similar quality.

In the $500–plus range, you can expect to find the work of well-known artists.

How much should you spend? That depends on two factors, only one of which is the size of your pocketbook. The other: your motive for buying.

Wait a minute, you say. I'm buying to decorate my walls. Isn't that what this chapter is all about? Well, yes. But you can buy original prints not only to decorate your apartment, but also as an investment.

Quality prints by well-known artists (or even by rising stars) can—and have—significantly appreciated over the years. And more and more people are buying them with this in mind—especially people who have given up on the stock market or real estate.

The idea of owning something beautiful that not only covers a vacant wall but also doubles as an investment is an appealing one. Only rarely in this life can you simultaneously demonstrate good taste and financial acumen.

But art investment isn't a game for amateurs. As with most investments, there are winners and losers. And the art investment winners are those who know what they're doing—or who hire people who do, to help them. Our point: Before you buy prints for investment purposes, learn what it's all about.

You can buy original prints in art galleries, at auctions, and through catalogs (found at framing shops). But we'd advise against buying at auctions unless you're an expert. The ideal way to buy a print is to see it before you make your purchase. But buying from an illustrated catalog is also acceptable, so long as you can return the print if you don't like it, and get a full refund.

You might also consider original paintings (by which we mean individual works of art, rather than prints—in mediums such as pastel, charcoal, ink, oil, acrylics, etc.).

Quality paintings are almost always expensive. That means they attract investors as well as art lovers. It also means that you probably shouldn't get involved with them unless you have the bucks, the expertise, or both.

But there are two types of original paintings that are within practically everyone's budget: those art works painted by unknowns and sold at local streetfairs and those sold at cut-rate "art galleries" in big cities.

The works of gifted amateurs or semi-pros can sometimes be very nice indeed—and they are individual creations, one-of-a-kinds, with their own character. And who knows—that unknown may be famous someday and if you've bought one of his paintings, you may find yourself with a valuable work of art.

The same can't be said of paintings from cut-rate galleries. These are often mass-produced for the decorating or hotel market. They're no more original than an Arrow shirt, and almost as common.

Obviously, you should consider paintings by unknowns if the price is right and if you like them. But what about the mass-produced type? Well, we feel that if they're inexpensive and you like them, it's no great sin to buy them and hang them on your walls. The snobs won't approve, but they never do. Just don't expect these paintings to quadruple in value before the decade is out.

PHOTOGRAPHY

Perhaps the most popular "new" art form these days is photography. It's fresh, it's interesting, it's attractive—and it's increasingly acceptable.

Today you can buy framable photographs at galleries, streetfairs, college shows, and dozens of other places. And you can often find works that you'd be proud to display, for less than $100.

As an art form, photographs are far less mature than paintings or prints. Only a few great masters have emerged from the pack —people such as Ansel Adams and Dorothea Lange. Many more remain to be discovered, and your chance of spotting one is just as good as anyone else's.

We can't tell you which photographic images to choose. That's purely a matter of taste. So is the choice between color photographs and black-and-white photographs (though color usually costs more). But there are some things to look for when buying photographs:

If you're buying a photograph, the first thing to check is focus. Unless the photograph is purposely blurred or soft-edged for artistic reasons, it should be in sharp focus.

Next, make sure that the photograph is well-finished—no spots, stains, or water marks.

At the same time, make sure it's well-mounted. Reject anything with curling (or bent) corners, or with air bubbles. Make sure the image has been mounted on acid-free mounting board, otherwise your photograph won't last long.

If the photo is framed under glass, make sure there is a space between the glass and the picture itself. If the two are touching, changes in humidity and temperature could cause the image to stick to the glass, with disastrous results.

And once you've bought the picture, don't hang it in direct sunlight or in places where the humidity is high (such as in basements or bathrooms). Both can cause quick deterioration.

CHOOSING AN IMAGE

As we've said, we can't tell you which pictures to choose. That's a matter of taste. But we can offer a few guidelines we've found helpful over the years.

Are your walls papered? If so, you'll probably do best with large-figured artwork—artwork that doesn't tend to blend in with the wallpaper. Do you have flowered wallpaper? Don't buy pictures of flowers. Is your wallpaper mainly striped? Don't buy pictures that repeat the theme. Aim for contrast—that's what creates interest.

Are your walls painted? If they're flat white, practically anything will work. But the darker they are, the more careful you should be. Once again: Aim for contrast. That's what will best set off the picture—and the wall.

Do you have an apartment full of naked wallspace? If so, don't rush out and buy a truckload of large pictures. You won't be solving your problem. You'll just be covering it. Instead, buy two or three larger items and lots of smaller ones of various sizes. Think of each wall as an opportunity to make an arrangement. Don't simply attempt to fill the space. Try instead to create interest, to catch the eye.

Are you seeking a predominantly red (or green, or blue, or brown, or whatever) painting? Are you trying to match the a) drapes, b) carpeting, c) livingroom couch? Don't. That kind of interior decoration almost always looks forced.

Besides, the prints, paintings, or photographs you buy are almost certain to outlast your furniture, carpet, and drapes (after all, how much wear does a painting get?) We both have pictures we purchased during our college days (which are more distant than we care to admit). Together, we've gone through 3½ generations of furniture, drapes, and carpeting since we bought those pictures—and we still like them well enough to keep them up on our walls.

Still in doubt? Forget the color, forget the size, forget the artist, forget the type of pattern—just buy what you really like. Chances are it will be a long and happy relationship.

FRAMING AND HANGING

So you've taken the plunge and bought yourself an armload of art items. Now what? Now it's time to figure out how to get them up.

Most art looks best framed. But you may not want to go that route, especially if what you want to put up on your wall is a large, inexpensive poster.

As millions of apartment dwellers have proved, it is possible to tape or tack pictures up on the wall. But even here there's a right way to do it and a wrong way.

If you're considering tape, avoid the following: cellophane tape (it yellows, cracks, and defaces everything it touches, sooner or later); double-faced "picture" or "carpet" tape (once applied, it never comes off—either wall or picture.)

Instead, use masking tape. It does all the bad things the other tapes do, but to a lesser degree.

And, whatever you do, *don't* stick it on the front of the picture. Roll it up in little circles and put the circles on the back of the picture—at the corners, along the edges, in the center.

Then, raise up the poster—with someone helping, if possible—and press it into place.

If you're considering thumb tacks, forget it. Unless you're hanging your picture on a wall covered with cork or wood, your chances of success are less than 50 percent. And even if you manage to get the picture up, you'll be putting holes in it at the minimum—and, more likely, tearing out the corners sooner or later.

If you've followed our advice and bought something you really like, you'll want to preserve it, even if it wasn't very expensive. And there's no better way to preserve your pictures—or to hang them on a wall—than a frame.

What, exactly, do frames *do* for pictures? Well, first they keep them from warping. If you have a mounted picture, warping is one of its greatest enemies. A mounted but unframed picture that's warped is practically impossible to hang, and difficult to frame. But if it's framed from the start, it will be unlikely to warp.

Second, if the frame includes glass, the image will be protected from dirt, dust, smudgy little fingers, scratches, and many other sorts of damage. Keep in mind that cleaning and repairing

Picture framing need not be a costly business. This apartment dweller has taken four matted prints and put them up between two long grooved holders. The same trick can be done even more simply with two strips of molding, available at your local lumberyard or building supplies store. Putting pictures together this way creates a powerful visual element and presents a more formal appearance than an arrangement of separate elements.

art works is a job for experts. It's a lot simpler—and cheaper—to frame them under glass, so that you can clean them in a matter of seconds with a rag and some Endust or Windex.

Third, framing increases the stature of practically any type of art, from bargain-basement posters to fine acrylics. Framing gives a feeling of quality and value. And well-framed pieces actually do increase in value, should you ever decide to sell them.

Fourth, framing adds its own element of interest. It's a way of characterizing the work of art. It's an additional decorative element. It's another way to use your creativity, to express yourself.

Sitting there, reading this, you may be saying, "All that's true enough, but who can afford to frame all of his pictures?"

You can. And if cost is a factor, here's how you can manage it:

Use precut wooden or metal frames. These assemble-it-yourself items can usually be found in framing shops, in hardware stores, and in dime stores and discount stores. All you have to do is pick out the right-sized elements, buy a sheet of glass cut to size at your local mirror or glass shop, and put it all together. The cost? About half that of custom framing, sometimes less.

Use ready-made frames. Your local discount or dime store has a selection of ready-made frames in about a half-dozen standard sizes. These are already assembled and they come complete with glass, inexpensive mounting board, and sometimes even hanging hardware.

Ready-made frames are about half the cost of the do-it-yourself variety—and that's cheap. They're not the most beautiful frames you've ever seen, but they'll do the job until you can afford better.

Used frames. You can find secondhand frames in many different places—"antique" (junk) shops, secondhand furniture stores, lawn sales, tag sales, garage sales, Salvation Army outlets, used-furniture auctions, etc.

On several occasions, we've found really beautiful frames at amazingly low prices. And not infrequently these nice old frames already contain nice old pictures, so you can kill two birds with one stone, so to speak.

By the way, if you're buying a used frame, beware of the one that's too small for your picture. It will be useless to you. But that's not the case with a frame that's too large. You don't have to be much of a handyman to cut it down to size.

But let's say that you have a dozen pictures or more and not enough cash to frame them all. What then? The answer is simple enough: Frame them one at a time, or as you're able. It will be a continuing source of satisfaction to see each picture go up.

What if money is no object, or not much of an object? Well, then, just trot on down to your local custom framer and start selecting frames for your pictures.

Different types of artwork require different types of frames—and we're not talking here about wood vs. metal, or carved vs. plain. For example, oils and acrylics generally shouldn't be glassed in, unless they're extremely valuable and it's more important to protect them than to let their full beauty shine forth.

On the other hand, watercolors, prints, and photographs should be covered by glass. But, in the case of photographs, the glass shouldn't touch the image. If it does, damage could result. Make sure your framer understands this and leaves what's called "air space."

Now, what style frame should you choose? And what materials are right for which pictures? Once more, these are mainly matters of taste. But there are some general guidelines you can follow:

- Like goes with like. Traditional pictures generally look best in traditional frames, modern pictures generally look best in modern frames.
- The larger the simpler. If you have a picture that occupies half your wall, keep the frame simple and slender. Ornate or heavily carved frames around large pictures often look silly. And they cost a mint.
- Let the picture dominate. Choose your frame to complement the picture, not to compete with it. Frames should set off the pictures they display. After all, it's the picture that's the work of art, not the frame—even if the frame costs more than the picture.
- Make sure the frames you choose don't conflict with each other. Many people base their frame choices solely on the pictures to be framed. But keep in mind that you'll probably have more than one picture on each wall. For this reason,

Fabric hangings are often a good deal less expensive than quality paintings or prints and the effect can be just as spectacular. What's more, these wall hangings add something that paintings can't: texture, which is a frequently overlooked decorative element.

there should be harmony between frames, as well as harmony between frame and picture.

- Avoid trendy, novelty framing. As we've pointed out, few household items last longer than framed pictures. So the ultra-stylish frame you choose today will inevitably be the badly dated frame of tomorrow. The solution? Choose classic, timeless, frame designs.
- Pay close attention to matting. The tinted cardboard matting inside the wood (or metal) frame can be an extremely important decorative element. It can pick up colors in the picture, it can contrast with the picture's dominant colors, or it can blend in.

Work closely with the framer to select the right color and thickness. Don't leave all the choices to him, since this is an opportunity to exercise your own taste and creativity—and you're the one who'll have to live with the result.

Incidentally, if you're aiming for elegance, double or triple matting can often do the job better than a heavier, more ornate, more expensive frame.

PUTTING THEM UP

All right, there you are with a roomful of framed pictures leaning against your couches, chairs, and tables, faced with the sort of decisions only museum directors make easily.

Which picture should go on what wall? How many pictures should go on a single wall? At what height should you hang your pictures?

Again, we're dealing in matters of taste. But we do have a few guidelines to offer, to help you bring order from chaos:

Put like size with like size. Got a big wall? Put your biggest picture there. Got a small wall? That's the place for you little jewel of a picture.

But let's say that your largest picture isn't all that big. Let's say that it will look small and lonely on that huge expanse of empty space above your couch. What then? Well, you can achieve the same effect with several pictures. Make an arrangement.

Incidentally, there are two ways to test out picture arrangements before you start putting nails or hooks in the actual wall in question.

One way is to make a sketch. Using graph paper, lay out the

Most people, unfortunately, are uncomfortable with pictures. They feel that one big one over the couch is just right. But, as you can see here, a lot of smaller pictures, attractively arranged, can have even greater visual interest, especially if they include several different types of images.

pictures you're thinking of putting up on any one wall. You can try several arrangements, then put up the one that works best.

Or use the floor. We've made our best arrangements by laying out pictures on the bare floor, as if it were a wall. This system lets you test out the effect before you commit yourself to it. It also allows you to make any adjustments or substitutions that seem right.

One friend of ours—he's a little on the compulsive side, but we still like him—lays out his pictures this way, gets up on a stepstool and takes a Polaroid picture of the arrangement he likes best. Then he duplicates the Polaroid shot of his choice on the wall.

Frankly, we think a sketch is sufficient. But memory isn't. We've proved that more than once, to our dismay.

Hang pictures at eye level. Now this sounds sensible enough— it's a well-known museum rule. But the more you think about it, the more it seems like nonsense. After all, eye level is a very specific spot. For standing people, it's generally about 5½ feet. For sitting people, it's about 3½ feet—less, if the chair is lower. Which level is right? And how can you hang a picture 4-feet square at a single level?

First, the eye-level rule refers to a single spot on the picture in question—the focal center. Nine times out of ten, this is located somewhere near the middle of the picture. This is the spot that engages and satisfies the eye, the spot to which the eye is led by the picture's composition.

Second, as for standing and sitting eye-levels, both are right, depending on the wall in question. In a foyer or hallway, where people are usually standing, the focal center should be about 5½ feet above floor level.

If you're hanging pictures in your livingroom or diningroom, use the sitting eye-level as your guide. (And if your seating is in several levels, plan around the eye level created by sitting on your main piece of furniture.)

But if furniture arrangements, heat registers, windows, thermostats and other impedimenta make eye level hanging impossible, it's no great sin to hang your pictures a bit higher. However, you should avoid mounting them much lower than three feet above the floor. Lower than that and they tend to get lost, or damaged.

Use art to bring high ceilings down. High ceilings give an apartment a feeling of spaciousness. But they can also create an empty, hollow feeling.

If this is your problem, pictures may be your solution. Take one large wall—your barest wall, if possible—and cover it with artwork from about three feet above the floor to about one foot below the ceiling. This will pull the ceiling down to a more comfortable height (visually, that is) and make the room cozier.

Now you have only one task left. Unfortunately, it's the one many people feel is the most difficult problem pictures present —hanging them up on the wall.

Practically everyone we know has had some bad experiences hanging pictures—shattered plaster, bent nails, broken picture frames, etc. But, with a little care, and the proper hardware, these problems can usually be avoided.

You must now determine what your walls are made of, if you don't know already. Are they wood paneled? Relax. You have nothing to worry about. Are they wallboard? Your chances of hanging your pictures successfully are excellent, providing you're willing to do the job properly. Are they plaster? Well, we want to take this opportunity to wish you the very best luck in your endeavors. We'll also give you some hints that might help.

Wood. Wood is tough, wood is sturdy. Wood can support pictures of practically any weight within reason. Wood doesn't crumble, chip, or tear.

Does this mean you can reach into your nail box, pull out a spike, and start pounding? No, it does not. You might get your picture up that way, but you might do irreparable damage to the wood paneling—which might lose you your deposit.

Instead, get a supply of standard picture hooks at your hardware store (they have several sizes, suitable for pictures of different weights) and nail one into a seam or crack between panels or in the design.

If you're hanging lightweight pictures on wooden walls, you might consider paste-up hooks. These devices consist of a small metal hook and a white fabric tab with glue on the back. Wet the glue, stick, up the tab and, *voilà,* you have a picture hook. You can buy this item at a dime store or stationery shop.

The greatest advantage of paste-up hooks: All you have to do is wet them to remove them. The wall surface usually isn't damaged. The greatest disadvantage: They can hold only lightweight pictures.

Wallboard. Wallboard or gypsum board often isn't strong enough to hold standard picture hooks. But there's a fairly simple solution: anchor bolts.

Anchor bolts are devices that go completely through the wall, then spread out on the other side and grip firmly. To install them you need a drill. Drill the hole, screw the bolts into place, then hang your picture.

All of this is a little troublesome. And if, like us, you have a lazy streak when it comes to such matters, you may be tempted to use standard picture hooks or even nails. Picture hooks (even the paste up variety) might work with lightweight pictures, but with framed objects of any size you're asking for trouble. What kind of trouble? A wall with a gash in it or a picture that gets smashed when it falls to the floor. Our advice: Take the few extra minutes it takes and put in an anchor bolt.

Plaster. Plaster walls are usually a decided plus in apartments. They're more solid and soundproof than wallboard—or even wood paneling. But they make picture-hanging a difficult proposition, because they crumble, chip, or crack.

How do you avoid damaging plaster walls but still get your pictures hung? Well, the paste-up hooks are one way, if you're hanging lightweight pictures. But if you're hanging anything substantial, you'll have to go into the plaster.

There are, essentially, two ways to do this:

1. Nail in picture hooks. Measure your wall carefully, keeping the picture wire taut and use a pencil to mark the spot at which you want to put the picture hook. Then, using masking tape, make an "X" at that spot. (This helps prevent surface cracking.) Then, using a fairly heavyweight hammer, briskly nail in the hook. (Tack hammers usually don't have enough punch. They require more strikes, and every strike increases your chance of breaking or cracking the plaster.)
2. Install expanders. Buy lead or plastic expanders at your hardware store, drill into the plaster with a masonry bit, push in the expander, then screw or nail in a picture hook. The expander will usually prevent wobbling.

What if you try either or both of these methods and you end up with a crater in your plaster wall? Don't panic—all is not lost. Move your location (at least two inches in any direction) and try

Must you always put pictures on the walls? Not at all. You can put up
anything you like. Three-dimensional objects are particularly interesting, as
you can see in this photo.

Many people feel that plants are good for filling up corners or for garnishing decors that are essentially complete. Actually, they can also be used effectively as a decorative centerpiece, as illustrated here. In this room, the plant on the bookcase serves as a focus and ties everything together.

again. If you've used the first method, try the second this time. If you've used the second, try the first.

But whatever you do, don't try to use the original hole again. Your first, unsuccessful attempt probably weakened the plaster too much for that. If you try the same location a second time, you could end up with a hole the size of a golf ball—and that's trouble.

As a matter of fact, if you've been following all of this picture hanging advice, you may already be worried about troubles like this. Drill? Nail? Glue? Tape? What would the landlord say? How much will it cost to repair the damage?

The truth is, all of these holes and pockmarks are much easier to repair than you may think. Even if you're a novice do-it-your-selfer, you'll probably be able to fix your entire apartment in an hour or so, with a little spackle and a little paint. Read the chapter on repairs and you'll see how it's done.

Meanwhile, don't worry too much about the holes, or the glue, or the tape. Don't even worry about the mistakes, unless they're so big you can't cover them up with a picture.

Instead, concern yourself with turning your bare walls into an interesting display of art, with imprinting your personality on your apartment, with expressing your individuality and creativity. After all, you're creating a place to live. What could be more important than that?

Putting Up Plants

Fortunately, when you decorate your apartment, you needn't rely entirely on your own resources. You can enlist that most powerful of allies, Mother Nature.

Natural greenery adds something to human living space that simply can't be provided by any other sort of decoration. It adds color, softness, and the kind of unpredictability that still can't be made artificially. It adds life.

Best of all, even if you can't afford artwork, you *can* decorate with plants. They're often very cheap—or even free. You can buy tiny plants for a dollar or so, and watch them get bigger. Or you can ask friends for pinchings from their ivies, root them in water, then plant them in a potting medium.

And you don't need fancy containers, either. You can use old mugs, pots, and glasses found at tag sales or junk stores. Even the traditional red clay pots don't cost all that much.

On the other hand, if you want to spend money, plants can also accommodate this urge. Every city and town has its nurseries filled with large and healthy specimens of everything from the common to the exotic. The possibilities are endless.

But that doesn't mean plants are for everyone.

For many, it's comforting to live with plants—to water them, to trim them, to watch them grow, to partake of their fragrance. Perhaps it's a primeval urge, stemming from the days when our ancestors swung from trees.

But for others, for those who travel a great deal, for those who don't have the time or inclination to take on additional responsibilities, for those who prefer their vegetation outside, apartment greenery may not be appropriate.

So, before you begin accumulating a household full of denizens from the vegetable kingdom, consider your true feelings. Think ahead. Will caring for your plants be a joy—or a chore? Will you be delighted, as they grow and prosper, or indifferent as they wither and die?

Evaluate your feelings honestly. And if you're the sort who doesn't have much feeling for plants, don't feel guilty about it. It's your relationships with other *people* that really matter, right?

And even if you're not the type to take on an apartment full of plants, you can still decorate your digs with enough greenery to soften it up substantially—air ferns, dried reeds and flowers, even artificial flowers and plants.

Now some people don't think much of artificial flowers and plants, and that's not hard to understand. As Joyce Kilmer once wrote, "Only God can make a tree."

But these days, people can make some pretty convincing imitations. The result may not smell like plants, but its decorative value is quite similar. And of course artificial plants don't need water, sunlight, fertilizing, or pruning—just dusting and an occasional washing.

This section, however, is addressed to those among you who want the real thing. Unless you're already an expert, you're about to find out that owning houseplants, if you do it right, is more complicated than you think. But it's also more satisfying than you'd imagine.

Everything in this apartment is light and airy—beautiful, to be precise. But the finishing touch—the potted plant—is what makes the whole thing come together. You're not sure? Just blot out the plant with your hand and see the difference.

When can plants serve both a decorative and a practical use? When you hang them in your window and let them double as window shades.

There's no room here to treat this subject in depth—dozens of books have been written about house plants. However, in the next few pages, we intend to give you the basic information you need to know where to buy, what to buy, and how to care for your purchases.

WHERE TO BUY

Almost wherever you look these days, there are houseplants for sale: at florists' shops, nurseries, plant stores, dime stores, discount stores, supermarkets, mail-order houses, overstocked botanical gardens, and amateur plant societies. And of course you can get cuttings from friends and acquaintances.

You can get good plants from all of these sources (although prices will vary dramatically). But you can also get losers, if you're not careful. Perhaps the best way to accumulate houseplants for your apartment is through cuttings from your friends. They're not just free, they're acclimated to your growing conditions and thus more likely to survive than those bought elsewhere and shipped in from other parts of the country.

Furthermore, the chances are your friends will be only too delighted to tell you all you need to know about light, water, feeding, and pruning. And if they have plants strong enough for cuttings, you can rely on what they say.

But if you don't have any friends with green thumbs, don't give up. Instead, join a plant society. Most major cities have several. Ask at the largest greenhouse. You'll soon find yourself with plenty of plantwise friends, each eager to share information —and cuttings.

Another good source of houseplants: dedicated amateur plantgrowers who've gone professional. Their offerings usually aren't expensive (comparatively) and they're adjusted to your climate. Check with local botanical gardens to get their names.

Plant stores are also good places to get your houseplants, as are greenhouses or nurseries if you can find one nearby. But florists' shops aren't recommended. To a florist, a houseplant is a sideline, at best.

Supermarkets, dime stores, and discount department stores can all be good plant sources—if their plant departments are tended by people who care, a rather rare occurrence these days. And mail-order is okay, too, if you're buying plants that

Got a nook or cranny that needs decoration, but isn't right for pictures? You can almost always use houseplants. Their leafy, green, natural shape lends interest and softens straight lines and angles.

can survive a lot of rough treatment, such as cacti, bromeliads, etc.

HOW TO BUY

In many respects, it doesn't much matter where you buy, so long as you get a healthy plant suitable to the environment you intend to provide for it. But how can you tell if a plant is healthy? We recommend that you follow these guidelines:

- Overall appearance. Make sure the plant has good color, overall, and that it appears generally healthy and full. If it's not, skip it.
- Insects. Check underneath the leaves, flowers, growing tips, in the soil, and wherever else bugs might lurk. If you find any, move on to the next plant.
- Roots. Pick up the pot and look underneath it. Any roots sticking out? If so, you've probably found a plant with a *permanent* home, one that won't take well to being repotted.
- Leaves. Examine the plant to see that it has all of its leaves. Plants that have lost leaves have had something happen to them. It might be fatal, it might not. Don't take any chances.
- Disease. Check stem and leaves carefully for signs of plant disease—whitish mildew deposits, brown-edged leaves, holes in the leaves, etc. If the plant you're looking at is sick or wounded, pass it by.

WHEN TO BUY

In general, the best time of the year to purchase houseplants is during the summer or, possibly, the spring. This is when plants are at their strongest and healthiest, and most likely to survive the trip from the store to your apartment.

On the other hand, the springtime is best when you're buying from a store that's air-conditioned in summer. Drastic temperature changes can kill most houseplants very easily. So can drastic changes in humidity. So the closer your apartment matches the store in this area, the better chance your new houseplants have of surviving.

Some people recommend that when you buy a small plant, you should carry it home in a plastic bag, to avoid drying it out. But, large plant or small, handle it as if it were a bottle of nitroglycerin. That will greatly improve its chances, once you get it home.

PROVIDING THE RIGHT ENVIRONMENT

The key to keeping your houseplants healthy is to give them all a healthy environment. That consists of the following factors: light, humidity, temperature, nutrition, grooming, and potting. We'll take them one by one:

Light. You can find a houseplant that will thrive in every room in your apartment—except the darkroom. But you probably won't have a room that's right for whatever houseplant you choose.

The truth is, each houseplant species is different. Some crave bright sunlight. Others are quite content with shade. It all depends.

Here's a quick rule of thumb:

For bright sunlight, try impatiens, sansevieria, coleus, beloperone and geranium;

For well-lit rooms without direct sunlight, try cyclamen, rhoicissus and cissus, hedera or monstera.

For shady rooms, try ferns (pteris and pellaea are usually good) and such foliage plants as helxine, maranta, and lilium (Easter lily).

For rooms with a little sunshine, most flowering houseplants will do. You might also try such foliage plants as ficus, dracaena, or chlorophytum (spider plant).

Temperature. Heat and cold, in excess, are fatal to most houseplants. But if you choose your houseplants carefully, you can usually find some that will survive most apartment conditions.

Let's say, for instance, that you don't heat your livingroom at night. In such a case, try philodendrons, aspidistras, ivies and chlorophytum.

Or, let's say that you're a cold-blooded sort (nothing personal intended) and that you keep the heat at about seventy-five degrees at all times. In that case, you'll do best with poinsettias, sansevieria (often called mother-in-law's tongue), hoya (wax plant), zebrina (wandering jew)—or, of course, cacti and succulents.

Humidity. This terms refers to moisture in the air—not rain, not the water you pour on a plant's roots. To put it simply, almost all plants like high humidity. Most require it for their survival.

And yet, during a typical winter's day, the humidity in your apartment may fall far below that needed for everything except cacti. That means where you're living, it's as dry as the desert.

How much humidity do your plants need? Well, that depends. Generally, a plant with thinner leaves needs more than one with thicker leaves, because it loses water faster (plants transpire, which is the vegetable kingdom's version of perspiring).

Also, plants need more humidity in warmer weather (and, correspondingly, less in cooler weather). Also, they need more water—and more food—in growing season.

If your apartment has low humidity—as it probably does—you have two choices: You can limit yourself to plants that like such conditions—cacti and succulents; or you can put your plants in high-humidity containers.

You can, for example, put your potted plant inside a larger pot filled with very moist peat, which retains water and emits plenty of water vapor (also known as humidity). Or you can put your potted plant inside a bowl resting on a shallow layer of stones covered by an inch of water. Evaporation will provide the humidity.

Or you can group your plants together on waterproof trays filled with a layer or two of medium gravel, three-quarters covered by water. These trays should be put on your radiators, to increase evaporation.

Or you can rely on two mechanical methods. One is the hand sprayer. You fill it with water and spray the plants directly, several times a day. This helps raise their environmental humidity, but it's a lot of work for you.

A better method—for both you and your houseplants—is use of the home humidifier, a gadget about the size of a hamper which has a pad-covered wheel within. The wheel turns, dipping continually into a reservoir of water and hastening its evaporation. A good one of these will raise the humidity to reasonable levels, which is healthy for your plants and for you, too. But they're expensive—anywhere from $75 to $150. On the other hand, you can take them with you when you move.

Watering. It would be lovely, indeed, if plant experts could put out charts that said, "Water this plant once a week, water that one every two weeks, water the other one once a day, and water the one over there every ten days." But the sad fact is, there are too many variables in keeping houseplants to create such a chart.

So, how can you tell when a houseplant needs a drink? The best indication is the soil or peat it's growing in. Stick your finger in. If the growing medium is moist, don't give the plant any water. If it's dry, add water—enough that some overflow runs out the base.

But, if your plant is standing in a tray or a little saucer, don't let it stand in more than ¼ inch of overflow. That much is okay, because it raises humidity. More than that can be fatal.

Still in doubt? Then let your plant tell you what it wants. If the leaves have gone limp, water it. If they're turning pale, cease watering for a while.

Despite what some might say, there's no reason to water from below unless the soil or potting medium seems caked on top (and you can always break through if it is).

But never, never use cold water. It should be room temperature, otherwise the plant will get the same sort of shock you do when you leap into a cold swimming pool.

Feeding. Plants eat. They need nutrition, just as we do. But that doesn't mean you have to give them three square meals a day. Far from it.

In fact, most plants you bring home have gotten enough food to last them for a couple of months at least. Besides, they'll probably be in shock because of the differences between their old environment and their new one. And feeding at a time like this could kill them.

After the plant has settled in, feed it with diluted liquid fertilizer (follow the instructions precisely) about once every fourth watering. But when the weather is chilly, do it once in every eighth watering.

Potting. You've just brought home your first houseplant. It's in a plastic pot. But you've heard, vaguely, that traditional clay pots are better. You've also heard that you'd better repot the plant immediately, if not sooner.

Nonsense. Plastic pots may not be beautiful and they may not counter-balance heavier plants, as clay pots can, but otherwise they're just fine.

Chances are, you can keep your new plant in its current pot for a couple of years, anyhow. You needn't repot until it starts to grow more slowly, or until you spot a root sneaking out of the bottom of the current pot.

When you're sure that repotting is in order, choose a container a size or two larger than your plant's present home. Clean it thoroughly. Put some "crock"—broken crockery or brick chips —in the bottom, so roots won't come through the drainage hole.

Then turn upside down the plant you're repotting, keeping your fingers over the soil. Tap the back end of the pot and it should come out easily. If it doesn't, scrape the inside of the pot with a knife.

Then gently loosen the soil that's clinging to the roots of the plant (but don't do this with delicate root systems, such as those on cacti or avocados). Now, lay the plant on a clean surface.

Next, add some soil mix to the new pot. After that, pick up the plant and put its roots in the new soil. Keep adding soil, pressing it down lightly, until it's up to the former level. Your plant has now been repotted.

Cleaning. Plants get dirty. The shiny leaves on most permanent house plants attract the stuff. But these leaves are coated with a waxy substance, so they can easily be cleaned with water, plus a trace of dishwashing soap. Sponge it on gently. But don't wash those plants whose leaves have a velvety texture.

If all of this is too much trouble for you, there's an easier way. Just leave all of your plants outside on the fire escape on a mild rainy day. They'll love it.

Vacations. What do you do with your plants if you go away for a weekend? A week? Two weeks? Well, if you take your trip in cold weather, you don't have too much of a problem with short vacations. Just take your plants off of cold windowsills, where they might get chilled, and put them on a table in the center of the room, in moderate light.

Then give them a good watering. To insure high humidity, you might also put pots of peat around the plants. They'll get by for a week or two.

In other seasons, however—especially in the summer— there's no substitute for a plantsitter, a friend or neighbor who hopefully has a feeling for plants, who'll come in frequently and water your little treasures. It's even worth it to pay a teenager to do the job, if you can find someone you know is reliable.

To make the job easier, label each pot with the name of the

plant. Then leave an instruction list that describes what should be done in each case. Also leave fertilizer and watering tools close at hand.

What—you can't get a plantsitter? Well, all is still not lost. Take your plants out of their pots and put horticultural wicks through their drainage holes. Then reinsert plants. Put the potted (and wicked) plants up on blocks that are standing in a bowl of water, in such a way that the wick is largely covered with water.

If you're only going to be away for a few days, you don't have to do such an elaborate job of watering. Just give your plants a good watering, then cover each with a baggie, taping it closed. Your plants will still be healthy upon your return.

No book that discusses houseplants, even in the brief space we can give them, can be considered complete if the authors didn't list a few of their favorites. So here are some of ours . . .

SOME POPULAR HOUSEPLANTS

There are umpteen zillion different varieties of houseplants—and that's a conservative estimate. And which ones you like best are a matter of, well, what you like.

But just to start you off, if you don't know much about the subject or you haven't developed any particular favorites, here's a selection to get you going. They're listed in alphabetical order.

Aphelandra squarrosa louisae (zebra plant). Everyone seems to like these plants—and why not, since they grow easily and they have great foliage. But they have to be renewed yearly, from cuttings.

Asparagus plumosus, meyeri, sprengeri. These are all asparagus ferns. But sorry, they're not ferns at all. They're members of the lily family. They need lots of water and lots of plant food, but not much sunlight.

Aspidistra elatior or lurida (Aspidistra or cast iron plant). Like dark green leaves 1- or 1½-feet long? This plant makes exactly that. Best of all, it can go in your dimmest corner and survive rather long periods without water. It isn't called the cast iron plant for nothing.

Begonias. These are great houseplants—everyone should have one. They come in many different varieties. Cane-type begonias, their stems slightly resembling bamboo, make fine houseplants. We like the "Preussen" variety. But beefsteak begonias (B. erythophylla), "Cleopatras," and semperflorens are also quite nice —the last being very popular, since they flower at the drop of the hat.

Chlorophytum comosum variegatum (spider plant). This popular and easy-care houseplant consists of a spray of broad, grassy leaves with white centers and green edges. One disadvantage: They grow quickly and need frequent repotting. But they're so likable you probably won't mind.

Cissus antarctica (kangaroo vine). Want a hanging-basket plant? You'll have trouble finding a better one than this. Doesn't need much sun, water, or humidity. And it can go two years between repottings. Short of a perpetual-motion machine, what could be better?

Coleus. Tired of old-fashioned, green houseplants? Well, chin up—coleus can come to the rescue, with velvety, heart-shaped leaves of every imaginable color. Got a friend who has one? Ask for a cutting—they're a cinch to grow that way.

Cyrtomium falcatum (Japanese holly fern). If you like ferns, this is one of the easiest to grow in your apartment. It needs quite a bit of water, true, but very little light. Treat it well and it will give you fronds 2 feet long, with large, glossy, rich green leaflets.

Gynura aurantiaca (velvet plant). This is the plant that produces the leaves you love to touch (but shouldn't). They're purple velvet, and the plant is perfect for hanging pots. It needs good sun and regular watering, though not soaking—but it's not difficult to maintain.

Mimosa pudica (mimosa or sensitive plant). Speaking about leaves you love to touch, this plant produces finely cut, fern-like leaves that practically snap shut when you touch them. They're fascinating and fun. And if you have young visitors to your apartment, you can count on this plant keeping them occupied for fifteen to twenty minutes, since it takes about ten to twelve minutes for the leaves to reopen.

Nephthytis afzelii. You say plants die when you look at them funny? You say you can never remember to water anything? You say you can't be bothered with fertilizer? You say you'd still like some houseplants? Well, give this one a try. It can survive just about all you can dish out and its arrow-head shaped foliage will still look good.

Philodendron scandens (Sweetheart vine). If you're not familiar with houseplants, this is the one you'll probably think of if someone mentions the subject. It has shiny, rich green leaves and it is usually potted so that it can run up a stick in the middle of the pot. The philodendron oxycardium is another popular variety, and both are very easy to keep. About the only way to hurt them: too much sun or too much water.

Sansevieria (snake plant). This succulent, with its stiff, swordlike leaves, is one of the easiest houseplants to maintain. In fact, you can't do much to hurt it, short of shoving it down the disposal.

Sinningia speciosa (gloxinia). This one isn't a cinch. It requires high humidity and good lighting. But if you can create the right environment for it, it will give you some spectacular flowers. It grows from a bulb, which costs a dollar or so.

Tradescantia (wandering Jew). This is an excellent plant for a hanging basket, happy in sun or shade, cool room or warm. Don't overwater them and they'll be with you for years, with their lovely, oval leaves and their freely flowing stems.

BONSAI AND BOTTLEGARDENS

In addition to normal houseplants, of which the above are only a tiny sampling, there are a number of specialized houseplants and houseplant environments. We've choosen two to describe in a little detail: bonsai and bottlegardens (terrariums).

Bonsai. Bonsai are tiny trees in tiny containers, an art perfected by the Japanese. At their best, they're miniatures of the real thing, perfect in every detail, and trained to grow in particular, mystical shapes. At their worst, they're dwarves—and not attractive at all.

Unless you really know what you're doing, you probably shouldn't attempt to grow one from scratch by yourself. It takes at least two years to get one off to a good start.

Unfortunately, they're not exactly a picnic to keep, either. They require very cool temperatures, much air and light (but no direct sunlight), frequent leaf misting, and watering.

Bonsai aren't exactly cheap, either. But if you buy one—particularly a fairly well-grown specimen—and take care of it, it will be an interesting and charming house companion for many years.

Bottlegardens (terrariums). Terrariums are ideal for the person who's willing to put himself out once, to a considerable extent, but who never wants to be bothered again. They're also excellent if the temperature and humidity conditions in your apartment prevent you from growing other houseplants.

In essence, bottlegardens or terrariums are their own private worlds, sealed away from ours, existing on their own, sustaining themselves in every way without help, providing beauty under glass.

When completed, terrariums are quite beautiful, even magical. Your local plant store will show you how to make them.

VEGETABLE GARDENS

Before we move on to other matters, there's one more subject we should touch on, at least briefly: edible plants.

If you have a patio or a large window with lots of sun (and a sturdy floor in front of it), you might consider growing potted vegetables. We know several couples who do this quite successfully.

Of course, it's an open question as to whether or not they actually save money by growing their own vegetables. But it's impossible to doubt the satisfaction they get from feeding themselves from their own garden—even though they don't own a square foot of the great outdoors.

If this idea interests you, you should know that there are several breeds of tomatoes, lettuce, cucumbers and peppers that thrive in pots. And, of course, carrots and radishes do well in any container.

If you have a big, sunny window, you may be able to get your vegetable plants to produce year round. If not, you can start a new crop when the winter months approach.

Just remember, vegetables need lots of root room and plenty of water. The seed package—or the nursery where you bought the seedlings—will tell you each variety's requirements.

So much for plants, terrariums, and vegetables. We think they're the ultimate finishing touch in any apartment and we're confident you'll find them worth the effort.

Chapter 11

APARTMENT
SECURITY

Ever since time immemorial, people have been searching for a place where they could feel completely secure, a place to live where there were no threats of any kind.

They're still looking.

Even the great feudal lords, sitting in their huge, stone castles, protected by legions of knights in shining armor, no less, still thought it wise to surround their magnificent homes with moats, with drawbridges for access.

Today, in an age without castles, moats, or knights in shining armor, we continue to face problems of security, of how to protect ourselves and our possessions from burglars, intruders intent on doing us physical injury—and fire.

Of course, the security problem varies from location to location, from neighborhood to neighborhood, from city to city. But there is no apartment, no matter how remote, no matter how well-protected, that has a guaranteed lifetime immunity to fire and theft.

We're not advocating paranoia. Unless you know you've chosen an apartment in a high risk area, we don't think you should continually think about security. But there's nothing at all wrong with some sensible precautions. Even if they're never put to the test, they'll give you peace of mind.

Burglars and Intruders

You've heard stories—scary stories—of how people, upon returning home for the evening, have discovered burglars at work in their apartments, or how they've heard a noise in the night, only to find there was an intruder in the apartment.

Too often these stories are true, even in relatively low-risk areas. And in big cities, they're so commonplace that they're seldom reported in the newspapers. But security experts say that burglars and intruders can be stopped nine times in ten before they even get through the front door—if tenants take the proper precautions.

Broadly speaking, these precautions fall into two categories: locks (and other means of keeping unauthorized strangers out of your apartment), and habits—a series of simple acts, practiced regularly, with unvarying consistency, that lower your risks and make the most of what you've done to make your apartment intruder-proof.

But, if you live in a building that has many other apartments and if you share a common front and back door (and perhaps even a door leading to the garage), your security—and that of the other tenants—will inevitably be a cooperative effort.

This is because the best place to stop any burglar or intruder is before he even gets into the building. Once in, his choices and opportunities will be many.

For this reason, there should be a set of security groundrules which you and every other tenant in your apartment building follow religiously. Here are some suggestions:

- When entering your building, never let a stranger in when you unlock the front door.

  You may find, for instance, someone waiting outside the door, as though they've just buzzed a tenant or spoken with a tenant on the intercom and are waiting to be admitted. This might be legitimate—but it could also be a burglar's ploy. Some "deliverymen," especially, aren't what they seem.

  In such a case, before you unlock the door, inquire—*helpfully*—whom they're visiting and in what apartment. Then buzz the tenant yourself. If the visitor is legitimate, he'll be grateful. If he's not, he'll vanish.
- When you're sitting in your apartment and someone unexpectedly buzzes you, don't automatically push the button that unlocks the front door. Use your intercom to find out who's downstairs and why they want to come in. Some burglars or intruders simply buzz every apartment until they get someone to admit them. But if everyone insists on knowing who

their unexpected visitors are, that entrance avenue will be closed.

- When leaving your building—from any exit door—make it a habit to reach back and make sure the door has closed and locked properly. If it hasn't, contact the superintendent immediately. Burglars often find their way into apartment buildings whose front or rear doors are inadvertently left ajar.
- If any outside door to the building is loose or if the lock doesn't work well, contact your superintendent immediately. And if you find any door forced open, call the police. There's a chance the intruders are still somewhere on the premises.
- If you notice that the lights over the door have gone out, tell your superintendent. Brightly lit entrances discourage thieves, who need to work unnoticed.
- If you notice any strangers walking around the building, ask politely if you can help them find the person they're looking for. And if the answer doesn't satisfy you, don't make a big deal about it—just go to your apartment, lock the door, and call the superintendent or the police. Maybe the strangers have a good reason for being in the building, maybe they don't. But it's worth a few false alarms—and even some embarrassment—to make sure.

If you and all of your fellow tenants agree to follow these simple rules, you'll substantially reduce the risk of someday finding your apartment burglarized.

But in addition to these security rules, there are some precautions you can take in the building that will help assure your personal safety—and the safety of your possessions:

- Be alert around your building's storage and laundry areas. They're a favorite spot for intruders. If there's something wrong with the lights or if there's a potentially dangerous stranger around (we're not referring to someone's visiting granddaughter), keep on going.
- If, when you come home, you find the lobby lights are out, don't use that entrance (or, at least, don't use it alone). Go around to another door. Sometimes intruders unscrew lobby light bulbs so they can hide in the shadows.
- Be alert when you must use apartment building stairways or

other public areas where there's not much traffic. These spots are among the intruders' favorites.
- Elevators are another danger spot. Once you get in one and there's a stranger inside, there's little you can do to summon help, even by screaming. The solution: If there's a potentially dangerous stranger in the elevator—and no friends or acquaintances—let the door close and take the next car.

If you and all of the other tenants in your building follow these suggestions rigorously, burglars and intruders won't find your building an easy mark.

But that doesn't mean you're home free. There's still a possibility that unwelcome guests with unpleasant intentions can find their way to your front door or one of your windows.

To keep them out, you're going to have to take some well-thought-out precautions.

Doors and Windows

Take a look at your apartment doors and windows. Chances are they look quite secure. There are probably two locks on the door, and the windows no doubt at least have some simple twist locks. A burglar or an intruder, however, may see them quite differently.

He may see, at a glance, that your front door can be opened in a matter of seconds, with very little fuss and no noise at all. Or he may find that your windows can be opened almost as easily from the outside as from the inside.

How can you make both openings truly secure, without bricking them over and without putting up so many locks that it takes ten minutes to get inside your door, even with keys in hand? And how can you do all this without making such a large investment that it might be cheaper to let the thieves clean you out?

Well, that's what this chapter is about.

DOORS

Before you even start thinking about new locks and the like, take a look at the door itself. It could be a security risk no matter how many deadbolts and chains you install on it.

Check the following items:

Hinges. These should be on the *inside* of the door. Otherwise a canny burglar will able to open your door by removing it entirely. This is true even if your door has "tamper-proof" hinges. They *are* harder to pop open, to be sure. But if your apartment is out of sight of the others, a skilled burglar might have plenty of time to take off the door and empty out your apartment before anyone is the wiser.

If your hinges are on the outside of the door, and easily accessible to anyone who might walk by, have them changed. This isn't a very difficult carpentry job, but if you don't want to attempt it, you might be able to get your super to do it. Otherwise, hire a carpenter. It will cost you much less than, say, replacing your hi-fi set.

Even if the hinges are on the proper side of the door, tighten them and make them secure in the wood. Otherwise, they may spring free with a couple of good kicks.

The door frame. Your door should open inward. And when you close it, it should come to a rest, at all edges, against a strong frame—hopefully metal, hopefully an integral part of the doorjamb itself. This frame should be designed so that it's impossible to insert anything between the door and the doorjamb.

If there's a crack between the door and the doorjamb, many a thief will be able to gain entry just by manipulating a credit card in the opening. And if that fails, a thin hacksaw blade can be inserted, with which practically any lock can be cut.

The door itself. Your apartment door should be made of either solid wood (the thicker the better) or of metal, with a wooden core. But many apartment owners economize by installing hollow wooden doors—the type used within apartments between rooms.

Hollow doors are fine for privacy, but practically worthless for security purposes. A sturdy ten-year-old boy could break one down in about two minutes.

Incidentally, your door should have a peephole—a wide-angle telescope about the size and shape of a cigarette. Installed through the door at eye level, peepholes let you see who's knocking without opening your door. They usually have little covers on the inside, so that the person on the outside can't see in.

Glass panels in the door. Country-style or "garden" apartments sometimes have decorative glass panels in the door. They may be attractive, but they're practically an open invitation to thieves. All they have to do to gain entrance is break the glass, reach in, and unlock the door.

If your door has glass panels, ask the landlord to board them up, inside and out, and install a peephole instead. This will give you the view you need without endangering your security.

Some intruders, by the way, try to avoid your gaze by standing just outside the range of the lens. If that happens to you, just ask whoever has knocked or rung to step in front of the door. Then look. If your visitor passes muster, open the door. If not, don't—not even if you have a chain. (More about chains shortly.)

Sidelights. Sidelights are those rows of glass panes that are sometimes mounted on either side of an outside door. They're intended to admit light and to let you see who's at the door. But, like glass panels in the doors themselves, they're more convenient for burglars than they are for tenants. All they have to do is break the glass, reach in, and unlock the door, and whatever you own is theirs.

There are two ways to cope with sidelights. One is to board them over. This works, but it can be unsightly and it can damage the woodwork. The other way involves your door lock, which we'll discuss shortly.

LOCKS

There are two basic types of door locks—and you'll want them both: locks that are installed inside the body of the door and locks that are installed on the door's surface.

Chances are, your apartment came with a lock mounted inside the body of the door. The outside probably has a keyhole, the inside a turnbuckle. This is known as a mortise lock. It's set in a rectangular cavity cut into the door from the edge.

Mortise locks close the door in two ways. First, they have a spring latch beveled on one side to let the door close. Second, they have a deadbolt—a rectangular chunk of metal that, when you turn the key, protrudes through the lock's faceplate and fits into a hole in the doorjamb. The spring latch does nothing more than hold the door closed. The deadbolt is intended to prevent the door from being opened, except by the key.

In addition, your apartment may have a key-in-the-knob lock. Most of these have spring latches—and no other closure. Thieves find them very easy to jimmy, with a credit card or piece of celluloid. And if that method fails, it isn't much trouble to break off the handle, exposing the lock mechanism itself.

Your apartment may also have a rim lock. In this case, you have a cylinder that goes through the door, giving you a keyhole on the outside. On the inside, on the door's surface, you have a deadbolt that fits into a plate on the lock. (One common make: the Segal lock.)

You may also have a simple deadbolt, a rectangular or circular shaft of steel imbedded in the door which can be engaged in a plate on the doorjamb by turning a turnbolt on the inside of the door. This lock may have no cylinder or keyhole on the outside, which will make it useful only when you're within the apartment.

Your apartment might also have a chain lock. These gadgets allow you to open the door partway, but are designed to prevent someone from forcing his way into your apartment.

Each of these locks has its advantages and disadvantages. But expert locksmiths agree that a "vertical bolt" rim lock is the most secure.

Unlike mortise locks set into the body of the door, rim locks don't weaken the door's basic strength. And their deadbolt locks can't be opened with a credit card. With a pickproof cylinder, no ordinary lock is better.

But they're not perfect. Many rim locks with inside turnbolts are downright dangerous if mounted on doors that have decorative glass panels or sidelights.

If this describes your situation, however, you can restore the lock's security by getting a double-sided cylinder—one that must be opened with a key no matter which side you're standing on. That way, if a burglar breaks the glass, he'll find no turnbolt to twist with his fingers, only another keyhole.

But even a double-sided cylinder has its disadvantages, if you don't do your part. First, don't leave the key in the inside keyhole for the sake of convenience. If you do, you might as well have a turnbolt. Second, keep the key in a spot that's obvious from the inside but invisible from the outside. That way, it will be handy if you need it in a hurry—in event of fire, for instance—but a burglar won't be able to get to it.

A mortised deadbolt is also fairly secure, but it has one disadvantage over a deadbolt rimlock: Because it's mounted within the body of the door, it weakens the door. This means it's far more vulnerable to a good solid kick. Also, if it has a turnbolt on the inside and it happens to be mounted on a door with a glass panel or sightlights, it's very vulnerable, should the burglar break the glass.

Chain locks are very dangerous—partly since they seem like such a good idea, letting you leave your door unlocked, but simultaneously open, so you can see who's there.

Just think about it for a moment and you'll see why chain locks aren't very secure. How many times have you seen someone kick in a chain-locked door on television? Sometimes the kicker is a rapist, intent on attacking the beautiful heroine. Other times, it's a policeman, bursting in to make an arrest in the nick of time. But the chain is never much of a barrier.

But after all, that was television and this is real life. Are chains that flimsy and breakable in real life? The answer is yes. The average person—and that means you—can muster enough force to pull the screws out of the wood, snap the chain, or break the slide mechanism.

We know, because we've done it. Twice. We've set the chain in the front door, then stupidly walked out the back door and locked ourselves out. Then we've trotted around to the front again, put a shoulder to the door and broken in, to our own apartment. And neither of us is likely to be mistaken for a strongman or weightlifter.

There is another device that lets you see who's there without forcing you to open the door. We've discussed it already. It's the peephole. We advise you to have one installed and forget about that chain lock.

KEYS

Even the best lock has a weak point. It's the key. With the proper key, any lock can be opened almost instantly, assuming it's working right.

Well, you might ask, what's wrong with that? Isn't that the way it should be? What's wrong is that you may not be the only person to have a key to your apartment.

Unless yours is a brand-new building, there've been other tenants before you, using the same lock and the same key. And the fact that the landlord has now given you a key is no guarantee that the previous tenant hasn't given copies to several other people, or even retained a copy himself.

For this reason, you should *always* have a new lock installed in your door (or doors, if you have a back and/or side door). The only case where that isn't true is when you're the first person to occupy the apartment.

We have an aunt and uncle who may have saved themselves from a considerable amount of grief by doing just this. Mark and Cissy, we'll call them, moved into an apartment under an odd set of circumstances:

The previous tenants hadn't even moved out of the apartment. They'd just called the landlord to say that they were leaving the state. They told him to mail them the deposit. They even left their furniture (not to mention a good deal of garbage and spoiled food and much of their clothing).

The landlord, who wasn't exactly a trusting soul—fortunately for Mark and Cissy—hauled the furniture away, then changed the locks on the doors and windows.

About a month later, when Mark was working late and Cissy was home alone, the previous tenant showed up. But Cissy didn't know that at first. She just heard someone trying to open the door, apparently with a key that didn't work.

She ran to the peephole and looked out. A total stranger was outside—a very angry, total stranger. When the key didn't work, he pounded on the door. Frightened, Cissy asked the man what he wanted. He told them he'd come for his furniture and belongings. She told him to talk to the landlord.

The pounding stopped, but then Cissy spotted the man near the back door. She called the police, who arrived within minutes. They picked up the man, who turned out to be a wanted criminal who'd fled town to escape prosecution.

Even if you're certain that only you—and the landlord or superintendent—have the keys to your apartment, they can still be a security risk, if you do something careless with them, or not so smart.

For instance, do you put a key under the mat? Or in the mailbox? Or over the doorjamb? If you do, you may be leaving it not for a friend or relative, but for a burglar. Burglars, after all, have families and friends and apartments and keys of their own. And they know all the common hiding places.

If you must leave a key for someone, put it someplace unusual

—in the bottom of the standing ashtray by the elevator, for instance, or under a rose bush, or buried in the grass one foot left of the edge of a certain piece of flagstone.

Then there's the problem of the lost keys. Many people try to protect themselves from the genuine inconvenience of losing a keyring by attaching a tag with their names and addresses. This is fine, assuming they're found by a boy.scout who turns them into the police station. But what if someone less noble finds them?

There are better ways to make sure you get your keys back. Some veterans' groups, for instance, mail out miniature license-plate tags for this purpose. The keys are sent back to them and they send the keys to you. The finder of the keys never knows your address. This service is also offered commercially by some AAA clubs.

SLIDING GLASS DOORS

Many suburban apartments have little patios or porches, with sliding glass doors for access. They're unbeatable when it comes to convenience, light, air, and view. But they're the pits when it comes to security. The little locks that come with them can usually be picked in a few moments. Some suitcase locks are better.

But you can make your sliding glass doors reasonably secure. Just go to the hardware store and get an adjustable metal bar that braces the sliding part of the door against the opposite frame. This locks in place. And even if the door's lock is broken, the bar is immovable.

If you don't want to spend the money, you can improvise a bar of your own, out of wood or pipe. But the type you buy comes with nonskid pads on each end, so the window frame won't be marred. Incidentally, a similar device exists for smaller sliding glass windows.

If we had our way, all sliding glass doors would come equipped with this bar. It's an excellent deterrent to thieves— unless the thief is willing to break the glass (a very noisy, attention-attracting act) to gain entrance. Few are.

WINDOWS

Because of their very nature, windows are a greater security risk than doors. Window locks are rarely as elaborate or as effective as door locks. Indeed, because windows are made of glass, it's practically impossible to create a lock that's anywhere near as burglar-proof as, say, a dead-bolt, mortise lock. And burglars can always break a window.

On the other hand, there are some precautions you can take to minimize the possibility of unauthorized entry through your windows. The first one involves the lock.

Most windows come with simple twist locks. These serve to keep a window closed. But they don't much bother an experienced burglar. By forcing a long knife blade between the sashes, he can easily open such a lock.

But there are better window locks. The next step is a twist-type lock with a key. When locked, it can't be pried open with a knife. In fact, it can't even be opened if the window glass is broken out of the pane.

A twist-type lock might not suit your needs, however. What do you do, for example, if you like to sleep with the window ajar? How can you get your fresh air without risking your security? Well, there is a way—in fact, a couple of ways.

First, you can get yourself something called "ventilation locks." These are mounted on the lower sash and they have key locks. You can raise the window a bit, then lock it in place, so it won't go up any further.

You can also accomplish this with two long nails and an electric drill. All you have to do is to drill a hole through both sash frames about ½ inch from the glass and near the top of the lower frame, on both sides, then drill another set of holes in the outside (upper) sash 3–10 inches higher. You can even drill several sets, for varied ventilation.

At night, when it's time to sleep, just raise the window to the height you prefer and insert long nails into the holes. They'll keep the sash from falling. And no one on the outside will be able to raise it any higher, either.

If you're living in a high-risk area, however, all this talk of locking windows won't mean much to you. Your problem is how to prevent burglars, thieves, or other criminals from breaking through your windows to get at your valuables—or you.

There are several ways to do this, but none are totally without their problems. For instance, you can buy steel versions of the accordian devices that are used to keep infants from wandering up or down the stairs or into rooms they shouldn't enter. These spread out across a window and are then padlocked to one side.

Or if you like you can buy decorative iron grillwork and have it permanently installed in front of your window, your landlord willing—and landlords usually are, if you're willing to spend money to improve their property.

Lastly, you can put in iron bars or heavy steel mesh, cementing them in place. But these are often easily removed by a crook who has a pry bar and time to use it.

The main problem with all of these devices is that they're just as good at keeping you in as they are at keeping the bad guys out. And, in the event of fire, that isn't so good. For this reason, many building codes forbid the use of grillwork that can't be opened from the inside. And if it can be opened from the inside, chances are it can be opened from the outside, too—so what good is it, anyway?

Perhaps the best solution to this problem is screw-in mullions —the cross-members that divide, or appear to divide, a window into panes. If your windows have one large pane, you can get screw-in mullions at a hardware store, lumberyard, or home-supply store.

Once installed in combination with a good, key-type window lock, they'll discourage all but the most professional and persistent burglars, since even if they break the glass, there won't be an opening that's large enough to crawl through.

Another way of accomplishing the same general purpose is to install acrylic plastic sheets over your windows (or even use them to replace the original glazing). They're more expensive than glass, but they're very difficult to break, and therefore more secure. They also provide an additional benefit: Their insulating qualities are quite good. On the other hand, they scratch easily —something to keep in mind during installation or if you have a dog or cat who scratches at your windows.

Of course, if you're not on the street floor—and most apartments aren't—you don't have to worry much about window security. Circumstances that call for vigilance, however, are:

1. If your building has exterior fire escapes; and
2. If your apartment is on the second floor and the second floor of your building is within reach of a ladder.

In such cases, you should treat your windows exactly as though you were living on the ground floor.

ALARMS

Do you have a valuable stamp collection? Coin collection? Collection of antique postcards, china, firearms, first editions? Do you own a considerable amount of jewelry? Silver? Fur coats? Do you keep a lot of cash in your house? Do you have a little of everything—but quite a bit, if you add it all up?

If you've answerd yes to any one of these questions, you should definitely consider an alarm system. If fact, your insurance policy, if you have one, may even require an alarm system. And if you don't already have insurance, an alarm system may get you a lower rate when and if you decide to buy insurance.

Alarm systems come in all sorts of shapes, sizes, and capabilities. At their simplest, they're designed merely to wake you up if anyone tries to get in. They're little battery-operated boxes that hang from doorknobs or windows, that start squawking if jiggled. But you can achieve the same effect with cowbells, if you prefer.

After this come photoelectric beam devices (break the beam and the alarm sounds), ultrasonic motion detectors (if anything moves in the room they're guarding, the alarm goes off), and pressure-sensitive mats (they sound off if someone steps on them).

All of these gadgets work well enough, although they're somewhat limited, protecting only the room in which they're installed. But all present a serious problem if you have a dog or cat. Think about it a moment and you'll see what we mean.

Perhaps the best of the lower-priced alarm systems involves foil tape installed around the windows (and an electrical connection at the doors.) This stuff sounds off if it's broken anywhere along the line—something pets aren't likely to do.

Some of the fancier and more elaborate alarm systems can be wired into the desk of an alarm-monitoring company. If this company receives a signal that there's been a break-in at your apartment, it calls the police, who hop in their cars and immediately drive over to investigate.

This system works well—although it's very expensive. But it has one major disadvantage: No matter how careful you are, it sometimes goes off when it shouldn't.

Our friends David and Iris had one of these put in their home.

It was tied to a photoelectirc beam system that criss-crossed most of their main rooms.

This system worked well enough; then, one summer, it started giving a series of false alarms. At first, the alarm company suspected that the culprit was our friends' golden retriever. But the man who'd installed the system insisted that he'd been very careful abut aiming the beams above the dog's height. But the dog was shut up anyway.

Oddly enough, the false alarms persisted. And each time, the police came, dutifully—although their enthusiasm waned as time went on. Finally, an expert was called in. He surveyed the house and spotted the trouble.

It seems that during the summer one of the bedroom windows was left open for ventilation. This window happened to be near a bulletin board. When the wind blew, papers on the bulletin board flapped, breaking the beam of light—and setting off the alarm.

Many alarm systems come with decals for pasting to doors and windows, with the thought that the mere sight of such a warning would deter most thieves. This is true, within limits. Thieves don't like to work where the odds are against them.

But then some "clever" people decided that if the decals were what was scaring off the thieves, all they needed were decals— not alarm systems. As a result, for every working alarm system in place, twenty or thirty residences have decals on their windows and doors. The crooks know this and have lost their fear of the warnings.

VACATIONS

Your apartment is at its most vulnerable when you're not there. And the risk is highest, naturally, when you're away for the longest period—such as when you take your annual vacation to Florida to see the in-laws or when you go camping in the mountains. How can you minimize the risks?

Start by telling your landlord or superintendent when you'll be gone, and for how long. You might even consider giving him a telephone number at which you can be reached in the event of emergency (but that depends on your feelings of privacy, etc.).

Next, call (do *not* leave a note) your milk delivery service, diaper delivery service, newspaper delivery service, and tell them when to stop deliveries and when to begin again. Just to make sure they get the message, set a period beginning two days before you actually leave (one day to notice the problem, one day to make sure they've corrected it), and one or two days *after* you get back (it's always best to err on the safe side). Go to your post office two days before you depart and arrange to collect your mail after you return.

The day before you leave, set up a couple of timers in rooms that can't be seen through your windows. These timers should be attached to lights and arranged so that the lights go on and off at the hours that would be expected if you were home.

One of our favorite security measures is to set a timer on a radio. We make sure that the volume is up fairly high, so that it can be heard from outside the door or window. You can do the same with a TV set, which will also provide a light, by the way —a flickering light that may be interpreted as someone walking about the room.

Even if crooks know about this trick (and there are none they haven't seen), they can never be sure your apartment isn't occupied. And that means they're less likely to break in, since most burglars merely want to grab as many of your goodies as they can, with a minimum of fuss.

If on your return you see any signs of disturbance, don't touch anything, don't even go inside. Call the police immediately. There's always the possibility the thieves are still inside. And even if they're not, they may have left clues.

One last notion about protecting yourself from burglaries:

If you are robbed, you have a far better chance of getting your property back if you've identified it in some way. Perhaps the best way of doing this is to use a small, motorized, engraving tool to carve your social security number or your driver's license number in some inconspicuous (and nonremovable) spot on each of your valuables.

Many police stations now offer this service. And they also provide decals for your doors and windows that note you've marked your belongings this way.

These decals actually discourage burglars, because valuables engraved with their owners's identifying numbers are harder to sell or to fence.

Should you enter your apartment and find a burglar at work,

or should you wake up to hear burglars, the police advise you to get out of the apartment in the first case and immediately call the police, or, in the second case, pretend you're asleep and call the police from your bedside phone, if you can do so without attracting attention.

The main rule: Don't confront a burglar. Burglars want your property. They're not there, 99 times out of 100, to harm you. But if they feel you represent a threat, they may react by attacking. And however valuable your property may be to you, your life is certainly more important.

Fire Protection

Unfortunately, your property—and your life—are at risk from a hazard other than burglars and intruders: fire. Fire can strike anywhere, in new building or old, in good neighborhood or bad, in a high-rise building or a garden apartment—anywhere.

But, according to the experts, most residential fires could have been prevented. And even those beyond the control of a building's occupants can be minimized. With the proper precautions, you and most of your possessions can survive.

COMMON HAZARDS

What causes apartment fires? The causes break down this way:

- Fires from cooking and heating appliances   24.1 percent
- Fires from smoking cigarettes or pipes   17.7   "
- Electrical fires of all types   13.8   "
- Children playing with matches   9.7   "
- Faulty storage of flammable liquids   9.2   "
- Faulty chimneys, unguarded fireplaces   4.6   "
- Clothing fires, often from candles   4.2   "
- Other causes   16.7   "

In all, these hazards cause more than 1,500 residential fires in the United States every day, in homes and apartments where the occupants thought they were safe and sound.

What can you do, if anything, to make sure you and your apartment don't become part of these statistics? Well, your first defense is prevention, and there's a great deal you can do here. It's simply a matter of common sense.

Let's take the hazards one at a time and see.

Cooking and heating appliances. Kitchens and fires go together —that's a fact of life. The main culprit is grease. Under the proper conditions, it burns. And if there's a thin film of it on your range or on the kitchen hood, it can spread quickly. If a lick of flame reaches your kitchen curtains, the fire is off and running.

The best prevention measures are to keep the kitchen clean and greasefree. But common sense also suggests that you keep your grease bottles or cans far from the range—likewise from your frilly curtains.

Heating appliances also cause many a fire, by tipping over and causing a rug or carpet to start burning, by being located too close to drapes, by coming into contact with paper or wood.

The common sense way to prevent fires from heating appliances: Don't put them next to anything flammable, don't leave them going and unattended, follow all the safety instructions.

Careless smoking habits. That cigarette or pipe you're smoking is already aflame. And if you don't treat that flame with respect, you may find it spreading.

Once more, preventing fires from this course is a matter of common sense: Don't smoke in bed (or even in that favorite tilt-back recliner, if you tend to fall asleep there); don't empty ashtrays into wastebaskets—use the sink or toilet instead; put your cigarettes inside ashtrays, not on their edges, otherwise the cigarette may fall off and land on a newspaper, magazine, or carpet.

Electrical fires. Common sense can help you here, too. The best advice we can give: Don't tempt fate. Don't use worn, frayed, or broken extension cords or appliances; don't put more plugs into a wall outlet than it's designed for; don't bypass the grounding pin on three-prong plugs.

Of course, electrical fires can be the result of worn, frayed, or faulty wiring within your walls—wiring you cannot see. But very often, this wiring lets you know when there's trouble, by causing fuses to blow frequently. If this happens in your apartment, you should probably have an electrician check out your wiring.

Children playing with matches. You don't need to be told anything about this subject, do you? You know that matches should be out of reach of any children who might live in or visit your apartment. But the trouble is, *everyone* knows this—and yet, nearly 10 percent of all residential fires are caused by kids playing with matches. Clearly, someone is being careless. Don't let that someone be you.

Faulty storage of flammable liquids. Many of today's chemicals are flammable. In fact, when used in small rooms, their very *fumes* can be flammable. And rags soaked with them can catch fire long after you've put them away. How can you reduce your chances of being burned out this way?

First, make sure all household chemicals, cleaning fluids, solvents, paint thinners, etc., are stored in tightly sealed containers. Second, don't throw oily rags or mops into a closet. *Clean* them, then store them. Third, keep all flammable chemicals far from any heat source. Fourth, don't use flammable chemicals in poorly ventilated areas.

Faulty chimneys, unguarded fireplaces. Very few apartments these days have fireplaces—or chimneys. So this is mainly a problem of houses. But, if you're fortunate enough to have a fireplace and chimney, a little common sense will help prevent fire from this source.

To begin with, have the chimney cleaned when you move in. You have no idea how often previous tenants used the fireplace. The natural, normal use of a fireplace causes creosote to build up. That's one of the by-products of log burning. And it's flammable under the right conditons.

You may think, so what? If the creosote in my chimney catches fire, well, chimneys are designed for fires. This isn't so. Chimneys are designed to vent smoke.

Chimney fires can cause house fires if the chimney is weak, or the mortar broken, or if it passes through dried-out wood or wallboard. The best way to prevent them: periodic cleanings. We recommend that you have it done at least once a year—more often if you use your fireplace several times every week, as some people do in the colder climates.

Unguarded fireplaces are another too-frequent cause of residential fires. Residents put the logs in, start the fire, then walk into the other room for a while. Then a spark leaps out past the hearth and lands on the rug—and before anyone knows it, there's a full-blown blaze.

Clothing fires. As far as we're concerned, these are the most tragic of all, since they all too often involve children. We have some friends whose little boy barely escaped serious burns at his own birthday party when his clothing touched a candle and caught fire.

This particular source of fire can be easily eliminated. All that's necessary is to bring out the cake with candles lit, supervise the blowing out (which should be immediate), then remove the candles. That way, there's nothing to worry about.

But, no matter how much common sense you apply, there's always the possibility that a fire may break out that no one could have anticipated. At that moment, the safety of your life and your property depends not on prevention, but on preparation, warning measures, and extinguishers. Separately and together, these measures can spell the difference between life and death.

PREPARATION

What should you do if there's a fire in your apartment? It's a simple question, but without a simple answer, since each apartment presents a different situation.

For this reason, should the worst actually happen, very few people know how they should meet the threat—what actions come first, which can wait. They haven't worked out any procedure.

So the first step you can take to protect yourself for fires—outside of reducing the hazards as much as possible—is to work out some sort of procedure, a series of steps that automatically go into effect in the event of emergency.

This emergency procedure should either be worked out with the cooperation of everyone who lives in the apartment, or in the case of children, carefully explained to them.

The first priority in any fire—that is, anything beyond a small, momentary flare-up in a wastebasket or an oven, that you can put out easily in a minute or less—is to get out of your apartment. But how?

If your apartment is on the ground level of your building, you have a number of choices—the windows, the front door, perhaps a back door, or a garage door.

On the other hand, if you live in a high-rise building, you may think your only way out is through the front door, which is probably the only door you have.

But even in a high-rise building, even if you live as high as the eighth floor, you can escape through your windows—if you have a little courage, and the proper escape ladder.

Roll-up rope or chain escape ladders are now being made that permit safe exits from eighth-floor apartments (and, of course, those on lower floors).

The best of these have something called a stand-off device, which holds the ladder away from the outside wall so that those descending it will be able to get a toehold on the rungs.

High-rise ladders are available from Exitable, G.A.M.A., Inc., 1800 Worcester Road, Framingham, MA. 01701. Their longest models sell for about $200—expensive, perhaps, but worth the price, should you ever need one. If you live on a lower floor, say two or three stories above ground level, you can get a much more reasonable emergency ladder from Rival Manufacturing Co., 36th and Bennington Streets, Kansas City, MO 64129. The two-story lengths are $26, and the three-story lengths $36.

To figure out which exit to use in the event of fire, begin by imagining an outbreak in each room, one at a time. Is there a fire in the back bedroom? Decide, in advance, which way its occupants should exit. Or is the fire in the kitchen? If so, which way should you leave—by means of the front door or, say, the escape ladder in the bedroom? Or is the fire in the hallway? Then, would it be better to go out the garage door or the bedroom window?

Figure out the fastest way to exit for every member of the family, in every room, in every conceivable circumstance. Then discuss it with the others who live in your apartment, and hold a fire drill—especially if there are children, elderly people, or invalids living with you. Such fire drills should be held no less frequently than once every six months.

Having a fire drill isn't simply saying—"Okay, let's pretend we have a fire. Who goes where to get out?" Every possibility should be considered, so that all occupants know the smartest response—and that is to vamoose, leaving everything behind, not bothering to dress, not even stopping to call the fire department (at least not from inside your apartment). True, your apartment may contain personal items that are irreplaceable—but you're the most irreplaceable item of all.

Once you're out you should immediately call the fire department (or use the nearest alarm box). Make sure everyone in your apartment knows where it is, or what number to call.

During your fire drill, you should also discuss what *not* to do.

Tell everyone, for example, not to take refuge in a closet. That can be a fatal decision. Also, if your apartment is in a high-rise building, you shouldn't use the elevator to get to the ground floor. The fire may affect the machinery or the elevator's electrical supply, in which case you'd be stuck, with who knows what result. Use the stairs instead.

Also, do not go back into your burning apartment once you've gotten out, with the thought of rescuing your color TV set, your checkbook, your citizenship papers, or anything else—with the exception of another human being.

But to make sure you know what people have escaped and which remain within, arrange a preappointed spot for everyone who lives in your apartment to meet, once they've gotten out. Make sure that even the youngest member of the family (if you have children) knows that this is where he or she should go, immediately after leaving the apartment.

And every time you have a fire drill, discuss all of these matters. That way, should a real fire break out, your plans will already be in place. And, instead of panicking, you and those who live with you will be more likely to do the right thing—and to survive.

Smoke and fire detectors. According to the National Safety Council, 70 percent of all fire deaths occur at night, when people are sleeping. By the time the fire, smoke, or sounds of burning awaken the sleepers, it's too late for them to escape. And sometimes they never wake up.

But in the last few years a group of smoke and fire detectors has come onto the market designed for home or apartment installation. Their sole purpose is to awaken sleepers at the earliest possible moment, to greatly increase chances of survival.

There are basically two types of smoke detectors, those that operate by means of a photoelectirc cell and those that detect the ionization of the air (something that occurs when there's smoke in the room). Both are the size of small, ceiling-light fixtures.

The photoelectric type responds earlier—in some cases, as much as twenty minutes earlier—to slow, smoldering fires, such as the type that can occur when a cigarette is dropped into the carpet or when a mattress or piece of upholstered furniture catches fire.

The ionization type is fastest at detecting a rapidly flaming blaze—such as the sort that occurs when the kitchen curtains catch fire, or paper or inflammable liquids flame up. It beats the photoelectric detector at this sort of thing by about twenty to thirty seconds.

When either one of these ceiling-mounted, battery-operated gadgets detects smoke, it lets off a piercing scream—enough to wake most sleepers, especially if the unit is mounted near the bedroom.

You might think that your best bet is a combination unit, one combining both technologies. But, according to the consumer magazines, few of these are very good. Instead, we recommend that you buy one (or more) of each. A good ionization model can be purchased at your local catalog department store for less than ten dollars. Photoelectric units cost about twice that.

The best place for your ionization detector is probably right outside your bedroom door, on the ceiling. The photoelectric detector is probably better nearer the livingroom, where smoldering fires are more likely to take place.

Most of these devices have audible signals to tell you when the battery has run down (it should last about a year). Some have little flags that drop down. To be sure they're working, however, you should test them every couple of weeks.

When testing a smoke detector, by the way, it isn't really enough to push the test button, hear the scream, and walk away, content that you are being protected. All you've really determined is that the battery is okay. Dirt may be obstructing the mechanism in such a way that it can't detect smoke. So you should test it with smoke—a lit cigarette held about six inches away, in the case of a photoelectric detector, and a flaming match in the case of an ionization detector.

Fire extinguishers. If there's a small blaze in your apartment, you can put it out yourself—but only if it's truly small—a wastebasket fire, for instance, or a grease fire inside an oven, or a little blaze in front of the fireplace where some sparks jumped out, or a small fire at a faulty electrical plug.

But, according to the Fire Association of America, you don't have much time. The temperature of a fire can jump from 135 degrees to 1,000 degrees in one minute's time. And soon after that, it will be totally out of control.

On the other hand, if you have the proper fire extinguisher

close at hand, you can douse a small fire in a matter of seconds. But there are many different kinds of fires, and many different types of extinguishers. Use the wrong one on your fire and you'll find yourself in serious trouble.

The Underwriters Laboratories (UL), which sets the standards for devices of this sort, classifies fire extinguishers according to the type and size of fire they're capable of putting out.

Class A extinguishers, for instance, are designed to put out fire fueled by ordinary combustibles: paper, wood, cloth, plastic, rubber, and other nonliquids.

Class B extinguishers are designed to extinguish fires fueled by flammable liquids—gasoline, paint solvents, flammable chemicals, grease, and cooking oil.

Class C extinguishers are intended to put out fires involving electrical appliances or electrical current—any appliances connected to household wiring, for instance.

There is another class—Class D, for fires involving combustible metals, such as phosphorus. But you're very unlikely to encounter that sort of fire in your apartment.

Extinguishers are also rated as to the size of a blaze they can put out. This is paired with the type of blaze they're intended to fight. For instance, an extinguisher rated 1A must be able to put out a test fire of 50 pieces of 20-inch-long wood 2x2s. And a 2A extinguisher must be able to put out a blaze twice as large.

A 1B model should be able to extinguish 3¼ gallons of naphtha burning in a 2-square-foot pan. A 10B model can handle a fire ten times that size. But C-rated fire extinguishers aren't rated that way. The "C" simply means the extinguishing material doesn't conduct electricity, so it's suitable for use on electrical fires.

For household use, we recommend that you buy at least one extinguisher with a UL rating of 1A:10BC. These usually weigh less than five pounds and are usually about 3 inches in diameter and 16 inches long. With mounting brackets, they cost about $25.

Also available are 2A:10BC models, which weigh between eight and ten pounds and are just slightly larger than the less powerful models. They cost about $45.

All of these extinguishers work more or less the same way—you release a safety mechanism, then either squeeze two handles together or push down on the upper handle with your thumb. Most are capable of about ten seconds of firing, either all at once or in short bursts.

Almost all models now on the market use ammonium phosphate powder to extinguish A-type fires. This also works on B- and C-type fires. It's driven out of the extinguisher by pressurized gas, and almost all fire extinguishers have dials showing if the pressure is up.

Once an extinguisher is used, even for an instant, it must be recharged, since powder left in the discharge valve can cause the pressurized gas to leak away. Fire-extinguisher dealers can recharge most units for less than $10.

It's not enough, of course, merely to own the proper fire extinguisher. You must also keep it handy, in a place where it's likely to do the most good. Many an apartment has burned even though the tenant owned an excellent fire extinguisher, because he left it on the top shelf in a closet.

Perhaps the best place to keep your fire extinguisher is in the kitchen, mounted on a wall bracket. If you're getting two units, we'd suggest that you keep the other one near your bedroom, so you can grab it on the way to a fire, should one break out.

When you get your extinguisher, read the instructions carefully and make sure that everyone who lives with you reads them, too. Then, refresh your memory every time you have a fire drill.

Insurance

No matter how careful you are, no matter how well protected your apartment may be, something could happen. If you've taken the necessary precautions, you'll probably escape unharmed. But what about your property? How can you replace what's burned or what's been stolen? There is a way. It's call insurance.

For many years, only homeowners could get insurance that covered the valuables in their dwellings. But recently, more and more insurance companies have been offering renter's insurance.

As you might guess, renter's insurance doesn't cover the building you're living in. But it does cover all of your possessions—your clothing, your furniture, your valuables.

For perhaps $200 a year, you can get the following coverage:

Fire, wind and other perils. Your tenant's policy can insure you against financial loss of your furniture and personal possessions, even while you're away from home—in a hotel or motel, for instance. It can cover such hazards as fire, lightning, windstorms, hail, explosions, smoke, vandalism, plumbing leakage and freezing.

Theft. Many renter's policies cover practically every type of theft loss, both within your apartment and while you may be traveling. Your personal possessions and those of your family can be covered.

Fire legal liability. This feature can give you added liability protection for damage to any rented premise or house furnishing, caused by fire, explosion, or smoke from sudden unusual and faulty operation of any heating or cooking unit. This could cover, for instance, your legal liability for damage to the dwelling or apartment you occupy or to the summer cottage you rent.

Personal Liability. This essential coverage provides financial protection in the event of liability suits arising from accidental injury to others while in your apartment, or accidental injury to others caused by your personal activities, including sports, or accidental injuries caused by your children or your pets.

Medical payments. When such accidents involve bodily injury to others, in most states medical bills up to $500 per person can be paid, regardless of your legal liability.

Improvements. As a tenant, you may have spent a good deal of your own money in decorating or making alterations. Under some policies, up to 10 percent of the total coverage on the contents of your apartment can be applied to losses to such improvements.

Damage to property of others. Many renter's policies will make payments for damage accidentally caused by you to another person's property while it's in your care.

Credit-card and check forgery. Some policies allow you to add this coverage, protecting you up to the limits you choose, in the event of forgery or lost or stolen credit cards, charge plates, and checks.

Additional living expenses. Many renter's policies pay up to 20 percent of the insurance on your personal property for necessary extra living costs (hotel bills, meals, laundry, etc.) incurred while your damaged apartment is being repaired.

As we've said, a policy where we live that covers $20,000 in contents and $200,000 in liability will cost about $200 a year. But the provisions—and the prices—vary widely from state to state. Check out two or more insurance companies in your immediate area to find out what's offered and how much it will cost you. Ask about HO-4 coverage—renter's insurance.

If you live in a high-crime area, however, you may have trouble getting insurance from a private company. For this reason, the federal government now makes available up to $10,000 of burglary insurance to tenants in certain areas. This costs from $60 to $80 a year. But you can't get this particular insurance if you don't have the proper locks. If you think you may be qualified, write to: Safety Management Institute, Federal Crime Insurance, P. O. Box 41033, Washington, D.C. 20014.

Even if you are well-insured, be prepared to collect less than your belongings cost, in the event of fire. Insurance companies will instead reimburse you for the actual, depreciated value of each item—considerably less than its current new price, unfortunately.

And if you want to avoid arguments and speed the reimbursement process, you should at least have a list of the major items within your apartment. What we do, instead, is take a set of photographs (Polaroids are fine) of every room, from several angles. We have it on deposit with our insurance agent (although you could leave a set with a friend or in a bank safety deposit box —but don't keep it in your apartment, for obvious reasons).

Incidentally, if you have anything that's unusually valuable —antiques, jewelry, furs, stamp collections, and the like—you may need special insurance. Discuss this with an insurance agent.

Before we leave the subject of security and move on to other matters, we have one final word: One of the best ways we know of to protect yourself against both fire and theft is a watchdog— an animal who barks when strangers approach or when something goes wrong.

One St. Louis couple we're friendly with, Ann and Dick, have a very friendly Border terrier who's been trained to bark if anyone he doesn't know approaches the apartment, and at the smell of smoke.

When they first told us they'd had their dog trained this way, we were very dubious. We knew watchdogs sometimes frightened burglars away, but we weren't so sure they were of much use in the case of fire. But one night, Butch (that's the dog's name) started barking at about 2:00 A.M.

Dick got up and checked the doors and windows. He was

about to give Butch a good scolding when he thought he smelled something. He went into the kitchen and found the toaster cord sparking and smoldering. The plastic counter top it was resting on had melted down to the wood, which was beginning to char.

Ann called the fire department, which got to their apartment in about three minutes and put out the fire without further incident. Now Dick and Ann both believe that if they hadn't had Butch, they could have been involved in a serious electrical fire —one of the worst kind.

We think Butch may very well have saved their lives. And we think a good watchdog could do the same for you, if your landlord allows you to have pets.

Chapter 12

MAINTENANCE
AND
REPAIRS

You're in your new apartment now. It's furnished and decorated. The medicine chest is full. So is the pantry. The drapes are up and so are the shades. All the furniture is in place. Likewise the rugs, carpeting, and linoleum. The walls are filled with pictures, and houseplants abound. The kitchen is humming, the bathroom fine, the locks great.

You're finished, right? All you have to do now is simply live here. Rise 'n shine, come 'n go, prepare the meals, clean, dust, and change the sheets occasionally—and just, well, occupy the space.

Sorry. There's more to it than that. There are also maintenance and repairs.

Wait a minute, you say, surprised and disturbed. Isn't that for landlords? Aren't they the ones who must handle leaky roofs and broken-down furnaces? Don't they have to get the lawn mowed and the snow shoveled? Aren't repairs and maintenance the province of the owner? After all, I haven't purchased a house. I'm just renting an apartment.

Well, we have some bad news for you—and some good news. First the bad: Things do go wrong in apartments. And many of them are your responsibility to get fixed. You can hire someone to do the fixing, of course, but when will they come and how much will they cost? Or you can argue with the landlord or superintendent, but you won't always win. And even when you do, it may be more trouble than it's worth. That's the bad news.

Now the good news. Even if you have ten thumbs (and even the most ham-fisted of us rarely have more than three or four), you can handle most of the normal maintenance and emergency repairs that are within your province, as an apartment dweller. Most of these repairs don't require any substantial technical skill or even innate handicraft talent.

But what can go wrong in an apartment that's your responsibility—and within your ability to fix? Well, these are the most common problems:

- *Plumbing.* Clogged drains and toilets that won't stop running;
- *Electrical.* Popped fuses (or circuit breakers), broken light bulbs, faulty electric plugs, faulty lamp sockets;
- *Walls.* Holes large and small;
- *Doors and windows.* Sticking and squeaking, broken windows;
- *Appliances.* Problems with small appliances, dishwashers, ranges and ovens, refrigerators, washing machines, dryers, vacuum cleaners, irons;
- *Thermostats.* Malfunctions or dirt;
- *Ceramic tile.* Cracked or loosened tiles;
- *Household pests.* Mice, squirrels, and other uninvited guests.

Does this list frighten you? Are you worried because you can't tell a frammis from a doohickey? Well, relax. It's easier than you think. Much easier. Just take it a step at a time and you'll see.

Plumbing Repairs

Your guests are arriving in half an hour and you hear a steady burbling. You go into the bathroom to check and, sure enough, your toilet is running on. You jiggle the handle a few times without result. What now?

Well, don't panic. Chances are you can fix the problem in a few moments. Here's how:

- Remove the top of the toilet tank.
- Look at the black rubber ball or trap door at the bottom of the tank. It covers the drain. Is it seated properly? Roll up your sleeve and give it a nudge, to make sure (don't worry—the water is clean).
- Check the flush handle, the lever it's connected to, and the drain that's connected to the rubber ball/trap door. Is everything connected? Is the chain tangled or loose? Untangle or connect and flush again.

- Does the trap door fall smoothly back into place? No? Perhaps the lifter's out of alignment. The toilet may work better if you move the chain to another hole in the lifter. Or the lifter lever may require a little bending. Try one (or both) of these, then flush again.
- Does the lifter lift the trap door properly? Does it allow the trap door to fall back in place, securely closing the drain? If not, you may need to reposition the lifter hook on the lifter arm.
- Now, flush again. Some lifters have guide arms, little brackets through which the lifter moves up and down. If these are out of alignment, the little trap door won't close properly and the toilet will run on. Try realigning the guide arm. It's just a matter of loosening the set screw, then tightening it again, once you've made the adjustment.
- Hear a splashing inside the tank? The refill tube may not be discharging directly into the overflow tube. This makes refill water flow directly into the main part of the tank—and splash. Solution: Bend the refill tube slightly (or the spring that holds it in place), so that it leads directly into the overflow tube, the large open tube coming up from the middle of the tank bottom.
- Still splashing? Flush the toilet to see if there's a leak around the top of the inlet valve (the assembly the refill tube comes out of). If there's a leak, unscrew the top of the inlet valve and replace the washer or O-ring. That ought to do it. If that doesn't work, wait until your guests are gone (the next morning will be fine), go down to the hardware or plumbing supply store, and get a new intake valve assembly. Turn off the water lines leading to the toilet and flush it. When the tank is empty, unscrew the old valve assembly and put in the new one.

Here's another common plumbing problem. You're standing in the shower, singing away, when you suddenly notice that the shower bottom is filling up with water. Or you're doing dishes and it's time to drain the water. You lift the drain, but nothing happens.

What you have, in both instances, is a case of drainclogitis, a common but rarely fatal plumbing disease. Here's how to fix it:

- If the trouble is in a sink with a stopper (such as a bathroom sink), first remove the stopper. If it isn't loose, unscrew the connection below the sink, near the drain trap and pull it out. You may have to turn it in one direction or another. Now look inside the drain hole. See any hair, paper, or chunks of soap? Scoop 'em out and run the water again.
- Let's say that the water drains, but very slowly. In that case, go get your plunger, or plumber's helper. Set the bell over the drain and push hard, forcing air in. Repeat a few times, or pump it up and down for a minute or so, as fast as you can. That will do it, in most cases.
- Still got a problem? Okay, it's time for Liquid Plummer, Drāno, or some other chemical. Put on your rubber gloves (you don't want to get the stuff on your hands—it's very caustic) and pour the chemical into the sink, following directions. Wait the prescribed length of time. (Incidentally, do *not* do this before trying your plunger, or your plunger may bring up some drain chemical and splatter you with it.)
- If this fails, you have a seriously clogged drain and mechanical intervention will be needed. Ask if you can borrow a plumber's snake or a pistol-grip auger from your superintendent. We're sure he'll have one, even if he doesn't often use it.
- If your clog is in a sink, place a large pan under the trap (it's that U-shaped bend in the pipe right below the sink) and open the trap plug with a wrench. The trap plug is that large screw at the bottom of the U-shaped bend. No trap plug? Then you'll have to remove the entire U-shaped piece with a wrench. Do this carefully or you'll strip the threads and create work for your local plumber.
- Now take your plumber's snake and force it through the drain opening in the sink. This should break up the clog. Do this several times, until whatever is blocking the drain has come out through the open trap plug. Then reassemble. Your difficulties should be over.
- If it's your toilet that's blocked, force the plumber's snake through the trap and work it back and forth vigorously when you reach the obstruction. When it seems cleared, flush.

Do you still have a drain problem? Are several drains clogged? If so, the problem is a main plumbing line. This needs professional attention. Call the superintendent and/or the landlord to arrange for it.

Electrical Repairs

You're sitting in your favorite chair, reading, waiting for your nighttime snack of rye bread to toast, when the lights suddenly go off.

Or, worse, you're cooking dinner for twelve. You turn on burner number three of your electric range and everything in the kitchen that's electrical suddenly dies.

What you have, almost certainly, is a fuse problem. You've overloaded a circuit. And the fuse—the purposely weak link built into the circuit—has given way.

Incidentally, this may well have prevented an electrical fire. Fuses pop only when the load is too heavy for the circuit—a condition which, if it continues, causes overheating of the wires and can cause electrical fires.

But what should you do?

Well, if your apartment fusebox is in the basement and it controls all of the apartments in the building, all you *can* do is to call your superintendent and ask him to take care of it. But if you apartment is separately fused, you can fix it yourself.

Here's how:

Get your flashlight out, go to your fusebox, and open the door. (Your apartment, if older, may have several fuseboxes, by the way, in which case you'll have to repeat this process.)

Now, shine your flashlight into the fusebox. If you're lucky, you may have circuit breakers instead of fuses. If one of these has popped, you'll see either a readout on the switch that says "off," or you'll be able to see that one switch is in a different position than the others.

To turn everything back on, all you have to do is flip the switch to the on or reset position, by pushing a button or moving a toggle switch. (Of course, if you haven't reduced the electrical overload, it will snap off again.)

If you don't have a circuit breaker, you'll have fuses. They're the little screw-in objects that look like lightbulbs without the bulb part. To see which one has popped, you look through the little window on top. You'll find a small copper strip there, under the plastic. It will go from one side to the other—and it will have a narrowed portion in the center. In a "blown" fuse, this narrowed portion will be missing—"blown" out. If the window is black or discolored, and you can't see the metal strip, that's probably the "blown" fuse.

You might instead find another type of fuse—a plug-type with an opaque top out of which sticks a little button. This is a circuit-breaker-type fuse. If the button has popped out, push it in again and the circuit will come to life.

To change a fuse, follow these rules:

1. Locate a new fuse of the *same* amperage. If you've blown a 60-amp fuse, replace it with a 60-amp fuse. If you put in one of higher amperage, it will hold, all right, but your wiring might not. It might catch fire.
2. If the floor near the fuse box is wet, put down a piece of dry wood and stand on it while changing the fuse. You shouldn't have to ask why.
3. Don't hold on to the pipes or the hot air ducts or anything else while changing a fuse. Put your free hand into your pocket.
4. Don't try to do your fuse-changing in the dark. You don't want to stick your finger into the hole.
5. If you don't have a fuse of the proper amperage, go to the hardware store (or the nearest all night drug store) and get one. Don't put a penny in the socket. If you do, you're asking for trouble.

If you follow these steps, your lights will come on again—and stay on, unless you overload the circuit once more. If these steps don't produce the desired results, however, get professional help. Electricity is dangerous.

Here's another common electrical problem: You've burned out a light in a ceiling fixture and gotten out a bulb to replace it. But try as you might, you can't unscrew the old bulb. Even worse, the old bulb breaks off, leaving the screw part still in place. What to do?

First, turn off the power—not just the switch, but the power at the fuse box or circuit breaker.

Next, let the socket cool for a while. Experts recommend thirty minutes.

After that, try removing the socket while wearing a thick leather glove.

Still can't do it? Try using a needle-nosed pliers on the inner working parts of the socket, twisting them counterclockwise.

If that fails, try whichever one of these remedies is close at hand: an old tennis ball pressed hard into the base of the bulb; a tightly wadded ball of newspaper; a bar of soap; a big cork.

If you still can't get the thing out, you have two choices: changing the socket altogether or calling an electrician (who'll probably do the same).

All right, here's another electrical problem you may run into: You plug a lamp into an outlet and nothing happens. You plug it into another and it lights up just fine. So you plug something else into the first outlet. Nothing. Your problem: a faulty outlet. The solution: Replace it.

Here's how:

1. Cut off the power to the circuit by removing the appropriate fuse or flipping the proper circuit breaker;
2. Remove the wall plate;
3. Unscrew the outlet (it has a screw at either end) and pull it toward you an inch or two, or until the terminals are exposed (these are the screws to which the electrical wires are attached).
4. Remove the wires from the old outlet and screw them onto the new outlet in the same arrangement (if each terminal has two wires, just treat them as though they were one).
5. Push the new outlet back into the wall and attach with screws,
6. Replace the wall plate.
7. Turn on the electricity and test.

If it doesn't work, call the superintendent or the electrician. But 99 times out of 100, it will.

Now, here's another common household electrical problem. One of your lamps has a socket that flickers and buzzes. Something's wrong here. To right it, you must replace the socket.

Here's how:

1. Unplug the lamp, take off the shade and remove the harp.
2. Unscrew the socket (you may have to reach inside the lamp

base to do this, or you may be able to do it at the bottom of the lamp.)
3. Pull the socket out.
4. Pop off the base of the socket (if yours has a "press here" pressed into the metal, press there and it will open.) This is rather like cracking open an egg, but less destructive.
5. Carefully disassemble the socket (it's made of soft metal, usually, and will bend all too easily).
6. Unscrew the wires from the old socket and screw them into the new socket, bending the wires around the screw in the same direction it goes when it tightens (that way, each turn of your screwdriver will make the connection better).
7. Reassemble everything.

If you have a frayed cord, by the way, you can replace it in much the same way. Screw the wires into the socket, feed them back through the lamp, then install the plug. To make your life easier, get the sort of plug you can install by sticking the wire into it and closing a snap.

There are a few other minor electrical repairs you'll have no trouble doing—installing a new wall switch (it's just the same as replacing an outlet), changing a ceiling light (ditto) or replacing a plug. But that's about it. If you have any other electrical troubles, call your superintendent—or an electrician. And don't monkey with anything behind the wall unless you happen to be a certified electrician. As we've said—but it bears repeating—electricity is dangerous.

Holes in the Wall

Let's face it, accidents do happen. Sometimes, while moving furniture or putting up a picture, you may crack or chip a wall. If this happens, you have three alternatives: You can leave it for your landlord to fix (in which case you'll forfeit part or all of your deposit), you can call in a professional—or you can do it yourself.

If you've made a small hole or chip—the sort of thing that happens while hanging pictures—you'll find repairing it a very simple job indeed.

Go to the hardware store and pick up the following: spackling or crack repair compound (it comes in paste form, in a can), a pointed tool (an old can opener will do if you happen to have one lying around), and a small trowel or putty knife. An old toothbrush is also useful.

Clean out the hole or crack with the pointed tool, getting all the loose plaster or wallboard pieces out. Blow out or brush out any remaining dust. Then fill the hole with spackling compound, using the trowel or putty knife to feather it into the surrounding wall.

This is a good time, by the way, to check all of your other walls, and similarly fill any other holes or cracks.

Once you've done this, let the repaired areas dry overnight. Then, the next day, sand them so they're even with the wall. Allow another 12 hours for complete drying, then repaint. That should take care of it.

But what if you've made a considerably larger hole—something, say, the size of a golfball? Well, if your apartment walls are built of wallboard, you shouldn't have too much trouble.

Here's what to do:

1. Using a razor knife, incise a square around the original hole.
2. Cut out the inside of the square, leaving yourself with a square hole with four clean edges.
3. Cut yourself a square of wallboard about an inch larger than the square hole.
4. Cover the "extra" inch of this new piece with glue and screw a large woodscrew into its center, tightly enough to hold firmly.
5. Insert this "back patch" through the square hole, diagonally, holding on with the screw.
6. Fit the back patch so that it's square and so that the glued inch comes into contact with the back of the wallboard. Pull on the screw for a few minutes, until the glue sets.
7. After a few days, cut yourself another patch, this one just slightly smaller than the hole.
8. Remove the screw.
9. Put a thin but adequate coat of glue on the back of the "front patch," then insert. Let dry.
10. If the "front patch" is slightly depressed, when compared to the rest of the wall, don't worry about it. If it protrudes slightly, sand it so that it's level with the rest of the wall.

11. Now fill in the cracks around the edge with spackle. If necessary, coat the entire patch with spackle, to bring it flush with the wall. Let dry a few days.
12. Paint.

If your walls are made of plaster instead of wallboard, clean the area out until the lath—a latticework of wooden strips that supports most plaster walls from behind—is exposed.

Next, using platter or spackle, fill in the hole, starting from the outside edges and working toward the center. If the hole is really a dilly, you may have to fill in a little, then let it get hard, then fill in a little more, until the hole is gone.

Use your trowel or putty knife to level and smooth the patch as well as possible. Bring it out flush with the wall. After it's dry, sand it and paint it. The hole will be gone. In fact, after a while, you'll have trouble remembering where it was.

The Broken Window

You hear a commotion outside. You go to the window to look out. It's only some kids, having a snowball fight. You go back to your seat. But no sooner have you begun to relax again, when something comes crashing through one of your windows. It's a snowball. You rush to the window again, but the kids have scattered.

Now you look at your window to assess the damage. Only a single pane has been broken, but that's bad enough. There's glass all over the floor and there's plenty of cold air coming in. What do you do now?

Well, first things first. You have to take care of your immediate problem before you do anything else. Find yourself a piece of cardboard—the kind that comes in freshly laundered shirts is ideal—and, using masking tape, put it up over the hole. Then clean up the broken glass. Wrap the big chunks in newspaper for safety, then throw them into a wastebasket. Then vacuum. Otherwise, you'll never be able to walk around that room barefoot again.

Now, measure the broken pane, taking the distance from one inside edge of the window frame to the other, lengthwise and crosswise. Then go to a hardware store or home center and get yourself a piece of replacement glass about ¹⁄₁₆ inch smaller in both directions.

Next, using a thick glove, pull out the remaining broken glass pieces—from the outside, if you can. Then, using a screwdriver blade or a chisel, scrape out the old putty. You may have to chip away at it if it's hard, but be careful not to gouge the wooden sash.

Very likely, your window was held in place by little triangular pieces of metal—glazier's points. Pull them out with pliers. If you're working with a metal frame, you'll have metal clips instead. Knock them free.

Next, brush the groove with boiled linseed oil, or thinned exterior paint, to give a better bond when you apply new putty. After that, apply a thin layer of putty or glazing compound in the groove where the glass will lay. This will cushion it and help hold it.

Now lay the glass against this putty and, using the little tool that comes with a box of glazier's points, drive them in on each side—one very two to four inches. Make sure they're below the line of the glazing compound.

After this, put down the putty or glazing compound in thin strips, trimming as you go. Let it dry for a couple of weeks, then paint the putty with exterior paint, running it up onto the window pane slightly, to seal it.

Sticking Windows and Doors

You have a beautiful, double-hung window overlooking a beautiful lawn or flower bed. You go to open it, to get some fresh air, but it doesn't move.

Now you get serious and give it a good push. Still nothing. You bend down and put all of your weight into it. It stays put. You don't want to give up, but what choice do you have?

Does this sound familiar? Do you have this sort of problem? Well, if you do, don't give up. Chances are you can free up your window so that it will provide not only a nice view, but also a fresh breeze.

Here's how:

Take your putty knife and run it along the sides of the window, in the crack between the window and the frame. Your object: to cut through the layers of paint that may be holding the window shut. If the paint layer is especially thick, you may have to tap your putty knife with a hammer. But be careful not to damage the woodwork.

Now try once more to lift the window. Still doesn't move? All right, repeat the process described above, only on the outside of the window if you can. That should do the job. But if it doesn't, try the same thing at the top of the window, between the sashes.

Let's say that your window *does* open, but it's so sticky that every time you open it you're afraid you're going to throw your back out of joint. Any solutions to this problem?

Here are two: First, use steel wool to clean off any paint, dirt, or corrosion on the metal channels the window rides on. If that doesn't work, try lubricating. We recommend WD-40, a spray-on, silicone lubricant. We prefer it to household oil, which is a magnet for dust and dirt—which will eventually cause the window to, you guessed it, stick.

Of course, windows aren't the only household openings that stick. Doors often do the same, and nothing can be more annoying.

At first thought, most people are sure that sticking doors must be taken off their hinges and sanded or planed down. But this isn't always the case.

Very often, when doors stick, the problem is in the hinges. So, before you do anything else, check them to see if they're loose. We do that by first checking the hinge screws. If they all seem okay, we close the door and run a piece of paper down the crack. Where the paper drags is where the door sticks, and the hinge opposite this spot is often the culprit.

Open the door wide and unscrew one of the hinge screws (the ones going into the jamb are more likely to be loose than the ones in the door). Insert a couple of wooden toothpicks, break them off flush with the hinge surface, then put the screw back in. Do this, one at a time, to all of the screws in the hinge.

Now try the door again. Still sticks? Unscrew the screws, one at a time, insert another toothpick or two, and replace the original screws with longer ones.

If that doesn't work, locate the sticking spot (using the paper trick) and sand it down, using a piece of sandpaper wrapped around a block of wood. Don't take off too much, however—

doors usually stick because they're swelled up with moisture. When the doors dry out, you may find yourself with a gap if you've done too much sanding.

And if this doesn't work, it's time to take the door off the hinges and take a plane to them (but it's at this point that we would call the superintendent, especially if there's no experienced handyman in the house).

Appliance Problems

Just when everything is going along perfectly, the toaster conks out. Or the TV set goes haywire. Or the mixer dies. Or the dishwasher stops draining. Or the refrigerator stops refrigerating. Or something goes wrong with the washing machine, the clothes dryer, the iron, or the vacuum cleaner.

Life being what it is these days, we all tend to depend on our labor-saving appliances. But all too often, they break down. And when they do, everything comes to a stop, because we really don't know how to get along without them.

Now there's nothing made by man that can't be repaired by man—but at what cost? And how long will you have to do without it? Or should you replace it with a new one? Or should you call the super? And what about doing it yourself?

Well, in this section, we want to answer these questions:

• Repair or replace?
• Whose responsibility is it?
• Can you fix it yourself?

Let's start with . . .

Small appliances. Small appliances are what you got for wedding presents or what the guys at the office got you when you left. They're not normally provided by your landlord, unless your landlord happens to be your mother. For this reason, getting them fixed is entirely your responsiblity (although if you have a very friendly super, you might consider asking him for help).

Each particular small appliance has its own weaknesses and problems, so they must be taken one at a time:

HAIR DRYERS   Is the problem in the switch or the fan? Toss it out. It will cost you more to fix it than to buy a new unit (and probably a smaller, more modern one at that). But, if the problem is a frayed plug, that's easy to fix. Just snip off the old one with a scissors and put on a new clip-on type plug. (Your hardware store has them).

MIXERS Is your mixer operating erratically or slowly? All it may need is a good oiling. Put a couple drops of household oil in the coils near the motor housing. Still doesn't work right? You have a motor problem. Some more costly mixers have motor "brushes" that can be replaced. In others, you'll need a whole new motor. Take it to a repairman. That should be less expensive than getting a new one.

ELECTRIC FRYPANS Cord frayed? Get a new one. Don't fool around with the insides. They're not as simple as they look. If it doesn't work, toss it out.

ELECTRIC SHAVERS First, clean it out. Whiskers can accumulate and cause the motor to run slowly. If that doesn't fix the problem, change the cord. If it's still giving you trouble, get a new one. Repairs are nearly as expensive as new units.

RECHARGEABLE APPLIANCES (SHAVERS, TOOTHBRUSHES, CARVING KNIVES, ETC.) The weak point in these units is the recharger. Sometimes, the terminals corrode. Other times, the batteries—which are not *infinitely* rechargeable—wear out. Which problem do you have? Clean the terminals with alcohol (use a soft cloth) and see if the unit charges. If not, chuck it—repairs will cost you more than it's worth.

TOASTERS If it's not the cord, which you can fix, don't consider repairing your toaster unless you have one of those fancy toaster ovens. Simple toasters can be purchased at discount stores for less than it takes to repair them.

TELEVISION SETS Old set isn't working right? Check the antenna connection. Is it tight? Are any of the little copper wires from one lead touching the other screw terminal? Is the lead wire broken anywhere?

If you have none of these problems, take your set to a serviceman (or, if it's a heavy color set, have him come to you.) Unless you're an expert, you won't be able to fix it and you shouldn't even try, since taking off the back of a TV set can present a shock hazard, *even if the set is unplugged.*

BLENDERS This is a 50-50 proposition. It will probably cost you as much to fix your blender as it would to buy a new one. In such situations we recommend replacement, since you'll have a newer, more modern machine and you'll have it immediately (who knows how long it would take to repair your old one).

VACUUM CLEANERS   As far as we're concerned, this is most troublesome household appliance we know of. However well it might have worked the last time out, we're never sure it will work the next time we try it.

On the other hand, many common vacuum cleaner problems are easily fixable without professional help. Among these: over-stuffed bags (if they're more than half full, throw them away), wrong bags (tsk, tsk—follow the instructions), broken rubber belt drives (get new ones—they're cheap), worn brushes (replace them), dirty filters (change them, wash them in water, or, at least brush them off thoroughly), blocked hoses (unblock with a wire hanger or plumber's snake), brushes clogged by hair or excess carpet fibers (pull them out or cut them off, so the brushes are free).

If, after all of this, you continue to have troubles, it's probably worth your while to take your vacuum cleaner to your friendly neighborhood appliance repair man, unless it's an antique.

One last word about small appliances. If they're less than two years old, there's a good chance they're still under warranty. That means it could cost you nothing at all to get them fixed. Check the warranty and original receipt—two items which, of course, you should save.

Large appliances. Most of the other appliances in the rest of your apartment are probably your landlord's property, not yours. But since you're the one who's inconvenienced if they break down, you should know how to perform simple repairs.

One appliance you just might own, if you've bought a portable one, is a:

DISHWASHER   These are fairly reliable appliances, but when they go wrong, it's very disturbing. And they can go wrong—leaving your dishes dirty, wet, or spotted, failing to drain, not pumping enough water, making a racket, or just not working at all.

If the dishes are dirty after they've gone through a normal cycle—and you've given them a reasonably good scraping before putting them into the dishwasher—the problem may be no more than a clogged filter.

To check, take out the bottom basket, remove the impeller (it looks like a propeller) and pull out the strainer. You can clean it in the sink.

If the dishes don't dry, that's probably a heating-element problem—something for a serviceman to fix.

If there are spots, you may be using the wrong detergent or not enough of it.

If the unit doesn't drain, you either have a clogged filter or something worse, which only a serviceman can fix.

If not enough water is entering the unit, the water inlet may be clogged (unclogging it is a job for a serviceman) or you may not be getting enough water in your apartment. Or you may be taking a bath or shower at the same moment you're trying to wash dishes. Don't.

If your dishwasher sounds as though Mount St. Helens is erupting inside it, it's probably one of three not-very-serious problems: the dishwasher isn't level (you can probably fix this, if you have access to the little screw-type legs that are used for leveling), dishes are hitting each other during the cycle (stack them more carefully) or a spoon has fallen into the bottom of the dishwasher and is hitting the impeller (turn off the machine, reach in, and pull it out).

If it doesn't work at all, your fuse may be out, or your unit night not be completely latched. Check both. If you still have a problem, call a serviceman.

ELECTRIC STOVE   Got problems here? Check the fuse box. And if that doesn't do it, your problem is no doubt with a faulty burner (heating element). These can be easily replaced, even by someone who's not handy. Just unplug the range before you do any work on it.

GAS RANGE   Don't worry if your soup splashes and puts out your pilot light. Just light it up again, with a match. But if it keeps going out by itself, call a serviceman.

OVENS   If your food isn't getting done soon enough—or it's getting overdone—you probably have thermostat problems. This is a job for your serviceman. But your landlord should pay.

REFRIGERATOR   In our experience, this is one of the most reliable appliances you can have—especially if it's less than ten years old. Nonetheless, it sometimes presents problems.

Among the most common refrigerator problems: interior either too cold or too warm, motor runs most of the time, frostless freezer collects frost, makes a racket when it runs, smells bad inside, won't run at all.

If the temperature inside is wrong—either too hot or too cold —check the thermostat and adjust it properly. If it still doesn't work, you may be opening the door too often and keeping it open too long, or the weather may be just too warm for the machine, especially if it's an older model.

If the motor runs most of the time, start by cleaning the coils and grill on the back or bottom. A vacuum cleaner usually does the job. Also, make sure the thermostat is properly adjusted. If this doesn't cure the problem, you may have to have the door switch replaced.

If you've got frost in the freezer—and it's a frost-free refrigerator—the chances are there's something wrong with the defrosting unit. This is a fairly major repair. Your landlord should pay for it.

If the refrigerator makes a terrible noise, it may not be sitting level on the floor. You should be able to correct this problem, by adjusting the little legs at each corner. On the other hand, the problem may be simpler than that—it could be dishes banging against each other to the vibration of the motor. If neither of these is the problem, it's a job for the serviceman.

If the inside smells bad, it's probably your fault—not covering strong-odor food you're storing or letting the defrost or evaporator pan get dirty. Or it might be the previous tenant's fault, for the same reasons. In either case, you'll have no trouble correcting the problem. If it persists, however, call the serviceman.

If the refrigerator stops running, check your fuse box. If that doesn't provide an answer, get in touch with the superintendent quickly. You'll be able to keep food for several hours if you don't open the door. But after that, spoilage will begin to set in.

CLOTHES WASHER   These, too, are fairly reliable machines for the most part, especially the newer models. But, nothing built by man is perfect.

Here's what to do if you have problems:

If there's too much water, either you have a plugged hose or strainer—or a job for the serviceman.

If the water is too hot or too cold, check the supply valves and temperature controls. That should take care of it.

If you're not getting any water, clean the filters, make sure the water is on, and check the intake hose for sharp bends. Also, in cold climates, make sure the pipes aren't frozen. If this doesn't solve your problems, call for help.

If you're getting a slow drain, the chances are you've put in too much detergent, or the wrong detergent, and the suds are going down the tube in slow motion. Also check the lint screen.

CLOTHES DRYER Here's another very reliable appliance. In fact, if you have problems, it's probably because the lint filter is packed solid, or because you're trying to dry your entire wardrobe at once.

Ceramic Tile

Ceramic tile is that wonderful stuff in the bottom of your shower, or on the floor and walls of your bathroom, that shrugs off heat and moisture, that cleans easily and always looks good —except when it cracks, loosens, or crumbles.

Normally, fixing the bathroom tile in your apartment is a job for your superintendent. But if he isn't the helpful type, or he's a study in slow motion, this is something you can do yourself.

The commonest ceramic tile problem is crumbling or missing grout—the mortar between the tiles. This is something that should be fixed promptly, since it allows water to get in, which will cause tiles to loosen and fall out.

Here's how to accomplish the repair:

Buy yourself some prepared grout at the hardware store. Then, using the edge of an old screwdriver or putty knife, scrap out as much of the old, crumbling grout as you can. But don't pry or put pressure against the tiles—you may pop one out that isn't really loose.

Scrape the joint in a straight line, then brush out all of the dusty debris and small chunks, getting the joint as clean as you can. Then wet down the edges of the tile and the joint, using very little water.

Now, mix the grout, following instructions, and put it into the joints with your putty knife—or even a fingertip, if the crumbling area is small. Make sure there are no air bubbles. When the new grout is in place, smooth it out with an old toothbrush handle. Sponge off the surrounding tiles, so that no excess grout will dry on them—and your repair is finished.

If you have to replace a tile completely, that's a bit more complicated. First, you must get the tile out—a hard job, if it's only cracked. This is done with a hammer and chisel, starting at the center.

After you've removed the cracked tile or tiles, scrape off the grout on the edges of adjoining tiles and scrape out the old cement that held the previous tile in place.

Replacements for most common tiles are available at the hardware or flooring store—as is premixed tile cement. Put a coating of the cement on the back of the new tile, but not so much that it will ooze out the sides when you put the tile in place.

Then, put the new tile down, pressing hard with the palm of your hand to get it seated properly. If you have trouble getting it evenly spaced, use matchsticks on all four sides.

Once the new tile is in place and dry—it takes two or three days—put in new grout. No more cracked tile.

This same procedure, by the way, can be used to replace built-in soap dishes and toothbrush holders made of tile, that have broken off. Simply get replacements at the hardware store and proceed as though you were replacing a tile.

But, since soap dishes and toothbrush holders are heavier than individual tiles and since much of that weight hangs outward, you'll have to find some way to reinforce the new tile while it's drying. One easy method: adhesive tape.

Run two pieces of adhesive tape vertically over the soap-dish or toothbrush-holder tile, once it's in place, making each strip long enough to reach the tile above the new one and below it. Stick the top part of the tapes to the tile above the new one and the bottom part to the tile below the new one, then run additional strips of tape across both the top parts and the bottom parts of the two vertical strips.

Leave the tape in place for at least a day and a night, then remove. You'll have a perfectly operational soap dish or toothbrush holder.

Incidentally, if you can't find an exact replacement for the broken tile, you might try a contrasting or complementary color.

Thermostats

There's nothing worse, we think, than a cold apartment on a cold day. Nine times out of ten, unfortunately, the solution to this problem won't be within your means—it will be a furnace problem, a radiator problem, or some other major difficulty that the superintendent must fix.

But sometimes, especially in new apartments, your individual thermostat may be to blame. Thermostats are those little wall-mounted gadgets that tell the furnace how much heat to send your way.

The main cause of malfunction in a thermostat is dirt, plain and simple. Is this your problem?

First, make sure your thermostat is properly adjusted. Then, if this produces no heat, remove the cover to expose the inner works. Now, using a soft brush (a clean paint brush is fine), remove any dirt, dust, or lint. Such foreign matter can easily prevent a thermostat from working properly.

Then, replace the thermostat cover and wait. Does the heat come up? If not, you have a more serious problem. And if it's not in the furnace, it may be in the thermostat itself. Call your superintendent.

Pests

When you move into an apartment, you may find that you're merely joining some nonpaying tenants who've already taken up residence there—moths, mice, rats, or squirrels, for example. (We've already talked about kitchen bugs in the kitchen chapter.)

Almost certainly, you'll want to get rid of these little pests. Even moths, the most innocuous of the bunch, lay eggs in wool clothing, which is eaten by the larvae (little greyish worms) when they emerge.

Most moths are small and grey and harmless looking. But if you find any in your apartment, take immediate action. Begin by taking all of your clothing to a dry cleaner. Tell him what the problem is—but don't have your clothing permanently moth-proofed, as that chemical can be absorbed through the skin.

After your closets are empty, spray them with a moth killer. Then, hang mothballs or cakes in your closet, or put in a box of cedar chips (they're almost as effective and they smell much better). Change every few months, or until you're sure the moths are gone for good.

Mice, rats, and squirrels are another problem altogether. If you find your apartment is home to one of these rodents, don't immediately tell yourself you're living in a slum, however. It can happen in the best of buildings.

How can you spot rodent infestation? Well, the surest way of knowing you have these little pests is to see them running around. But there are other ways.

Have you found any nibbled boxes in your pantry? Are there little BB-size droppings on the floors of your cabinets? How about hairs along the baseboard? If so, you've got a problem—and it's a problem you'd better tackle right away, since besides eating your food, rodents can spread disease.

First, remove temptation. Put all food in the refrigerator or in tins (breadboxes are good). Clean the apartment thoroughly. Take garbage outside immediately.

Next, consider getting a cat or a terrier. They're the most effective rodent killers around. Very often, mice and rats will vanish forever as soon as they smell one of these animals. Try to get a proven mousecatcher, or the offspring of one. But don't take the animal away from the mother too soon. Four-month-old terriers or cats have probably had a chance to learn the skill.

A good mousecatcher will proudly bring you his catch so you can dispose of it. And if he does, don't act repelled. Pet your animal and praise it.

If you have only a couple of mice in the house, the best answer to your problem may be an old-fashioned mousetrap. Bait it with something really strong smelling. We've had great success with a combination of peanut butter and dogfood.

Try to avoid using rat poisons, however. These will rid you of your rodent problem, but they may leave you with one that's even worse: a horrible smell coming from someplace inside your walls, where the pest went to die. It will be with you for many months.

For a genuine infestation—a tribe of mice or rats that have set up housekeeping in your apartment and brought hoards of aunts and uncles with them—contact your landlord immediately. You'll need a professional exterminator, and so will the rest of the building.

The Tools to Do the Job

All of this advice on maintenance and repair is well and good, but without a set of tools, without the basic handyman's implements, you won't be able to maintain or repair anything. After all, there isn't much you can do with a spoon, a fork, a knife, and a can opener.

Therefore, we've put together the following list, complete with explanations where necessary, of what to have on hand. There's nothing fancy here, nothing difficult to operate, nothing complicated, but everything you'll need:

- A slip-joint pliers. There's nothing better for gripping
- A standard screwdriver, with insulated handle
- A Phillips-head screwdriver (for those "x" shaped screws)
- A 4-inch adjustable wrench (this is what people mean when they use the expression monkey wrench)
- A medium-sized claw hammer
- A set of Allen wrenches (these are actually an odd type of screwdriver, fitting hexagonal, open-headed screws)
- A set of small-bladed screwdrivers (the tiny blades are perfect for tightening the screws in eyeglasses, etc.)
- An assortment of sandpaper and a sanding block
- Three paintbrushes, small, medium, and large
- A putty knife
- A small chisel
- A bottle of household oil
- A small can of WD-40 spray lubricant
- An assortment of wood screws (they come in a plastic, compartmented box with about a dozen different sizes)
- An assortment of nails (in a similar plastic box)
- A roll of black, electrician's tape
- A small trowel
- Some plastic and lead wall anchors
- A utility (razor) knife
- A quarter-inch electric drill and a set of bits
- A plumber's helper (plunger)
- A flexible tape measure (the type that snaps back into its case)
- A small, all-purpose saw
- A container of white household glue

Unless you have a true do-it-yourself penchant, this assortment should take care of you pretty well. We strongly suggest that you also buy a smallish fishing-tackle box and put all of the tools inside. Keep this in a particular location in the house—a kitchen cabinet, the shelf on the back closet, etc.—so you'll know exactly where to find it when you need it.

With these tools at hand, you should be prepared for all but the larger catastrophes. And, in the event one of those occurs, you'll want to call your superintendent or landlord, since their interests will be as threatened as yours.

One last word about maintenance and repairs and we'll leave the subject for more pleasant topics: We haven't discussed anything in this chapter that's beyond practically anyone's abilities, regardless of age, gender, or life experience. Many people are afraid of trying to fix anything around the house, but they needn't be. All you have to do is try. You'll be surprised at how easy it is. You may even find yourself wanting to do more—to try some do-it-yourself projects. And why not? All it really takes is the desire.

Chapter 13

THE PEOPLE
IN
YOUR LIFE

When you move from one apartment to another, or from a private home to an apartment house, you're changing more than your place of residence. You're also changing the people in your life. If you're moving from one state to another, you may be changing almost all of them. But even if you're only moving across the street, there's going to be a change in the cast of characters you deal with every day.

At the very least, you're going to have new neighbors—and a new landlord and superintendent. You may very well find yourself with a new set of friends, perhaps people who replace former friends where you lived last, perhaps new additions. And if you change jobs at the same time you move, you'll find yourself with new co-workers.

All of this adds up to a very considerable shock to the system, especially in combination with a new dwelling, a new neighborhood, new shopping patterns, new transportation patterns, etc. It's no easy task to absorb such sweeping and profound changes in your life and keep your feet on the ground.

This fact is now widely recognized by many psychologists and psychiatrists, in fact. Their studies have shown that moving ranks, as a major cause of anxiety, right up there with divorce, major illness, a death in the family, and a sudden change in family income (in either direction).

This chapter is intended to help you deal with the changes involving the people in your life, to give you some hints and suggestions, and, at the minimum, to make you aware of some of the problems you can expect to face so that you can start preparing for them right now.

There are, essentially, three groups of people we can talk about here: 1) your friends—old and new; 2) your neighbors (and their children and their pets); and 3) your landlord and his employees—the superintendent, the doorman, the sanitation man, etc.

The most important of these, by far, are your . . .

Friends—Old and New

All of us need friends, close companions, and confidants with whom we can share our joys and woes—people we can help, people who can help us. Few things in life are more valuable.

And yet, when we move, depending on the distance we go, our established friendships may be endangered, by lessened contact, by new friendships on either side, by shifting interests.

There are two proverbs that relate to this situation: 1) Absence makes the heart grow fonder, and 2) Out of sight, out of mind. In our experience, they're both right. The first proverb holds true —for a while. Then, as time passes, the second proverb begins to more accurately describe our feelings. But that doesn't have to be.

PRESERVING OLD FRIENDSHIPS

Is it possible to preserve friendships over the long run, despite lengthy separations, despite the fact that you and your friends may be separated by many miles? We think so. But it's not easy.

If you're moving from one city to another, or from one state to another, far enough from your present friends that you can no longer meet for lunch with no more than ten minutes notice, or spend two or three nights a week together socializing, you've got yourself a problem.

The problem is: It takes work to maintain a relationship, especially at a distance. And, what with your new friends and associates, you're only going to have so much energy to put into the task.

So, you're going to have to choose. You're not going to be able to remain close to the entire coffee klatch or bridge club. You'll have to narrow down your efforts to one or two people— possibly three if you're extraordinarily energetic.

We recommend that you make this decision *consciously*, that you think it out, that you tell yourself, "I'm going to do my best to maintain my friendship with Sally and Barbara."

To be sure, there are Susan and Judy and Joe and Ed and all the others. But the chances are they're not really close friends— they're friendly acquaintances.

Anyhow, we're not recommending that you cut off all the rest —but only that you let *them* make the effort to remain friends with you. You may discover, in fact, that someone you thought was a friendly acquaintance turns out to be a true friend. We've had that happen to us when we've moved. So, by all means, be open to it. But don't put your energy into keeping up all of your relationships. You don't have enough, not long distance. No one does.

Once you've choosen the one or two people you want to remain close to, you'll have to pursue the relationship energetically. There are many ways to do this:

Letters. It's always nice to find a letter from a friend in your mailbox. But letters are severely limited instruments of communication. Unless you're willing to write lengthy manuscripts, you simply won't be able to say much to each other this way, in terms of volume alone.

Furthermore, letters lack an essential element of communication: instant give-and-take, genuine interaction. And when you write a letter, you can't see your friend's face or hear his or her voice—and vice versa.

In addition, letters are a far more formal means of communication than, say, a face-to-face conversation. They're more studied, more edited, less spontaneous.

All of this doesn't mean we're against letters. We're not. We love them, in fact. There's nothing better for some special occasions, or for saying things that are difficult to say in person.

But they're not the best way to keep a friendship going.

Tapes. Cassette tapes are an interesting alternative to letters, overcoming several of their disadvantages. First, they let your friend hear the sound of your voice—and vice versa, when you get a tape from your friend. Second, fifteen to twenty minutes worth of talk on a cassette tape allows you a much lengthier, much more voluminous communication than does the average letter. Third, tapes can be far more spontaneous than letters. But the give-and-take is still missing.

Telephone calls. For us, the telephone is the best way to communicate long distance. It has everything going for it, except the chance to see each other's expressions. But someday Picturephone may even give us that capability. The only drawback: cost. But the expense can be greatly reduced by calling in off-hours, when rates are lower. The savings are really substantial.

Visits. There's no better way to maintain friendships than for the parties involved to see each other and spend time together. Of course, if you've moved from one coast to another, visits may be difficult and expensive. But they may offer vacation opportunities to either of you.

And if you've moved only a relatively short distance away from your friends—a couple of hundred miles, for instance, you shouldn't have too much trouble spending occasional weekends together.

If you're really serious about maintaining some of your current friendships after you move, you'll have to pursue as many of these methods as you can, as often as you can.

But there is one key to it all: No relationship can continue to flourish if all there is to talk about is the past—past experiences, past acquaintances. To nurture a relationship, you must share new experiences. Otherwise, sooner or later, you'll simply run out of conversation. You can't reminisce forever.

At the same time, you mustn't cling so closely to distant friends that you seriously diminish your opportunities for making new friends. Your old friends may be warm and decent and giving. They may understand you in the deepest way. But the same potential exists in people you haven't met yet—new friends, friends still to be made.

MAKING NEW FRIENDS

There you are in your new apartment, in your new neighborhood, in your new city, in your new state—just about alone. You look around and all you see are people in pairs or trios or foursomes. Everyone seems to have his or her set of friends already.

Well, 'tain't so. First of all, even in the smallest towns, there are lonely people—people who aren't attached to other people, people who'd like nothing more than having a friend and being a friend. And even those who already have friends are usually open for more. After all, it isn't really possible to have too many friends.

But where can you find a friend? At first glance, it seems as though our society is set up to help men and women find romantic partners, but that there's no mechanism to promote friendships. But if you take a closer look, you'll see that there are many opportunities to find frinds, wherever you may live. Here's a review of the most common:

Clubs and organizations. Have a hobby? Pursue a particular interest? We know of no better way to find sympatico people than by joining a club for people who share your pleasure in an activity —gardening, bowling, politics, theater, music, photography, local history, sewing, bridge—well, the list is endless.

What's that? You say you have no particular interest or hobby? Well, there's no law that says you have to have a preexisting interest. Sample the clubs and organizations in your area to find out what strikes your fancy. Go to some meetings. Consider joining a couple of organizations.

But one word of advice here: Unless there is a compelling reason to do otherwise, don't get involved with clubs whose membership is mostly much younger or much older than you are. You're more likely to find friends among people who share your life situation, more or less.

Work. If you're changing jobs at the same time you're changing dwellings, your most immediate opportunity for human companionship may present itself at work, where you automatically share interests with your co-workers.

Very likely, you'll be approached by some friendly, more established employees who are interested in helping you learn the routine and the rules. It's a short step from that to lunching together, and not a much greater step to shopping together, seeing a movie together, double-dating, etc.

If you're not approached, however, you may have to do the approaching yourself. And that's much easier than it may sound. It's just a matter of asking questions, of requesting some help, of starting a conversation. One hint: Don't ask questions that can be answered "yes" or "no." That's no way to get talk going. Ask open-ended questions instead, such as, "I really don't understand. Could you explain that to me?" Or, "Why is it done that way?" Or, "What do I have to watch out for when I do this?"

Adult education. Chances are, there's a community college—or possibly even a university—nearby. If so, the adult education courses it offers are an excellent opportunity to find friends—and to improve your mind in the process.

To check on the adult education opportunities in your community, look in the Yellow Pages of your telephone book under schools, or colleges and universities. Then, get catalogs from the institutions that interest you.

Not sure what interests you? Some colleges will let you sit in on a class or two—"monitor" it—to see if you like it. This will give you an opportunity to check out the subject matter, the teacher, and your potential classmates.

Church. If you're a churchgoer, this is an excellent way to find people who share at least one of your interests—and a very important one at that.

If you're not a churchgoer, we recommend that you give it a chance. You may be pleasantly surprised at the quality of the people you find and at the wide variety of activites offered. On the other hand, if you've been an atheist for as long as you can remember, don't force yourself into a situation in which you're sure you'll be uncomfortable.

Neighbors. There's no better place to find—or to have—friends than in your own apartment building or nearby. As with the other suggestions we've made, you automatically have a shared interest. In addition to that, there's that great friendship aid, proximity.

We found some friends in our first apartment building. The manner was a little unusual—but, who knows. It might happen to you the same way.

We'd rented a one-bedroom apartment in a new high-rise in the city. Among other things, it had a small terrace. We were standing on it a few days after we'd moved in. Our Siamese cat was with us, sunning herself.

Across the way—the building was L-shaped—we saw another couple out on their terrace—with their Siamese cat. After a few moments, they spotted us and we both smiled.

"Who's your vet?" I asked—and we were off. That was ten years ago, and we're still friends.

Friendships with neighbors have some definite advantages. You can help each other out, waiting for packages to come in the mail, watching each other's kids, lending a cup of sugar, etc.

And since you are close, you don't have to plan very far in advance to share social occasions—shopping, dinner, movies, whatever.

Besides, it's very comforting to know that there's someone

very nearby whom you can count on—and who can count on you.

Cold contacts. If you're a basically friendly sort and you don't have too much trouble starting conversations, even with strangers, you'll find that you have all sorts of other opportunities to strike up friendships—at bookstores, in libraries, at supermarkets, in specialty shops, etc.

These are all places where you can find someone who shares one or more of your interests. All you have to do, practically, is ask:

"Did you read such-and-such?"

"I see you're reading an Agatha Christie mystery. Do you like it?"

"Do you know of any shops around here that sell so-and-so?"

"You must live around here. I've seen you shopping in this store several times."

Of course, more times than not, all you'll get is a polite answer to your question. But every so often, you'll find someone who thinks it would be interesting to talk to you. And that's how friendships are born.

Contacts from others. Moving out of state? Moving to another city? Moving to another part of town? Ask your friends and relatives if they know anyone who lives where you're moving, anyone you might like to know.

Perhaps you have a second cousin in your new town, or your best friend's college roommate lives only two blocks from your new apartment. If so, get their phone numbers and give them a call. Tell them who you are, that you're calling to convey X's regards. Then ask some questions about your new city or neighborhood.

If an invitation is extended, accept it. If not, and the person seems friendly, call again. Make a lunch date. Everyone has to eat lunch.

Not all of these contacts are going to become lifelong friends, but they will help you feel less isolated. And they can tell you where to get the best cuts of meat, who has weekly sales, where to get your hair done, and which is the prettiest walk through town.

Whomever you're talking to, however you've made contact, don't expect—don't even offer—instant friendship. (That only happens on the rarest of occasions.) Instead, prepare for a relationship that grows gradually, that needs nurturing.

Also, be prepared for occasional rebuffs. Given the world we live in today, some people are just too suspicious to be easily approached. But stick to it. There are plenty of people out there just like you.

Neighbors

Even if you only move next door or across the street, when you move into your new apartment, you're going to find yourself with a whole new set of neighbors.

This will be true if your new apartment is in a high-rise building, where your neighbors reside behind the doors spread out along the hallways. It will also be true if you move into a garden apartment or even an apartment in a small house—except that your neighbors will live next door.

Who these people are, what they're like, and how you relate to them will play a major role in the quality of your life. Good neighbors can become good friends—and make your life in your new apartment a joy and a pleasure. "Bad" neighbors can make you miserable, even miserable enough to move.

Knowing all of this in advance will help you better deal with any problems that may arise, perhaps transforming a potentially disturbing situation into one that's neutral or even positive. It will also help you maximize your opportunities for getting the most out of the relationships you have with your neighbors.

TROUBLESOME NEIGHBORS

There are several sorts of people who, as neighbors, can make your life less pleasant. The worst of these, we think, are:

The noisemakers. There's probably no one who's ever lived in an apartment who hasn't at least heard stories about a noisy neighbor—someone with a hi-fi set nearly the equal of the Hollywood Bowl, or a world-class party giver, whose frequent celebrations sometimes shake the building's foundations and last for forty-eight hours at a time.

To be sure, this is the land of the free. People have the right to throw parties or to play the hi-fi loudly. But this right has its limitations—and these begin where your privacy and your right to the quiet enjoyment of your own dwelling starts.

What do you do with a noisy neighbor—not someone who transgresses from time to time and who responds to requests for peace and quiet—but someone who habitually intrudes on your privacy with his noise?

The traditional solution is to pound on the party-giver's door, demand some peace and quiet, and leave in a rage. But this solution often does more harm than good.

The party-giver is apt to take offense and bring the party to a resounding crescendo—just to get your goat. Meanwhile, you lie in bed, simmering over his audacity and unable to do anything about it. The result: You don't get any sleep. And he feels he can throw a big, noisy party whenever he likes.

A better approach is to telephone the party-giver while the party is taking place, to politely explain that the noise is keeping you up and to ask him if he'd mind turning it down a bit. This way, he isn't insulted in front of his guests. And you don't make a fool of yourself in front of a roomful of strangers.

One young couple we know tried this approach without success. So they wrote a note to the party-giver and taped it to his door. It said that they didn't mind the parties—it was his right to have them—but could he please adjust the bass on his stereo to prevent vibrations through the floor—and could he please ask his guests to leave at a reasonable hour—1:00 A.M., they suggested. That approach worked.

But we know of other approaches that have also worked. For instance, there's the retaliatory approach. This involves placing *your* stereo speakers against the wall or floor between you and your noisy neighbor and giving him fifteen seconds of the 1812 Overture at full bass and volume, at, say, 2:30 in the morning. After a couple of doses of this, many noisemakers are ready to call a truce. But beware, this tactic make convince your neighbors that you're a noisemaker, too.

Another approach that sometimes works is the "kill-'em-with-kindness" approach. This involves visiting the noisemaker and making friends, if possible. We know one couple who invited a noisemaker to one of their parties—and was invited to his, in return. Both parties were reasonably quiet, as were most of the ones that followed.

Then there's the calling-the-police approach. This usually works, but it doesn't exactly make for good will, especially if the party-giver knows who's called the cops. Also, if there's something going on at the party that isn't quite right, you may end up causing more trouble for the party-giver than you intend, with the risk of serious retaliation.

Once, while living in a high-rise building and trying to sleep through a party that would have awakened King Tut, and after making a polite telephone call requesting a reduction in the noise level, we took extraordinary measures.

As it happened, each apartment had a separate fuse in a box located near the elevator. We simply removed the party-giver's fuse. Since he didn't know exactly who'd asked him to turn it down, he couldn't retaliate. After half an hour or so, we put the fuse back in. The party was quiet thereafter.

Another approach, after polite requests fail, is to contact your landlord or superintendent. He can talk to the offending party, and his requests to keep it down will carry more weight than any individual neighbor's request.

Yet another approach is to speak to other affected neighbors and visit the noisemaker as a group of three or four people. It's the rare noisemaker who ignores public pressure of this sort.

One caution, however: While you certainly have the right to peace and quiet in your own apartment, your neighbors have the right to throw parties and play music, at least within reason. A little music, a little laughter, a little gaiety is part of life. And if you constantly complain about it, perhaps you'd better do some thinking about your own life, not the transgressions of your neighbor.

If parties get to be a chronic problem in your building, we have one final suggestion that usually works. Post a sign in the entrance hall that lists these rules:

It's time to go home when:

- Someone intentionally breaks a glass
- The beer runs out
- There's a woman crying in the bathroom
- Something big gets spilled
- An engagement is broken
- Someone falls asleep in the corner

- Someone offers to fight someone else
- Someone leaves with someone else's spouse

If this sign is prominently posted, the party-giver will read it —and very likely get the idea.

The slob. "There's a slob in every building," one well-traveled young woman writer told us recently. "I've lived in New Hampshire, Texas, Hawaii, and Vancouver in the last five years and there was always one tenant who left his garbage in the hall for a week, or put it on top of the trash can—not in it—and had a car full of hamburger wrappers that dribbled all over the parking lot.

"And it isn't always a guy. One girl in my last apartment building—she modeled for soap ads, believe it or not—had a Great Dane who used the hall as a toilet. Just disgusting. And she dropped cigarette butts all over the place. She was the sort who emptied her ashtray from her bedroom window."

If you find yourself with a neighbor like this—and the odds are that you will, sad to say—it's a situation you simply can't live with. Besides being visually unpleasant, it's downright unhealthy. Dog feces and garbage that isn't properly disposed of attract flies, cockroaches, and sometimes rodents.

Sometimes, you can shame a slob into cleaning up his act by setting a good example—keeping your own area clean, putting your garbage in the trash container, policing up after your pet, etc.

But if that doesn't work, sterner measures are called for—a gradual escalation from the mild and polite note or conversation to more vigorous measures, such as getting the landlord or superintendent in on the act, or forming a committee of concerned tenants to visit the offender.

In most cases, slobs are amazed to learn their behavior is unacceptable. They were raised that way and they just don't know any better—until they're told. And that applies to the well-to-do as well as the underprivileged.

Sometimes, however, sloppiness is an expression of hostility. In those cases, no amount of polite conversation accomplishes anything. And the entire building may start to slide downhill, as the rest of the tenants stop caring.

This is the time to talk with the other tenants you know disapprove of general sloppiness and bad sanitation and get them to act together, either to put pressure on the offender or to do some cleaning themselves. If you divide the labor, the slob may surprise you by cutting back on his dirty handiwork—or even joining the group. No one likes to feel left out.

You may get resistance to a joint effort at first. The other tenants may say cleaning up is the superintendent's job. But you can point out that if he doesn't have to spend all of his time cleaning up, he can spend more time making repairs and keeping the grounds in good shape.

The egotist. Here's someone else you'll find wherever you live. He's the fellow who parks anywhere he likes, regardless of what space he's been assigned. He's the guy who disobeys all the rules about locking the door after entering the building. He's the person who acts as though he owns the place.

In our experience, we've found that such people usually don't respond to polite requests. They may not even respond to letters, to visits from committees of tenants, to landlord's or superintendent's warnings. So, what do you do with them?

The parking lot offers an ideal opportunity to teach the egotist tht however he may feel, he simply can't do whatever he wants, that there are other people in the world, and that they, too, have needs—and rights.

If there's someone in your building who parks in other people's parking places, who hogs two spaces to himself, or who lets his guests park wherever they like, without telling him that your building has assigned spaces, you may have many delightful alternatives open to you.

For instance, park immediately behind him. That way, he won't be able to get out without asking you—at which time you can tell him that he's parked in your parking place and you'll be happy to move your car, so long as he stays in his space after this.

Or, if he parks across several spaces, put a few bricks, branches, or—better yet—concrete blocks around his car, so he'll have to do some moving before he can get out. Two or three experiences like this and he'll get the idea.

Alternatively, tape—better yet, *paste*—a note to his windshield explaining that he hasn't parked properly. Put it directly in his field of vision. It will be a pain to get off. So much of a pain he'll be reluctant to park in your space again.

If the problem is not with a tenant, but with a guest, make sure his host knows the parking rules and have him ask the guest to move. Also, be sure your guests park either in your spot or on the street.

As for the egotist's other acts of rudeness or lack of consideration, all you can really do is to make sure he's aware of your reaction to what he's doing. After a while, he should get the message.

Kids. Sometimes, the adult tenants in your building will be just fine, but their kids will be little monsters. You never can tell about kids. Sometimes they're little darlings, sometimes they're juvenile delinquents.

It's been said that there are no bad children, just bad parents. And that's where to start if you have trouble with one of the neighbor children vandalizing your property, harrassing you, your children, or your pet—or otherwise making your life miserable.

You'll find that most parents will be excruciatingly embarrassed, if you speak to them gently and politely, telling them you know their children aren't bad, just mischieveous. The parents will speak to their children and, nine times out of ten, the trouble will come to a screeching halt.

The tenth time, however, you'll get nowhere. You'll find that the parents hold the same values their children do, or that their little babies are incapable of doing anything wrong.

If this happens to you—and it may—you don't have many options. Just try to maintain as good a relationship as possible with the rest of the neighborhood kids (and even the bad egg, if you can). That way, when they go looking for trouble, they should look elsewhere.

Pets. It's been a hard day. You've had trouble sleeping, but you've finally drifted off—which is a good thing, because you have another hard day ahead of you. Then, in your dim, semi-consciousness, you hear it: barking. Loud barking. You wait for it to go away. It doesn't. It continues for—who knows how long.

You've spent all Saturday unpacking and throwing out cartons and boxes, carefully stuffing them into the garbage cans provided for such refuse. When you're finished, everything is neat and clean. Then, on Sunday morning, on your way out to get the newspaper, you see that the contents of all the garbage cans have been scattered across the apartment house lawn. A dog, gnawing at one of your boxes, runs off when he sees you.

You've decided to make a very special evening with a very special friend. You've put on that outfit you've been saving and slipped into your new shoes—the ones that cost you more than a week's salary. You walk out of the apartment house door and —squish. You don't even have to look. You know what you've stepped in.

You're watching your child out in the apartment complex playground. He's playing happily in the sandbox, with several other children. Then, a cat with a fancy collar strolls up, hops into the sandbox, and scratches away. You know what's next and you don't like it.

What you're up against is a pet problem—the sort of difficulty that has led more than a few landlords to prohibit dogs, cats, even caged pets such as rabbits, gerbils and birds (few disallow fish, but fish are more decorative than petlike.

If your building has pets and you're one of the pet owners, you can't expect others to be considerate of you if you're not considerate of them.

So, if your building has a dog-walking area, train your dog to use it. If you can't, be prepared to clean up after him (or her). If there is no specific dog-walking area, which is very likely, teach your dog to use the curb. The best spot is near a storm drain, for obvious reasons. Don't let your dog use other people's lawns or any area where people must walk or children like to play.

If your community doesn't have a "pooper-scooper" law like the one in New York City (a very successful ordinance, by the way), you can still do your neighbors a favor by cleaning up after your dog. There are several devices on the market that are sanitary and easy to use.

If you set a visibly good example, that alone will probably convince your neighbors to follow suit. If they don't, a polite request is usually enough to win their cooperation. If it isn't, you'll have to run the gamut of increasingly stern requests, with a call to the board of health as a last resort.

Barking dogs are the next most obnoxious pets. The dogs that bark for hours when their owners are away are especially disliked. One elderly woman we know finally called the police after listening to a neighbor's dog bark for a day and a half.

It turned out that the dog had been locked in the apartment for three days. The owners had left a bowl of food and a bowl of water, but they'd shut the dog in the bathroom, to prevent messes elsewhere.

When the owners returned, the authorities warned them that if they did not take better care of their pet, they'd be fined for cruelty and the animal would be taken from them.

If a neighbor's dog barks constantly—for more than thirty minutes at a time—speak to its owners. They may not realize that their dog is making a nuisance while they're gone.

If they can't train the dog to stop barking, suggest that they take the animal to an obedience course or get a book on dog training. If nothing else works, suggest they get a dog-sitter—or take the dog with them when they go out. Many dogs are perfectly content to sit in the car while their owners are at work, visiting, or shopping—so long as they have fresh air, clean water, and are exercised every three or four hours.

The last step you should take is to complain to the landlord. But if you're losing sleep or are unable to work during the day because of a barking dog, you owe it to yourself to do something about the problem. And if it's your dog that's doing the barking, see to it that he stops.

Just as shut-in dogs can be a nuisance, so can dogs allowed to roam. They raid garbage cans, chase small animals and, especially when they join up with each other, terrorize children and even adults.

If you're a dog owner, don't let your pet run free. Take him out on a leash, put him on a chain, or otherwise supervise his outdoor playtime. If dog packs or roaming dogs are a problem near your building, talk to your neighbors and your landlord about it. If they're not coming from within your building, you may have to call the police and file a complaint.

Cats don't present the problems dogs do—at least not to others. But if they're left to roam on their own, they may tend to kill birds or go after other small animals. This problem can be eliminated by putting a bell on your cat's collar.

Roaming cats also frequently use sandboxes for bathrooms. The solution is obvious enough: Provide your cat with its own litter box and keep it away from play areas. Ask others with cats to do the same.

ORGANIZING YOUR FELLOW TENANTS

One good way to handle almost any problem that might crop up in your apartment building is to make common cause with the other tenants.

Nothing can deal more effectively with noisy neighbors, slobs, egotists, dangerous or dirty pets, than a tenant organization. Properly constituted, these organizations have considerable power, not only through social pressure, but also through legal pressure. They're also useful in tenant-landlord relationships.

If you live in a large apartment complex, there may already be a tenants' association. Ask a neighbor. If no such organization now exists, think seriously about establishing one.

We know of one group that was established in a high-rise apartment building in a suburb of a large city. This particular building was inhabited mainly by older people.

Only on the rarest occasion did the organization have to deal with any external problem. But it provided a real service to its members by working out organized ways to deal with sickness, accident, and natural disasters.

For instance, one of the organization's activities was a round-robin calling service, where some of the more elderly tenants in the building were called regularly—once or twice a day—to make sure they were all right and to take care of their minor needs.

If your building has no such organization, you can be the catalyst that gets one started. Begin by talking to a few other like-minded tenants.

Then, set up a building meeting, giving each of the initially interested parties a list of tenants to invite personally. Arrange for two or three alternate dates, then settle on the one most people can make.

If possible, have the meeting in your apartment. Offer simple refreshments to all, since eating and drinking together lessens tensions and puts people in a good mood.

There are many ways to organize, depending on the number of tenants, the type and location of the building, the overall enthusiasm for the project, etc.

But we suggest that you begin by discussing what you'd like your tenants' organization to accomplish. Here are some suggestions:

- To provide a way to react in the event of illness or accident;
- To devise a way to deal with natural disasters or fires;
- To increase security throughout the building;
- To draw up a set of rules—as few as possible—to make apartment life more pleasant for all;
- To set up a plan for sharing the responsibility of looking after the apartments of those who are on vacation or are away;
- To draw up a list of emergency equipment owned by various tenants to use in case of power failure or other troubles (including a camping stove, lanterns, water containers, etc.);
- To set up an escort service, if the building is in a bad neighborhood, to protect those infirm or alone;
- To establish a system for checking in on those tenants who, for health reasons, might need help from time to time;
- To set up a committee to represent all the tenants in any negotiations or difficulties with the landlord;
- To set up a committee to work with the superintendent to make sure the building is well-maintained, well-lighted, and clean;
- To establish a committee for social events, entertainment, children's activities, etc.
- To establish communication channels between tenants—a bulletin board near the mail boxes, a monthly newsletter, a round-robin telephone system, etc.
- To set up a committee to oversee lobby decorations, plantings, etc.
- To set up a committee to meet with the police, the fire department, the public health department or any other public agency, in regard to matters of mutual interest to all tenants.

A small building, of course, may not need an organization this elaborate. But a large, multi-building complex may need even more—lawyers, doctors, security guards, etc.

Our point: There's no better way to insure good living conditions than with a tenants' organization. And, aside from all of its other benefits, it's a wonderful way to meet people and make friends.

The Landlord and His Employees

Wherever you move—next door, across the street, across the country, across the world—you'll find yourself dealing with a new landlord, at the minimum, and possibly a new superintendent, new doorman (or set of them), new janitor, new repairman, etc., etc., etc.

If you're renting an apartment in a small building, the chances are your landlord will also be your superintendent. With very few tenants, you may be able to establish a close relationship with him. He may be a warm and wonderful soul, always willing to help, always willing to see things your way.

If this is the case, offer thanks to the appropriate deity and thank your lucky stars. All too often, landlords and superintendents can't be described in anything like these terms.

It's really not surprising, if you think about it. Landlords, by nature, are worried, overburdened people. They've invested what's usually hard-earned money in an apartment building—an enterprise that is by no means safe or profitable.

And for their risk, they've been rewarded by complaints, suggestions, rising maintenance costs, tenants who are less than ideal, and all kinds of problems you can't even imagine.

On the other hand, they may be rewarded by some return on their investment, which isn't a bad thing, if you happen to believe in the capitalist system.

The question here is, how do you deal with them? There is no set formula, of course. But we'd like to take this opportunity to offer some advice:

Like yourself, your landlord is a human being. He has a wide range of problems and pleasures. He is concerned about you. He wants you to pay your rent, he wants you not to destroy the apartment or the building, he wants you to behave well—and he wants you to stay, if you do all the other things. But you are probably not his chief concern.

Your landlord knows, even if you don't, that what you've entered into is an agreement with *mutual* benefit. He's not doing you a favor by letting you live in his building and pay rent. He needs you exactly as much as you need him. Of course, if you leave, he can probably get another tenant. But then, you can probably get another apartment. For this reason, you should never be overawed by him.

If you're a good tenant (pay your rent, behave well, etc.), your landlord wants you to stay, probably very much. To make sure you do, he'll do everything reasonable to please you. Of course, "reasonable" has different meanings to different land lords. Some define it as any measure that doesn't cost money. This depends on the person.

Like other human beings, your landlord is likely to respond to kind and considerate treatment. Got a problem? Don't come into his office raging, as though he's determined to make your life miserable. Treat him as you'd like to be treated. Speak softly, be reasonable.

Your landlord, having many other things on his mind, would like to see all his apartment building's problems solved by his employees—particularly the superintendent. That's why he's hired the man. Therefore, don't go to the landlord with every small problem. In fact, don't go to him with *any* problem, large or small (unless it's an emergency, of course), until you've tried to get the superintendent to solve it.

This brings us to the superintendent, a man who probably lives in your building, whose job it is to solve every problem that may crop up (except, perhaps, legal ones), to fix anything that needs to be repaired, to keep the apartment building in reasonably good condition, and to keep the tenants happy—or at least not in a state of revolt.

Most of what we've said about the landlord also applies to the superintendent. But you have more leverage here, since part of his job is to keep you happy and since your building, most probably, is his only responsibility.

Our advice is to treat the super as well as he'll let you. Be considerate. Don't ask him to fix something immediately when next week will do just as well. Don't ask him to mind the baby. Don't give him extra duties—unless you're willing to pay for his help.

The relationship between the superintendent and the tenant, like the one between tenant and landlord, is built on a foundation of money. You're indirectly paying his salary. But that doesn't mean you're his employer. Good superintendents are harder to find than good tenants. So, if you make the landlord choose between his superintendent and you, chances are you'll be looking for another apartment.

In the buildings we've lived in, we've always gone out of our way to be nice to the super. We've baked cookies for him. We've tipped him when he's done special services for us (such as waiting for the telephone man and telling him where to install the thing). We've remembered him at Christmas. We've said good morning to him, to his children and his wife.

As a result, we've usually been able to get cooperation and good service. That doesn't mean our supers have dropped everything the moment we've called. But it does mean that they've taken care of our needs without serious complaint and without repeated prodding.

The one thing we've avoided doing is calling him unnecessarily—or at a bad time of day. Say, for instance, the built-in dishwasher doesn't work right. We discover it after dinner one night. Do we call the super at that moment? No. he's just finished dinner, too. We call in the morning. And we don't exaggerate the emergency.

Of course, if you're unlucky enough to get a super who shirks his duties or who is just plain incompetent, you may have to be more energetic about getting him to help you. You may have to go to the landlord. But if the super is truly no good, the landlord will recognize this and he'll be on your side.

Depending on the size of your building, your landlord may have other employees—specifically, a doorman (or doormen), a janitor, a security man, etc.

If so, you'll be in good shape with these people if you are kind and considerate to them, if you don't ask them to do anything that isn't their job without giving them an appropriate reward, and if you remember them at Christmas.

Unless you're dealing with people who are inherently grouchy, they'll warm to friendly treatment on your part. In fact, they'll do more than warm to it. They'll return it. And that could be very important to you when the post office unexpectedly drops a big package on your doorstep, when your great aunt Lil shows up without notice, when you arrive at the building's front door with more packages than you can carry.

This, then, is the new cast of characters in your life—your friends, your neighbors, your landlord, his employees. With a little bit of effort on your part, they can all contribute greatly to the quality of your life, to your feelings of well-being. As far as we're concerned, it's worth the trouble.

By now, if you've been following along through the chapters, your apartment should be in fine shape and you should be completely settled in. Now, at least, there's not much more to do with your apartment than to live in it. And in that connection, we wish you the best of luck.

And when it comes time to move again, we hope that your problems will be minimal. They should be just that, because after going through the entire process, after living in your own apartment for a year or two, you'll be an expert. Just wait and see.

Index